The Architecture of Public Space

Labics
Maria Claudia Clemente and Francesco Isidori
with a text by Marco Biraghi

PARK BOOKS

Preface

We'd like to express our gratitude to Marta Copetti, Alessandro Esposito, Giulio Marzullo, and (in particular) Giovanni Fabbri, who have patiently redrawn all the architectures presented in the book; to Giovanna Silva for the beautiful photos that have enriched the iconography; and finally, to Marco Biraghi for the precious critical contribution and for the constant encouragement.

Background

The opportunity to develop the thoughts from which this work has originated came in the form of an invitation to take part in a symposium titled "Common Luxury— Less Private Space, More Collective Space," organized by Andreas Ruby, the director of the Swiss Architecture Museum, in Basel in 2016. The title implied the idea that collective space, in a global context of urban transformations driven by prevalently private interests, represents an added value—the true wealth—that can be pursued by architecture. Andreas Ruby, who had previously visited our recently completed projects in Rome and Bologna— Città del Sole and Fondazione MAST—had perceived in both cases a particular attitude toward the construction of collective and shared spaces, partially attributable to the fact that those projects were designed by architects born and raised in Italy.

Preparing our contribution to the symposium, it seemed important to address the theme of public space from two different and complementary angles: on the one hand, the analysis of the role and meaning of public space in Italian cities, and on the other the role played by architecture in its formation.

These lines of reasoning, with their multiple nuances and interactions, have shaped the content of this book.

Objectives

While the first aspect constitutes the work's scenario of reference, the background in which the research can take on meaning, the second constitutes its operative content and, in our view, the most original contribution with respect to what is by now extensive literature on public space, which unfortunately often winds up being reduced to a manual of good common sense.

Starting with observations of historical Italian cities, their fabric, the relationship that is gradually established between certain works of architecture and public space, we have attempted to identify—like biologists or anthropologists who observe real phenomena to discern general principles—certain specific and recurring characteristics that have made those works of architecture into devices capable of granting form and meaning to public space; in substance, it is research that investigates typology and morphology in an attempt to understand how architecture can be capable of constructing the shared space of the city.

The objective of the work is not, then, to prepare a catalog of historic works of architecture, but to identify a series of typo-morphological solutions extrapolated from the historical context that generated them, enabling them to take on the character of models that can be repeated, notwithstanding their time and specific language of origin. The works analyzed should thus not be considered in their historicized character, like dead works to observe with the detachment of a scholar. They should be seen as living architecture to be studied

with the curiosity of the designer. Finally, the work sets out to build a strategy that can outline the essential characteristics of a way of making architecture that acts prior to and independently from language; it is the idea of an architecture that through the construction of public space and urban relations arrives at the formation of the city.

The method: the meaning of a classification

Pursuing these objectives, we have thought at length about the possibility of constructing a classification system, aware of the risks that can be implied in such a process. As we know, there are no rules, in abstract terms, of a taxonomic process, other than the rigor the scholar is able to call into play in the process of knowledge of reality. Classification, in fact, is first of all a technique, i.e., a means pertaining to knowledge, capable of granting general value to particular cases.

Of course, the construction of a classification system necessarily implies reductive choices, which stem precisely from the formation of the criterion of that construction. A classification system, in fact, can be evaluated in terms of the coherence with which the parameters assumed at the outset are respected, but the angle of observation and the criteria chosen, since they form the initial theoretical assumption, cannot be subjected to judgment.

The structure of the classification system

The construction of the classification system, in our case, has implied two consequent choices: the first has to do with the identification of categories; the second has to do with the selection of the case studies inside each category. It is worth specifying that the identification of the various categories or types, as well as the choice of the single cases inside each category, make no claim to completeness; often maximum clarity of assumptions has been sought, aside from the architectural language utilized or the historical period of the construction.

In the identification of the categories, which constitutes the structure of the classification system, a method has been applied that is both deductive and inductive at the same time: after having defined the categories in an abstract way, it became necessary to compare and verify them with real cases. This could imply, in fact, that the study of certain particular cases would lead to the redefinition of certain categories, or even the introduction of new ones. This back-and-forth process has been decisive: had we stopped at a merely abstract level, we would have run the risk of being ineffective in the knowledge of architecture which, as we know, is made of matter, space, real places; to instead substantiate it with cases that could be verified through direct experience, we felt the knowledge could also be enriched on a theoretical plane. Furthermore, by ordering the cognitive process through the filters of the classification

system, the individual cases were led back into a more general discourse, precisely thanks to the process of classification itself.

In the proposed taxonomy, some types are more widespread and already clearly encoded—including porticos, loggias or urban courtyards—while others are less widespread, such as inhabited bridges; some have been encoded for the first time—at least in the sense attributed in this research—such as steps, covered squares, frames, and city rooms.

After defining the macro categories, in the choice of the single cases we have not applied a chronological criterion, nor a merely qualitative standard, or one related to the historical importance of the artifact; the choice has gone to cases that from our perspective were able to best demonstrate the basic thesis of this work and the possible permutations or articulations inside each specific category. We are aware that there could be many other potentially interesting cases, including some that are much more famous than those selected—how could one fail to think, for example, on the subject of porticos, about the Fabbriche Nuove in Venice or the portico of Piazza San Pietro? Or, considering loggias, that of the Capitaniato in Vicenza or the Mercanzie in Bologna? But since this is not a manual of architectural history, the criterion of historical importance has not been utilized. The book thus contains certain acknowledged monuments alongside smaller or less famous specimens sharing in the same ability to narrate a point of view, and above all the bear witness.

Finally, once the cases were selected, they were all redrawn with the same technique, photographed in their present state and in the context where they stand, in the conviction that architecture is living matter that exists because it is space that can be utilized in the contemporary age. And since this is not a manual, as we have said, we have not lingered over the documentation of various historical phases—apart from brief remarks in the text—even when the buildings examined have undergone various alterations over time.

Table of Contents

Architecture of Public Space
Maria Claudia Clemente and Francesco Isidori

Public space in the contemporary city

According to the calculations of the Population Division of the United Nations, in 1950 for every 100 inhabitants of our planet only 29 lived in urban areas. In 1990 this quota had risen to 45 percent, while the urban population had more than tripled, reaching a level of 2.4 billion. Urban areas now contain about 3.5 billion people, and by about 2030, when the world population should reach 8 billion, it is estimated that 5 billion will live in cities, or 62 percent of the worldwide population. This incredible demographic thrust has caused rampant and extremely rapid growth in many cities. Just consider the fact that today (2021), 33 cities in the world already have populations greater than 10 million inhabitants.

The phenomenon of exceptional growth of cities, taking into account the differences regarding the historical-cultural and economic contexts of development, inevitably leads to the need to change our viewpoint regarding the way in which we can observe and interpret the city, or the ways in which we can study its evolutionary dynamics. This is a true paradigm shift[1] with respect to the tools—clearly obsolete, at this point—used in the past to understand urban phenomena and to govern urban growth.

The fact that large size could lead to a new way of thinking about architecture and the city was already clear from the early years of the 20th century, and became even clearer during the period of postwar reconstruction, when the logic of the *great number*[2] became inevitable.

Without delving too deeply into the cultural implications this paradigm shift can bring—reasoning that lies beyond the aims of this study—in this context we will simply observe that the problem of large size, or of the extraordinary expansion of cities, above all in this latest exponential phase, has had the side effect of a widespread loss of quality of urban space, seen as collective space. The obsessive repetition of buildings, aside from the specific quality of the individual episodes, is clearly not sufficient to generate a city. If we combine the phenomenon of urbanization with a parallel process of reduction of the role of public players in the growth and transformation of the city, the result is a progressive loss of quality of public space and a marginalization of the community as the main counterpart of urban actions.

All this may seem inevitable, but it is not: the logic that has guided the growth of cities over the last half century is not at all inevitable, but is the result of an impoverishment of collective awareness regarding themes of shared interest, accompanied by a weakening of government in response to these themes. Some see a clear political project in this phenomenon, based on a free-market worldview and its model of development; a project which, to be honest, has at times been cynically exploited by architects.[3] Certainly this model, which today seems like the only one possible, is a system that by urging a smaller number of constraints translates into laissez-faire urban policies and inevitably leads to the reduction of the role of public actors in the top-down control of the city, and the loss of importance of urban design and planning as a tool for governance of the territory.

The outcome is there for all to see: entire urban agglomerations of new construction in which there is a clear lack of interest in the building of the *res publica* in its various forms and expressions, where the foremost shortcoming is undoubtedly the lack of public space seen not only as empty space, but also and above all as a place of collective identity, endowed with specific qualities.

Paradoxically, precisely in the historical moment of the supremacy of life in cities with respect to the countryside, when therefore maximum attention and participation are needed on the part of the designated subjects—designers, administrators, intellectuals— the design of the city has gradually lost its meaning, and the "human invention par excellence"[4] is being progressively privatized.[5]

In this process in progress, the main loser is public space, which is increasingly split into two different, equally inadequate forms: on the one hand the leftover, undersigned void, which precisely by virtue of its lack of quality becomes "public;" on the other, the space of commerce, the shopping malls, outlets, privately owned places that artificially reproduce the idea-simulacrum of the Italian *piazza*.

The origin of a crisis

In cities of large size, as in many suburbs of the main European cities, an irreversible phenomenon can be observed that we might call the *pulverization* of the idea of the city itself: infinite episodes of construction are gathered in an incoherent blur, like the monads of a gravitational system, without form and structure. The public space around which the large European cities are built; the space of major community events, such as demonstrations or processions in squares; or simply the places of encounter with others—these places seem to vanish, yielding ground to a void without quality and without identity.

Beyond the inevitable paradigm shift required to describe the phenomenon, it is necessary to ask ourselves about the causes at the origin of all this, and the possible strategies for rethinking—if not of the very idea of the city—at least of its most representative element: public space.

To trace back to the origins of a crisis, then, it is necessary to take a step back and to analyze the relationship between the elements involved: city, architecture, and public space. Taking the *urbs* as the physical place constituted of the set of buildings and infrastructures that form the city, i.e., the machine to be governed; and the *civitas* as the symbolic and political place of encounter of the *cives* and of collective exchange; we can define the public space of the city as the material and immaterial infrastructure that grants visible form to the *civitas*. If the *urbs* can theoretically exist in the absence of the *cives*, it is only through the *civitas* that the space of the *urbs* takes on its meaning. In this regard, we could assert that the forms assumed by public space over time substantially reflect the various forms of *civitas* in line with the different political and economic systems in a given context.

Putting aside the analysis of these forms, we can observe that one principle remained without alteration in the city until the early 20th century: open space was defined and granted quality by the presence of architecture, and vice versa; and the two formed an inseparable pair. In this reading, open space has always been a *natural space*, to the extent that it naturally took formed with the growth of the city, constituting one of its characteristic elements. The structure of the city was therefore an *unicum* that held together—in a unified design—buildings and open spaces, inside an uninterrupted sequence. The form of the city was conceived in its entirety; the empty space and the architecture were part of a single project.

The crisis originates with the breakdown of the architec-ture-public space pairing, which happened during the Modern Movement, following the profound transformations in the form of the city and its system of values. These transformations can be traced back to three main factors. The first lies in the idea of the city itself: with the Modern Movement the thought of the city as an *efficient* place definitively asserted itself, a place where it was necessary to optimize the main functions of habitation, expressed in terms of mobility, productivity, residence, and free time, principles reiterated during the course of postwar reconstruction; cities were reconsidered on the basis of criteria that did not take the values of the *civitas* into account in any way, having the objective of making the *urbs* increasingly functional.[6] After all, it will suffice to recall Ludwig Hilberseimer (1927) when he stated that the design of the city consisted of two extremes: the overall map that systematically shapes the form of the city to the economic forces, and the definition of the individual inhabited rooms;[7] all else was marginal. While until the 1800s it was still possible to come across the expression of collective values in the tangible form of the public spaces of the city, with the Modern Movement the form of the city, abandoning the symbolic sphere, followed a logic of efficiency: the city—on a par with the house—became a *machine a habiter*. The second factor driving transformation in the understanding of the city during the Modern Movement has to do with the relationship between architecture and the city; the idea that the city was designed in its form by architecture was put aside; for health reasons the house, in the midst of greenery if possible, was distanced from the street, giving rise to an idea of architecture that was independent of the urban fabric: "The house will no longer be fused to the street by a sidewalk. It will rise in its own surroundings, in which it will enjoy sunshine, clear air and silence".[8] Finally, the third factor, a direct consequence of the first and second, has to do with public space and its loss of meaning. The claims of rationalization of the city advanced during the Modern Movement led to the separation of functions of production, commerce, residence, and service, compromising public space which, as we know, takes its vitality from a mixture of functions and the opportunities for encounter and relations generated by that mixture.

In short, during the Modern period we can see a split in which the logics of construction of the city and those of architecture become autonomous: to respond to the same requirements of efficiency, functionality, economy, and health, both lose any relationship of reciprocal necessity. The loser in this process is public space, which is impoverished, emptied of meaning, losing its central role as a catalyst of collective identity and a driver of urban dynamics.

While it is easy to assert that modernity "has destroyed the city as we know it,"[9] paradoxically it is precisely this model that is the most fungible and useful to the present liberal culture, within growth dynamics where the necessities of the *urbs* prevail over the values of the *civitas*.

Architecture, city, and public space

The break in the relationship between architecture and public space, or between architecture and the city—which is the same thing— is one of the most obvious effects of the of the new urban planning concepts that date back to the start of the 20th century. At this point we can investigate the consequences or repercussions on architecture and public space.

Balanced between a technical plane at the service of the market and a purely communicative plane at the service of the image, the architecture of the end of the millennium proved to be increasingly unable to address the community and to thus contribute to the improvement of the quality of urban space. It is a process that began many years before, at this point, since already in 1973 Manfredo Tafuri prophetically foresaw what was going to happen: "Arrived at an undeniable impasse, architectural ideology renounces its propelling role in regard to the city and the structures of production and hides behind a rediscovered disciplinary autonomy, or behind neurotic attitudes of self-destruction."[10]

But if this is well known by now, what has been examined less is the consequence of this break on the quality of urban space, namely the space of the *civitas*.

In the Modernist conception the city expands into the territory, conquering a dimension of landscape: its field of action becomes an open, potentially infinite space in which to move freely, where the buildings seem to float in the absence of a structuring relationship with the void. The backdrop of the city becomes an extremely expanded neutral territory, lacking a figure, in which architecture is no longer capable of defining and granting form to the emptiness.

So, in the Modern city there is a great deal of open space—even too much—but there is no public space; a fascinating tabula rasa—just as Brasilia and Chandigarh are fascinating—but more often than not lacking identity, incapable of generating intensity; a clean slate that is the result of a mechanistic vision of reality that has put the idea of *civitas* within parentheses.

As Bernardo Secchi clarifies, "What leaves us astonished and disoriented in many European cities of the 20th century is above all the lack of a meaningful and systematic experience of open space, seen as a place set aside for the sharing of a collective identity and the enactment of the public life of the city, which expands enormously, seeming to be pulverized in an episodic set of fragments connected to each other by spaces deprived of any clear status."[11] What is missing, then, is an overall project of public space, a holistic vision capable of expressing shared values that go beyond the single street and the single square. For this reason, the design of public space—the focus of this work—can in no way be treated as independent from the idea of the city and the relationship generated between architecture and public space inside the urban context.

Thus, urban architecture, with the aim of not becoming superstructure—to use Tafuri's terms—must be capable of constructing the public space of the city, taking its founding principles and rules from the city and its history. We cannot think of urban architecture as a monad extraneous to the fabric, as an object or a sculpture that finds its reason for being in an autonomous way with respect to the context in which it is inserted.

In a historical moment in which the debate on architecture is feeble and the debate on the city has been reduced to numerical questions pertaining to the specific discipline of urbanism, it seems useful to reach back to the reasoning of Aldo Rossi on a theory of the city from the viewpoint of architecture. The concepts of place, urban factor, monument, fabric, suitably updated with respect to the contemporary condition, are still useful tools for a project on the city; not in an abstract or ideological way, but in a concrete, real way. For Rossi, architecture and the city are interdependent parts of one single system: architecture constructs the city which, in turn, is an artifact, a work of architecture: "By the architecture of the city we mean two different things; first, the city seen as a gigantic man-made object, a work of engineering and architecture that is large and complex and growing over time; second, certain more limited but still crucial aspects of the city, namely urban artifacts, which like the city itself are characterized by their own history and thus by their own form."[12]

Public space as the core of democracy

Never before as in this moment in history, when the free-market policies shared by nearly all mature democracies are showing signs of difficulty, and are being challenged in both political and economic terms, has there been such interest in public space, seen in both literal and metaphorical perspectives. This is due to two orders of reasons that are worth examining here.

First of all, public space is the core of democracy, or the space in which to make different ideas coexist and be shared. In an essay for the Festival della Mente in Sarzana (Italy) a few years ago, Salvatore Veca stated: "I am convinced that one of the crucial earmarks of a political democracy is the dimension and variety of public space, in which to exercise the democratic freedom par excellence, that of sharing the ways of evaluating and proposing alternative or conflicting solutions to collective problems with other citizens. Public space, in this perspective, is a social, not an institutional space."[13]

These words bring to mind the meaning of public space and its political role in the thinking of Hanna Arendt. For Arendt, politics can achieve authentic expression only when citizens gather in a public space to discuss and decide on issues that have an impact on the entire community. The public sphere, then, designates the sphere where freedom and equality prevail, where citizens interact by means of discussion and persuasion. Arendt sees public space as the place of interaction, discussion and— if necessary—civil disobedience.[14]

This is a scenario that seems to be increasingly remote today; to the contrary, today's public space, full of limitations and barriers, packed with surveillance cameras, seems to be increasingly a space of control and fear; a space in which the liberty of the citizen is relegated to that of the consumer.

Second, public space is the space of reception, the space of encounter with the other.

As Zygmunt Bauman reminds us, for the construction of a truly multiethnic society an important priority is "the propagation of open, inviting and hospitable public spaces which all categories of urban residents would be tempted to attend regularly and knowingly and willingly share," because "the 'fusion' that mutual understanding requires can only be the outcome of *shared* experience; and sharing experience is inconceivable without shared space."[15]

In short, public space is a political space that measures the democratic breadth of a given community; a physical and at the same time metaphorical space whose presence is a guarantee of freedom of expression of the individual and the community.

An inversion: the design of emptiness

In the light of these considerations, we believe it is necessary to reflect on the state of the discipline, objectives, and aims that can be addressed by an architectural project, as well as the themes of language, the design of the city, over and above quantitative data.

We do not share the position of those who now say "the city no longer exists"[16] to justify the status quo as inevitable and unavoidable, making any discourse on the design of the city and the control of the territory futile; to the contrary, precisely this boundless growth and expansion beyond normative boundaries make it necessary and urgent to rethink the tools we have available, first of all on a political level. This does not imply a naïve and utopian rejection of the prevailing model based, as we have seen, on a strictly mercantile logic, but the awareness that alternative models, or at least intermediate solutions, do exist. Beyond the two extreme possibilities of unhesitating acceptance or radical repudiation, there is a third possibility that calls for the construction, through design, of a form of resistance.

To this end, we propose rethinking architecture and the city starting from an inversion of the viewpoint: what would happen were we to start with the design of empty space to construct a different vision for architecture and the city? Starting over from what has been most neglected during the last century, namely public space?

This inversion would imply assigning open space a role as primary infrastructure to revitalize the city as a whole; an infrastructure organized on different planes and levels to permit circulation, to encourage relationships, to allow exchange and trade, and the encounter with otherness; but also an infrastructure capable of bringing a different visual quality, of making the experience of outdoor space intense and meaningful, of bringing wealth to the common benefit, where wealth apparently pertains to no one.

Once the figures of open space have been defined, architecture would become the tool through which those very figures can take form; an architecture, then, that is at the service of empty space; an architecture not concerned with filling up all the available space—an utterly contemporary obsession—but willing to step aside.

In this way, the great misunderstanding of the modern could be overcome: that of architecture as an isolated figure that stands out against a neutral backdrop. At the same time, it would be possible to rediscover the urban fabric as a form of architecture in which void and full become cohorts, where the whole prevails over the individual objects. Works of architecture that arise to give form and quality to outdoor space, that generously open to a wider system; porous works of architecture that allow themselves to be crossed, to become part of the space that permeates the city, incorporating the civic values of the community to which they intrinsically belong.

But all this is nothing new: we can trace these attitudes back to the famous plan of Rome by Giovanni Battista Nolli in 1748, where the void of public space, represented in white, becomes the pervasive figure that surrounds the architecture, shaping it and in certain cases excavating it from the inside, to the point of absorbing it inside the urban fabric.

This plan, a faithful planimetric representation of Baroque Rome, has often been compared to the one made slightly later by the great architect and engraver Giovanni Battista Piranesi, *Ichnographia Campi Martii antiquae urbis* of 1762, an imaginary reconstruction of imperial Rome. The comparison arises because the two plans, though unwittingly, propose two models of the city that in some ways are antithetical: on the one hand, the *archipelago city*,[17] represented in the Campus Martius, composed of monuments set one beside the next, without an urban structure that holds them together, and thus without a project of open space; on the other, the *city as fabric*, that of the Nuova Pianta di Roma by Nolli, where the form of the empty space shapes the constructed space and vice versa, in which architecture contributes to the construction of the public sphere of the city.

Nolli's plan could be juxtaposed with the many photographs of everyday life in many historic Italian urban centers, in which the open spaces of the city, in a process of inversion, become internal spaces, theaters of social contact and civil coexistence: it is the image of an open and hospitable city, the only true antidote to fear of the other. In this sense, Nolli's plan is a political and, in some ways, visionary map, because by representing the total continuity of public space inside churches, courtyards, lobbies of the principal private buildings, it foreshadows and imagines a reality that goes beyond reality itself.

History therefore offers a different model, a model of integration between city and architecture, architecture and public space. It is not an escape into the past, but the comprehension of a way of operating, a way of thinking about the city that is different from that of the present.

Architecture of public space

The research and theories in the field of architecture and urbanism over the last century have almost always been based on a single theme: disciplinary concerns have been traditionally divided between studies on the city, the architectural object, or public space, examined separately as autonomous entities or topics. This separation, however, as we have seen, contains one of the problems of the current architectural and urban culture.

We have thus reexamined certain examples in Italian historical cities where this separation, in practice, does not exist, or at least is not explicit; examples where architecture, while asserting its autonomy, is nevertheless capable of taking part in the definition of public space; examples where public space is enriched and amplified by the possibilities offered by architecture; and, ultimately, portions of the city constructed through an uninterrupted sequence of works of architecture and public spaces.

We have thus begun to analyze certain particular cases where this readiness of architecture to construct public space is more outstanding, cases in which we can discover the existence of certain recurring typological and morphological elements that are normally seen as part of the architectural language, but could actually be included in an ideal catalog of tools or elements for the construction of public space. Let's take the portico, for example. Whether it is the portico of an agora of antiquity, a Renaissance palace or a 19th-century street, is it an architectural or an urban device? Does it belong to the building which it helps to support, or to the public space it amplifies and protects?

The same discussion could apply to loggias, steps or other elements examined in this research: are they urban devices, architectural parts, or structures of public space?

Architecture of Public Space is therefore a research project on the ways in which public space takes form, is structured and characterized, and the elements of which it is composed, through a process of selection and cataloguing of examples from the past.

Since in this research the accent, as we have extensively illustrated, is on empty space—negative space—and not on the figure-object of architecture, in the examples examined the internal space of buildings is never represented, except when it becomes public space, as in the case of galleries or arcades.

The selected works of architecture, as complementary figures of this mosaic, are those that have the ability to act at the service of the construction of public space, contributing to define its form and quality.

But how can architecture contribute to the quality of empty space? How can a single building amplify the public domain?

What characteristics should it have? It is hard to supply general definitions, though we can attempt to outline certain conditions: when architecture is capable of mediating between the private and public dimensions; when it is able to donate a part of its domain to free usage; when it contributes to a better definition of public space, increasing its quality and potential for aggregation.

We have thus attempted to identify categories and typo-morphological solutions that apart from the language they utilize can be repeated, becoming useful tools of design. It is important, however, to emphasize that these categories should not be seen as a mere catalog of formal solutions to be applied at will. Each of them, due to its history, is the expression of a given civil society, a vehicle of its underlying values. The comprehension of these values is essential to grasp their meaning, over and above aspects of form.

In conclusion, we believe that architecture—to get back to Tafuri's warning—should continue to play a driving role in relation to the city. And we believe that architects cannot give up on the political role played by architecture in relation to the context, hiding behind claims of disciplinary independence. Finally, we believe that the design of public space, as a bearer of collective values, can be the key of interpretation through which to reconcile architecture and the city.

1 One of the leading scholars on the paradigm shift of the contemporary city over the last 30 years is undoubtedly Rem Koolhaas, who has written various texts regarding this phenomenon that are worth mentioning here: Rem Koolhaas, *Delirious New York: A Retroactive Manifesto for Manhattan*, Monicelli Press 1997; Rem Koolhaas, *Junkspace: Per un ripensamento radicale dello spazio urbano, a cura di G. Mastrigli*, Macerata, Quodlibet 2006; Rem Koolhaas, *Singapore Songlines: Portrait of a Potemkin Metropolis... or Thirty Years of Tabula Rasa*, 1995; Chuihua Judy Chung, Jeffrey Inaba, Rem Koolhaas and Sze Tsung Leong, *Harvard Design School Project on the City: 1 Great Leap Forward*, Cologne: Taschen, 2001; and Rem Koolhas, *Testi sulla (non più) città, a cura e con un saggio introduttivo di Manuel Orazi*, Quodlibet 2021.

2 The theme of the *great number* as recurring during the course of postwar reconstruction; in 1964 Aldo van Eyck, together with his colleagues of Team X, called it "l'habitat pour le plus grand nombre." The great number was also utilized by Giancarlo De Carlo as the title of the 14th Milan Triennale in 1968.

3 Piervittorio Aureli, ed., *The City as a Project*, Berlin: Preface Ruby Press, 2013, p. 15.

4 As Lévi-Strauss wrote: "The city may even be rated higher since it stands at the point where nature and artifice meet. A city is a congestion of animals whose biological history is enclosed within its boundaries, and yet every conscious and rational act on the part of these creatures helps to shape the city's eventual character. By its form as by the manner of its birth, the city has elements at once of biological procreation, organizations, evolutions, and esthetic creation. It is both a natural object and a thing to be cultivated; individual and group; something lived and something dreamed. It is the human invention par excellence," in Claude Lévi-Strauss, *Tristes Tropiques*, Paris: Librairie Plon, 1955.

5 Koolhaas, *Testi sulla*, p. 194.

6 The term *urbanization* was introduced by the Spanish urbanist Ildefons Cerda (1867).

7 "The architecture of the large city depends essentially on the solution given to two factors: the elementary cell and the urban organism as a whole." L. Hilberseimer, *Groszstadt Architektur*, Milan: Clean, 1998, p. 98; original version: L. Hilberseimer, *Groszstadt Architektur*, Stuttgard: Julius Hoffman Verlag, 1927.

It is interesting to read *Groszstadt Architektur* as a response to the growth of cities after World War I—the book is from 1927—and to the need to find new growth models: "The city stems mainly from real needs, it is decisively influenced by economics and practice, structures and materials, the economic and sociological moment," p. 90. Manfredo Tafuri wrote about Hilberseimer as follows: "For Hilberseimer, the 'object' was not in crisis because it had already disappeared from his spectrum of considerations. The only emerging imperative was that dictated by the laws of organization, and therein lies what has been correctly seen as Hilberseimer's greatest contribution," in *Progetto e utopia*, Rome-Bari: Laterza, 1977, p. 99.

8 Le Corbusier, *La Carta di Atene*, Milan: Edizioni Ghibli, 2014. *La Carta di Atene, manifesto di urbanistica* was formulated during the 4th CIAM congress in 1933, and it had the theme of The Functional City. It was published anonymously in French in 1938 but not signed; only later was it attributed to its author. The first italian version is: *La carta d'Atene* / Le Corbusier; with a preliminary discourse by Jean Giraudoux, trans. by C. De Roberto, Milan: Edizioni di Comunità, 1960.

9 Koolhaas, *Testi sulla*, p. 125.

10 Tafuri, *Progetto e utopia*, p. 125–126.

11 B. Secchi, *La città del ventesimo secolo*, Rome-Bari: Editori Laterza, p. 58.

12 Aldo Rossi, *L'architettura della città*, Milan: CittàStudi, 1987, p. 17.

13 Salvatore Veca, "Spazio pubblico per le idee," text for the Festival in Sarzana, in *Sole 24 Ore*, August 28, 2016.

14 *The Human Condition*, published by University of Chicago Press in 1958, was published in Italy in 1964 with the title *Vita activa*. H. Arendt, *Vita activa*, Milan: Bompiani, 1964, p. 54–104.

15 Zygmunt Bauman, *Modus Vivendi. Inferno e utopia del mondo liquido*, Rome-Bari: Laterza, 2008, p. 105.

16 "Pervasive urbanization has modified the urban condition beyond recognition. 'The' city no longer exists. As the concept of the city is distorted and stretched beyond precedent, each insistence on its primordial condition—in terms of images, rules, fabrication—irrevocably leads via nostalgia to irrelevance." In Koolhaas, *Testa sulla*, p. 63.

17 Regarding the urban archipelago, see: Oswald Mathias Ungers and Rem Koolhaas, *The City in the City. Berlin: A Green Archipelago. A Manifesto by Rem Koolhaas with Peter Reiman, Hans Kollhoff and Arthur Ovaskam*, Zurich: Lars Muller Publishers, 2013.

Categories and History

Categories and history

During the research on the categories and their definitions, a strong relationship emerged between the categories themselves and the physical, economic, and social context in which they have taken form. We will not attempt to sum up the thousands of years of history of this relationship in a few sentences, but we do feel the need to underline the bond—which has always existed—between architecture and the form of the society, politics, and the territory.

Before delving into the narration, we can say that it is possible to identify two macro families: the *known* categories, which in some cases coincide with already encoded elements or types such as loggias or porticos; and the categories we can define as *new*, in the sense that they are types or architectures that exist in the city, but have never been analyzed in relation to public space; in other words, those that already exist but can be observed from a different standpoint through this work.

Covered squares, *urban courtyards*, and *loggias* are three closely interconnected types. Their birth coincides for the most part with the rise of the Communes, a phenomenon that developed in central-northern Italy starting from the end of the 11th century to meet the need to have places where the populace could gather to make political or administrative decisions, or more simply for trade. The relationship between these types and the form of the society is very strong. In fact, they are not found in southern Italy because this part of the territory had a totally different history, mostly connected with the presence of great monarchies until the founding of the Kingdom of Italy in 1860.

The *covered squares*, defined as such due to the public role implied in the use of these spaces, were conceived as places of gathering and trade, whether they coincided with the ground-level loggias of medieval public buildings of the *a loggiato* type, in which the life of the city took place, as in the case of Palazzo della Ragione in Milan; or whether the type was borrowed, successively, in buildings like the Palazzo della Loggia in Brescia. Only the Mercato del Pesce in Venice was made with a purely commercial purpose, but it is important to emphasize that in linguistic terms it substantially retraces the typology of the medieval palace, with a loggia at ground level and a loggia and hall on the upper level.

The *urban courtyards* are similar in terms of use and conception, and they too are often part of medieval public buildings, in the typology of the *broletti a corte*,[1] built in the communal era in northern Italy.[2] Besides that of Piacenza, included in the case studies, the term *broletti a corte* can apply, among others, to those of Brescia, Pavia, and Novara. There is a slight difference, though only as a question of image and not in terms of the intended public use of the space, in the courtyard of the Palazzo Municipale of Ferrara; built for the house of Este, the lords of the city of Ferrara, it was initially intended to be the courtyard of the ducal palace.

Likewise, the *loggias*, arising in the passage from a feudal society to the Communes, were created to contain gatherings of townspeople. Those of the first generation, according to Alessandro Merlo, usually coincided with the ground floor of medieval public buildings—defined in this work as *covered squares*—while those up against buildings or independent, indicated as the second or third generation,[3] began to appear when the political-administrative function separated from the commercial function, namely at the end of the communal era, with the advent of the seigneuries and the bourgeoisie. Nevertheless, for a long period nearly all loggias continued to have a hybrid function, not just for commerce but also as a place for public events, such as the Loggia dei Lanzi in Florence, or that of Castiglion Fiorentino; only later did the loggias begin to specialize as places of trade, as in the cases of the Loggia del Mercato Nuovo and the Loggia Pesce in Florence, or for functions of representation, like the Loggia dei Lanzi, which became an outdoor sculpture gallery, a tribute to the splendor and prestige of the Medici family.

The *porticos*, whose very ancient origins were consolidated in the form familiar to us with the stoas of the Greek *polis*, have had various connotations and roles over time, though always connected with the protection of a walkway at the ground level of a building: a space that although it ideally exists inside the profile of the building is offered as public. Porticos, unlike loggias, have always been places of transit, and have therefore never contained a specific function other than that of mediation between the internal and external space of buildings.

Nevertheless, starting from the Renaissance, with the spread of manuals, from Vitruvius to the treatises of Alberti and Filarete, the portico took on a new role that seems to stem precisely from its purpose in the context of the Roman forum or the Greek agora. This spread of knowledge of classical architecture coincided with the passage, in central and northern Italy, from the communal era to the phase of the lordships—the Medici in Tuscany, the Manfredi in Faenza, the Gonzaga and Sforza in Lombardy, and similarly the Badoer in the Veneto—and the necessity of powerful families not only to assert their presence in the city, but also to actively contribute to boost its quality and prestige. Porticos thus took on a new and important urban role as a device capable of granting eminence and unity to the main public spaces of the city, whether they appeared together with a building, as in the case of the Palazzo delle Logge in Arezzo or at Badoere, or were added to existing buildings, as in Faenza, Vigevano, Pisa, or many other Italian cities. The portico became a way to give a new guise to the medieval city, the expression of a renewed organization of the civil society.

The *galleries*, which can be seen as the natural evolution on a different scale of the Parisian *passage*s,[4] emerged with the rise of large-scale industrial production and the need for new urban spaces devoted to trade and to the social activities of a new bourgeois class. Somewhere between the square, the covered street, and the urban salon, the galleries had the character of hybrid, porous spaces that could be crossed, inside which there were a very wide range of functions: cafés, restaurants, bar, spaces of trade, but also book-stores, exhibition spaces, offices, residences.

The *steps* in front of the city's most important civic or religious buildings were devised to raise the building above the urban fabric and to thus grant it a monumental aura, as recommended in the manuals on classical architecture. At times, however, the topography of the site obliged the use of steps of such size as to make them become true urban devices, which besides connecting different levels of the city could also be involved in other uses. We are thinking, for example, about the role of steps in the Baroque era, as protagonists of the magnificent urban settings that enhance many Italian cities: from Piazza di Spagna in Rome to the steps of the cathedral of Noto.

The *inhabited bridges* are a category that fits into this re-search because like the steps they go beyond their original functional purpose—in this case the connection of two banks of a river—to become places endowed with their own formal autonomy, places where time can be spent. Inhabited bridges can be seen as squares overlooking the river, as in the case of Comacchio, as protected promenades as in Bassano del Grappa, or as open-air commercial galleries, like Ponte Vecchio in Florence.

The *urban terraces* constitute a category for cases in which the roof of a building or part of it can be utilized as public space. They are usually connected with the existence of a level shift or an embankment. This category, clearly linked to the topographical necessities of the territory, becomes a way to amplify public space on different levels in pursuit of an idea of a continuous city.

Finally, *frame* and *city room* are two categories in which architecture shapes and qualifies public space in a more pronounced manner, explicitly producing an inversion between inside and outside; categories in which the architecture, becoming concave, looks towards outdoor space so as to wrap it and redefine it. In the case of the city room—for example, the street-square of the Uffizi—the exterior becomes a true urban interior; in the case of the *frame*—such as the Domus Nova in Verona—the architecture shifts beyond its boundary to contribute to define the form of the space in front of it, sometimes mediating between the scale of the monument and that of the urban fabric.

1   The term *broletto* comes from the Latin *brolo*, meaning an enclosed court or garden, and until the Middle Ages, in the area of Lombardy, it indicated the space of citizen assemblies. Later the term was used to indicate the town hall.
2   Besides *broletto*, "there are in any case multiple terms with which to indicate these buildings: others include arengo, palazzo della ragione, arengario, palazzo della credenza, basilica, palazzo del popolo," in Alessandro Merlo, *Logge italiane. Genesi e processi di trasformazione*, of the series *Ricerche | architettura, design, territorio*, Florence: DIDA, 2016, p. 42
3   The loggias of the first generation are those located on the ground floor of municipal buildings. In Merlo, *Logge italiane*.
4   Starting in the second half of the 1800s, the *passage* had to face the competition of a new place of consumption: the department store. The department store, exploiting the possibilities of industrial production on an increasingly large scale, could offer products at lower prices than those sold in a passage. Unable to compete with the innovations offered by the department stores (such as the fixed price), the passages built after 1860 converted from being places of consumption to acquiring the status of monuments, becoming true urban galleries: "For the first time in history, with the establishment of department stores, consumers begin to consider themselves a mass. … Hence, the circus-like and theatrical element of commerce is quite extraordinarily heightened." In Walter Benjamin, Volume primo, *I "passages" di Parigi*, Piccola Biblioteca Einaudi, 2000, p. 50; original version: *Das Passagen-Werk*, hrsg. von Rolf Tiedemann, 2 Bände, Frankfurt am Main: Suhrkamp, 1983.

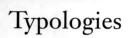

Typologies

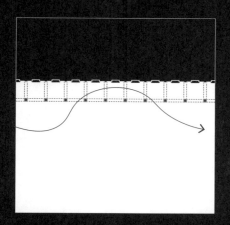

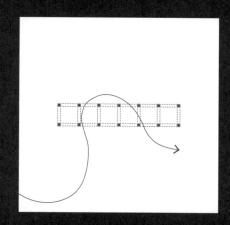

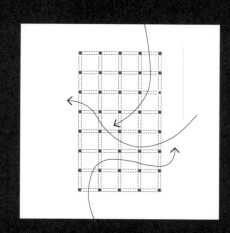

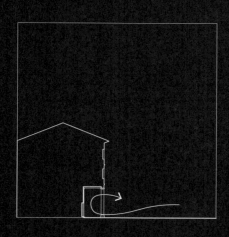

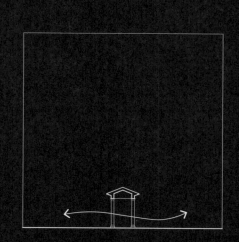

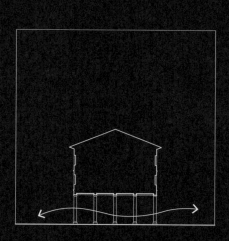

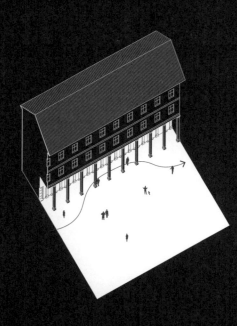

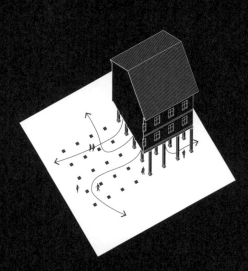

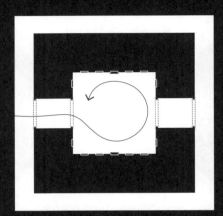
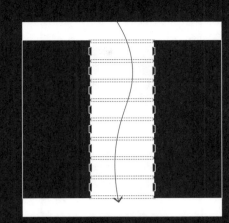
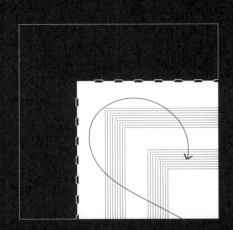

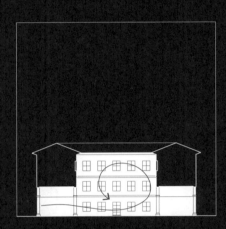
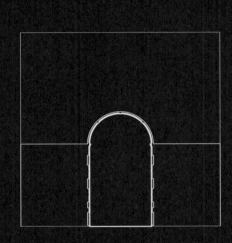
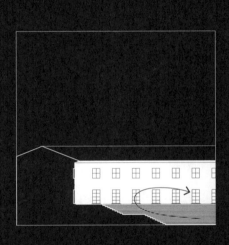

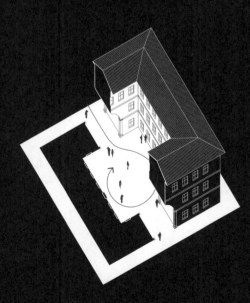
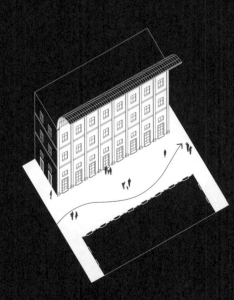
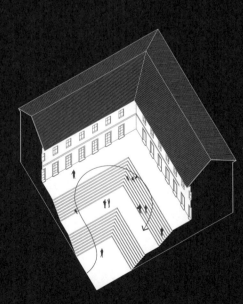

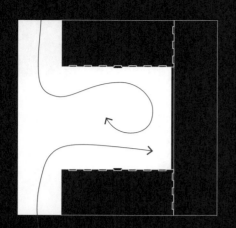
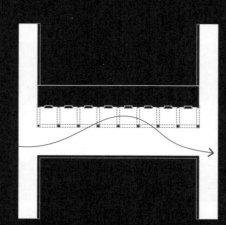
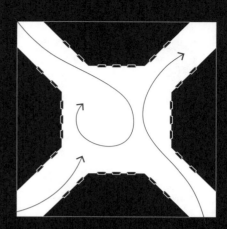

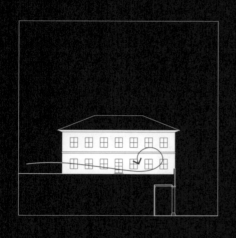
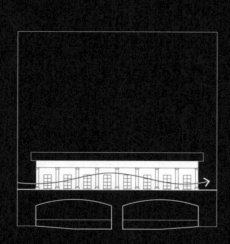
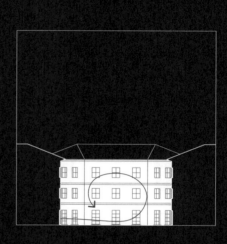

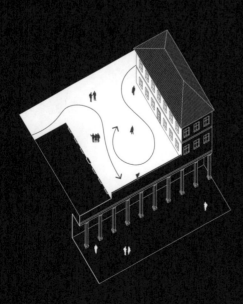
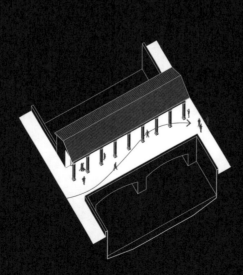

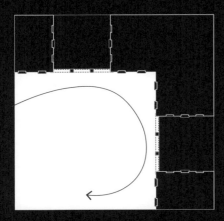

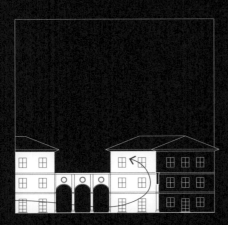

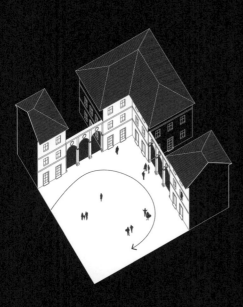

Case Studies

An area at ground level of which at least one side is composed of a row of columns or pillars, acting as a passage or a sort of hallway.

In other words, when a building donates a portion of the ground floor to public space, enhancing and impacting the street or the square faced by that building.

Portico

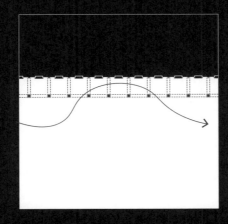

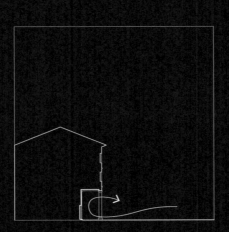

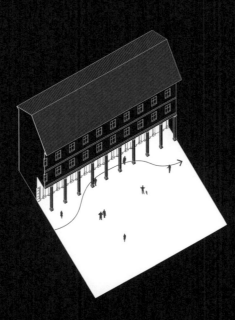

Palazzo delle Logge, Arezzo, 1573   38–49

Palazzo delle Logge in Arezzo is a Renaissance building designed by Giorgio Vasari in 1572, bordering the northeastern front of Piazza Grande, in the symbolic and administrative heart of the city.

The Palazzo, which was constructed to correspond to the upper part of the large space of the square, experienced a redesign of its northwestern front, radically altering its image: the long portico, extending for a total length of 125 meters, beyond the space of the piazza, formed a new urban backdrop that made a decisive leap of scale with respect to the fragmentation of the surroundings, still with a medieval character.

When Arezzo became part of the Grand Duchy of Tuscany, Cosimo I, who had become Grand Duke in 1569, commissioned major projects of urban transformation in the city, as happened for other centers in Tuscany. In Arezzo he ordered the demolition of the Palazzo del Comune and the Palazzo del Popolo from the medieval period. In 1572 he commissioned Vasari to reorganize the piazza, making it the true political center of the city. After Vasari's death in 1574, the construction was completed by Alfonso Parigi in approximately 1595.

The project takes on rhythm in the lower part thanks to a sequence of 20 arches, each with a height of 8.60 meters at the crown, repeated every 6.5 meters and topped by an initial order of windows and a mezzanine. The space of the portico—with a depth of 7 meters—is covered by cross vaults alternating with crosswise arches, below which workshops and venues open out, in keeping with the original purposing and conserving the old abutment form at the entrance with a central opening for passage.

The compact, regular, and symmetrical design of the building meets with several exceptions in the relationship with the context: in one of the central spans, a flight of steps interrupts the sequence of shops on the ground floor and connects Piazza Grande with the Piazza del Praticino above; the pavement of the portico is perfectly horizontal, and bends at the extremities with stepped connections to the bordering streets; finally, the northeastern side of the Palazzo terminates with a raised walkway supported by an arch, which acts as a pedestrian connection to the building in front, ideally concluding the perspective of the Palazzo, inserting the new project in the surrounding urban fabric.

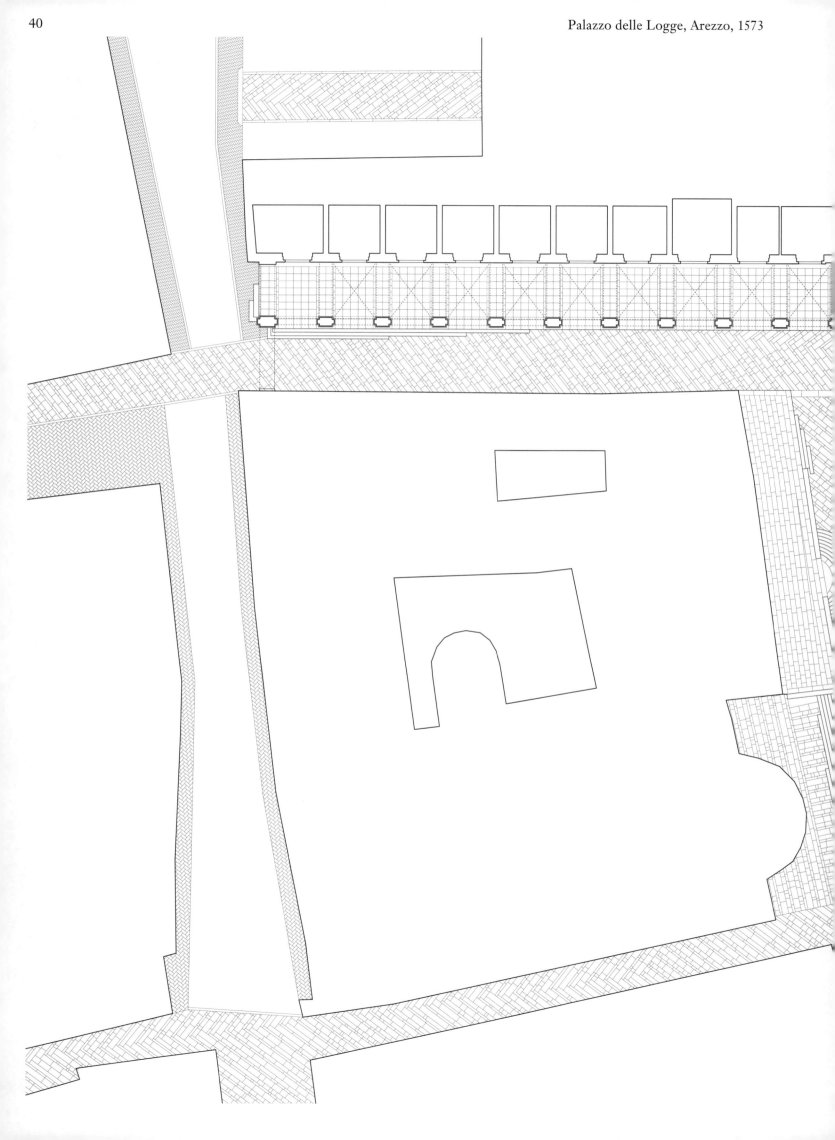

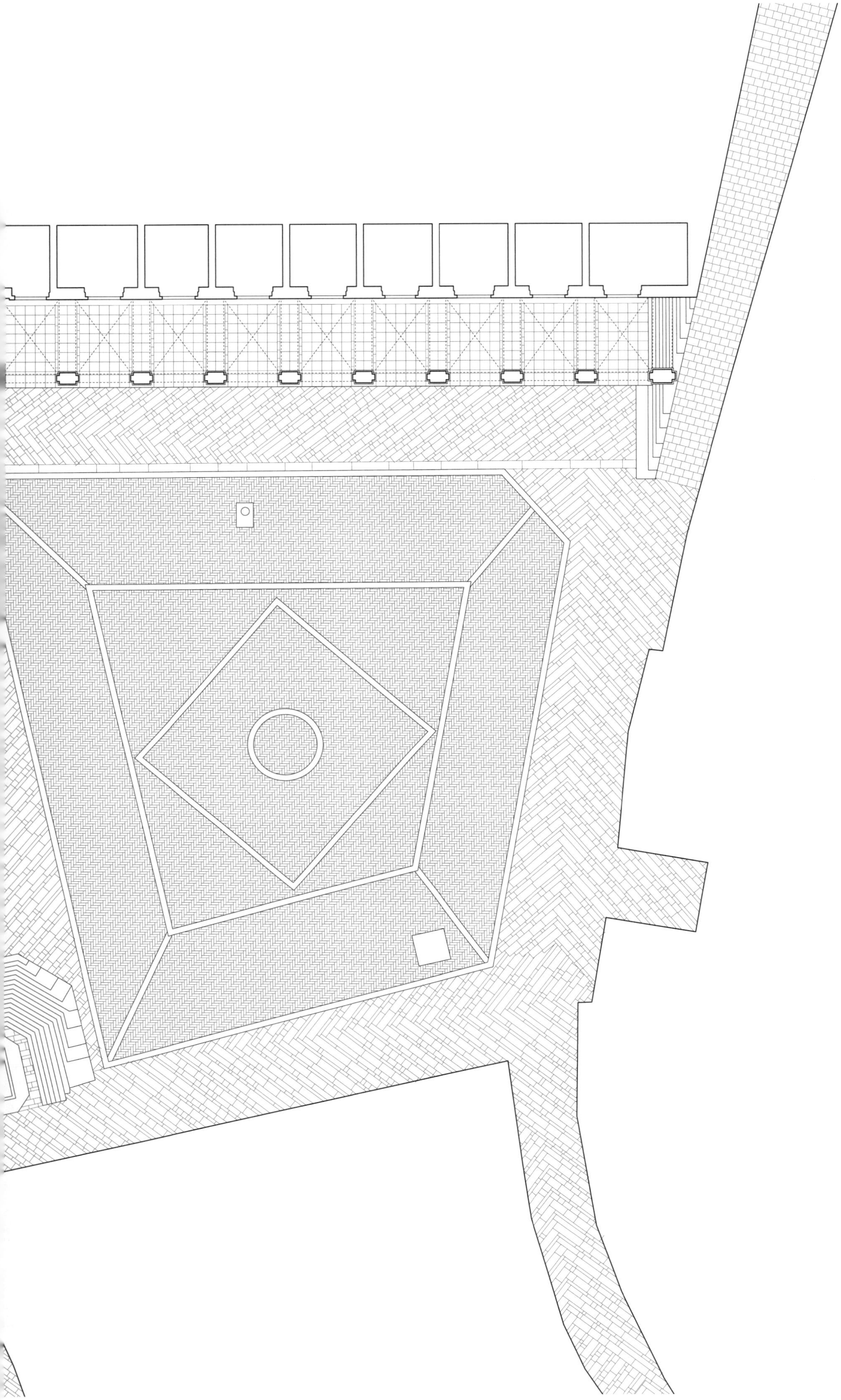

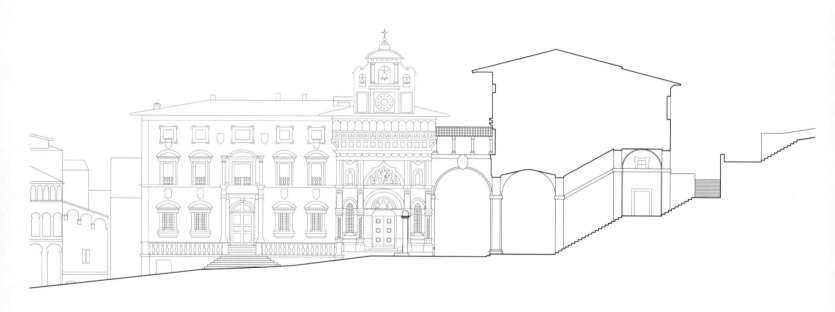

1:400

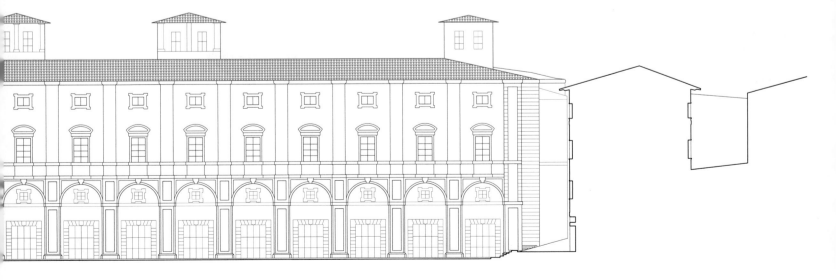

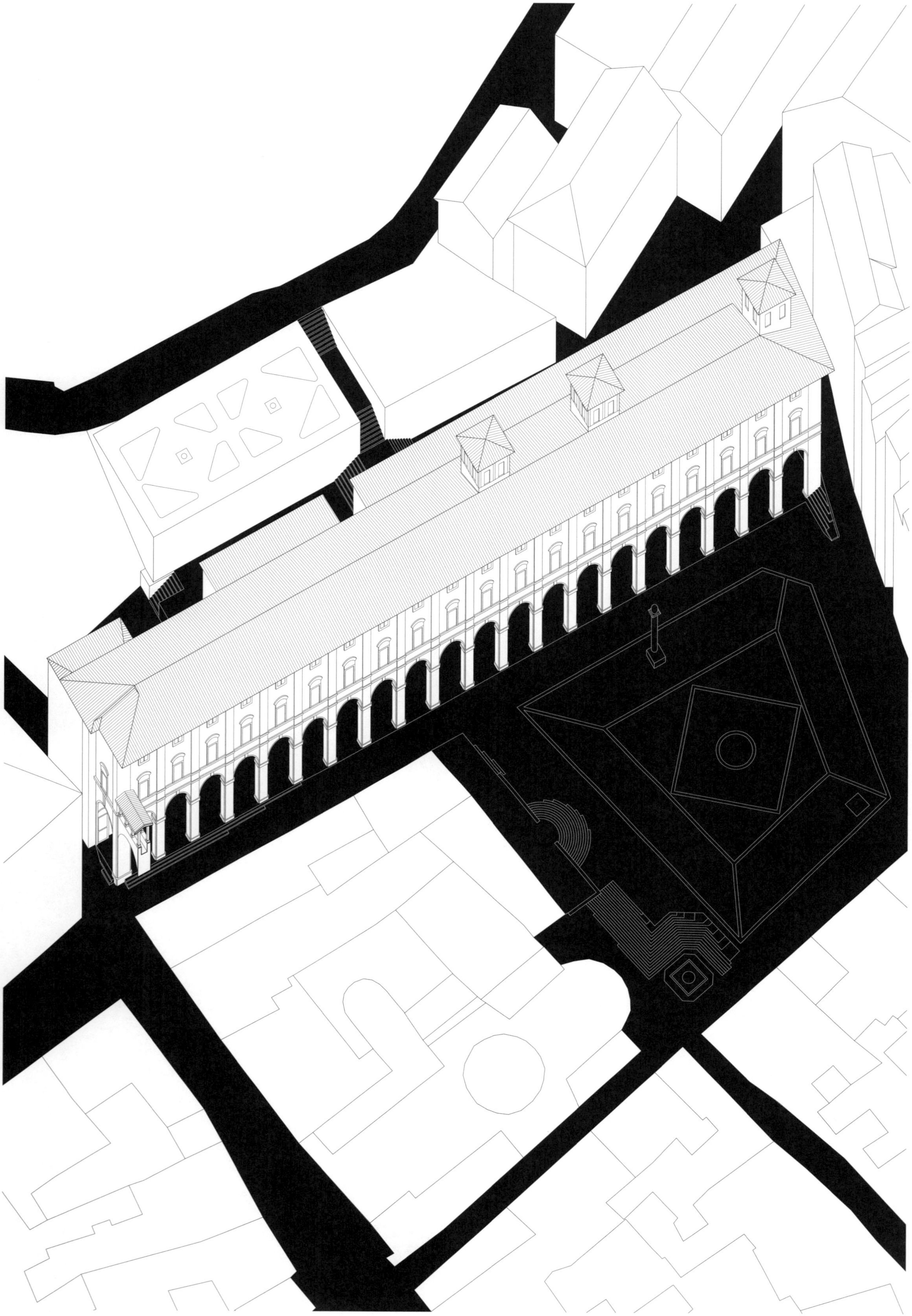

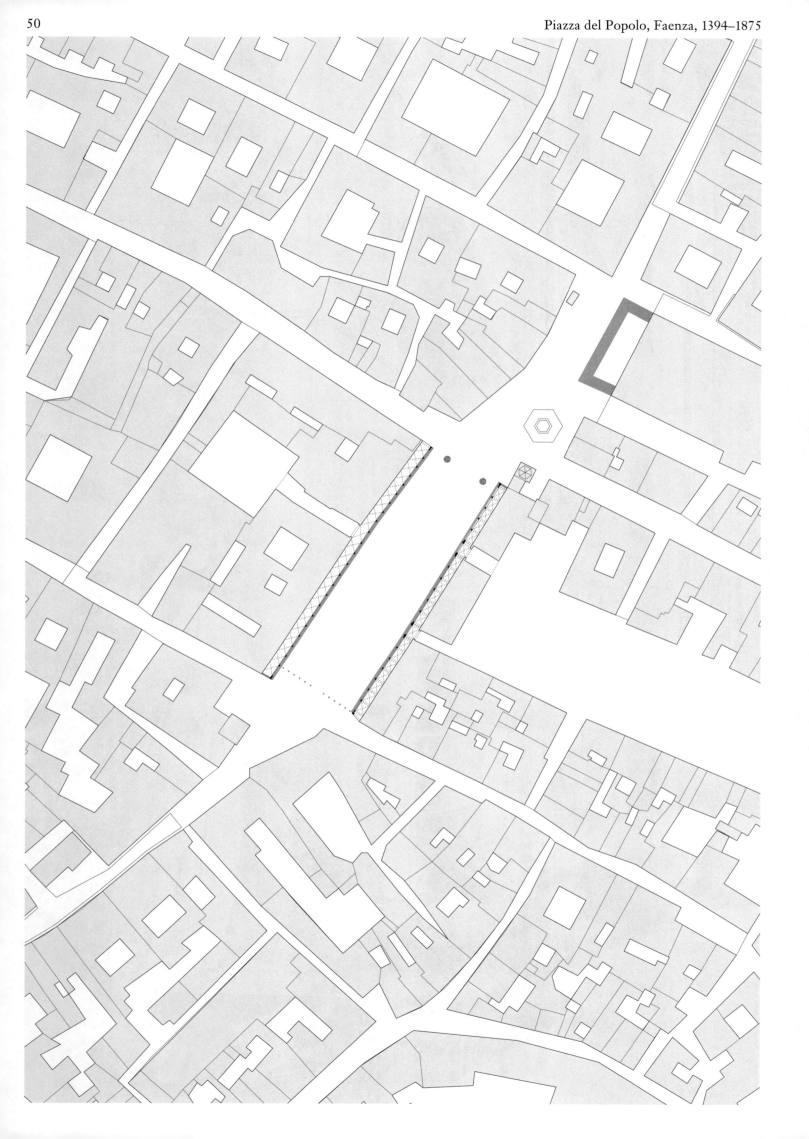

Piazza del Popolo, Faenza, 1394–1875   50–61

Piazza del Popolo is the most important and significant location in the city of Faenza, in terms of administrative functions and civic symbolism.

The piazza is a rectangular space bordered on the long sides by a system of porticos with upper loggias in neoclassical style. Added to the buildings behind them to grant dignity and importance to the urban space, the two porticos are similar in their forms, but very different in the backgrounds that led to their construction. It is interesting to note that the creation of the piazza in its present guise was not the result of a single intervention, but of a process of transformation that lasted over 300 years, across different municipal administrations and governments, though always reflecting the same ideal of the formulation of a symbolic place to enhance the image of the city.

The piazza is of age-old origin, but its present appearance is very different from that of 1394, when a wooden portico of seven spans on a single level made its appearance, also known as the Portico dei Sartori. The current arrangement is in fact the result of a long process of additions and replacements that began in 1470 with the transformation of the city into a *signoria* and the reconstruction, ordered by Carlo II Manfredi, of the portico facing the tower and placed against the current city hall, also known as the Loggiato del Comune; a loggia that in 1612 was extended along the entire side of the piazza and completely rebuilt in neoclassical style in 1859, with a design by Ignazio Bosi. The portico on the opposite side, known as the Loggiato del Podestà because it is placed against the Palazzo del Podestà (1177), was added—with the contribution of the shopkeepers— in 1760, with design by G.B. Campidori. It too was reconstructed in 1875 for structural concerns by the engineer Achille Ubaldini.

The last important modification of this loggia dates back to 1930, when for problems of stability the entire upper part was dismantled. At the time, a heated debate ensued between those who did not want the upper loggia to be reconstructed—permitting a view of the large windows of the Podestà—and those who wanted the columns to be put back in place, to conserve the visual unity of the piazza.

The two loggias seem similar but they actually have a number of differences. The Loggiato del Comune, rebuilt by Ignazio Bosi, presents some details that differ from the first one ordered by Carlo II, details which are still visible in the Loggia del Podestà: the double column at the position of the archways and the dado above the capital of the upper part of the loggia, both removed to add a more solemn air to the new project. There are also some differences in terms of cladding materials: the Loggiato del Comune has visible brick, while that of the Podestà is faced in stone.

The piazza measures about 106 × 30 meters, and features a pavement with a geometric motif in marble. The porticos rise 60 centimeters above the level of the piazza, and are supported by a system of columns with center-to-center distance of 4.5 meters. Behind both rows of arches a system of cross vaults reaches an overall height of about 6 meters, with respective depth of 4 meters in the Loggiato del Comune and 3 meters in that of the Podestà.

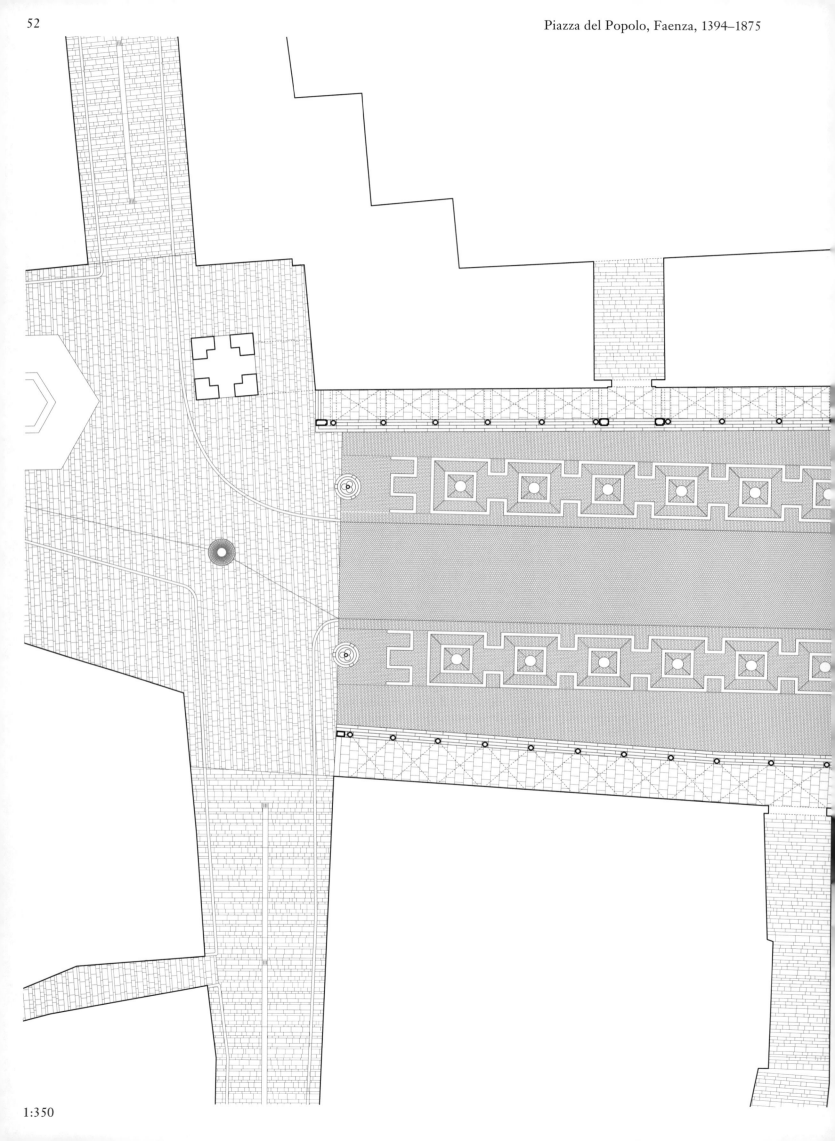

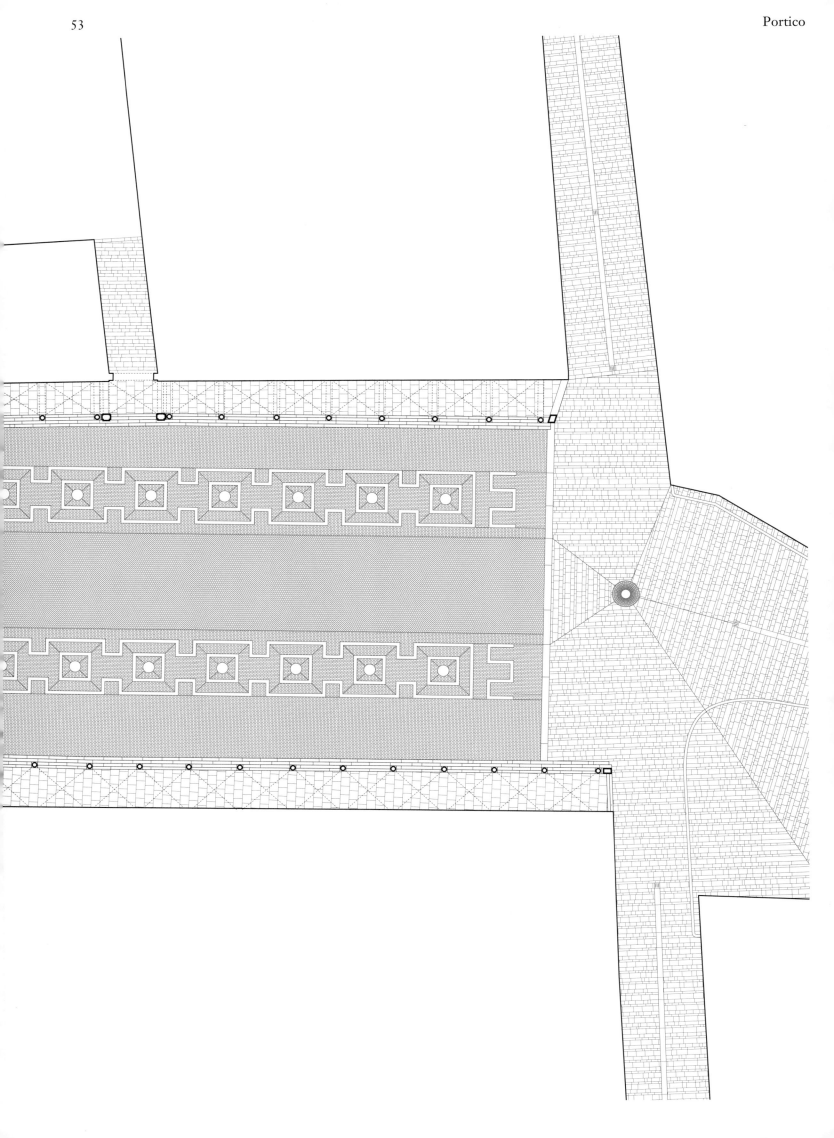

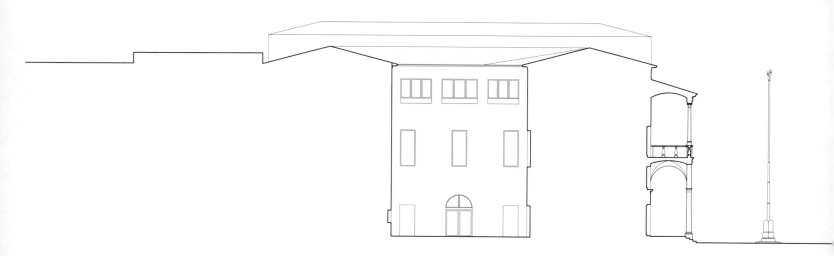

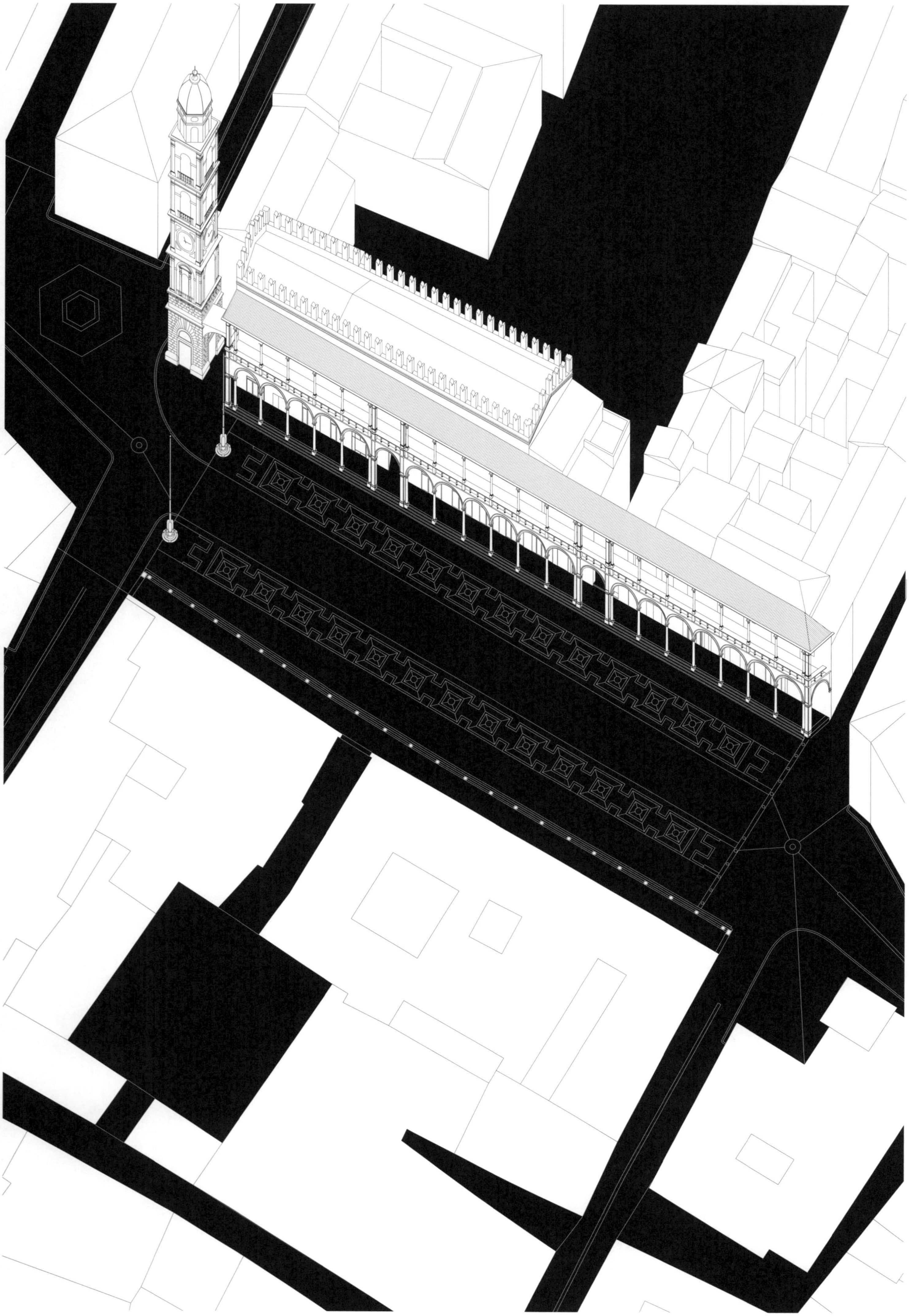

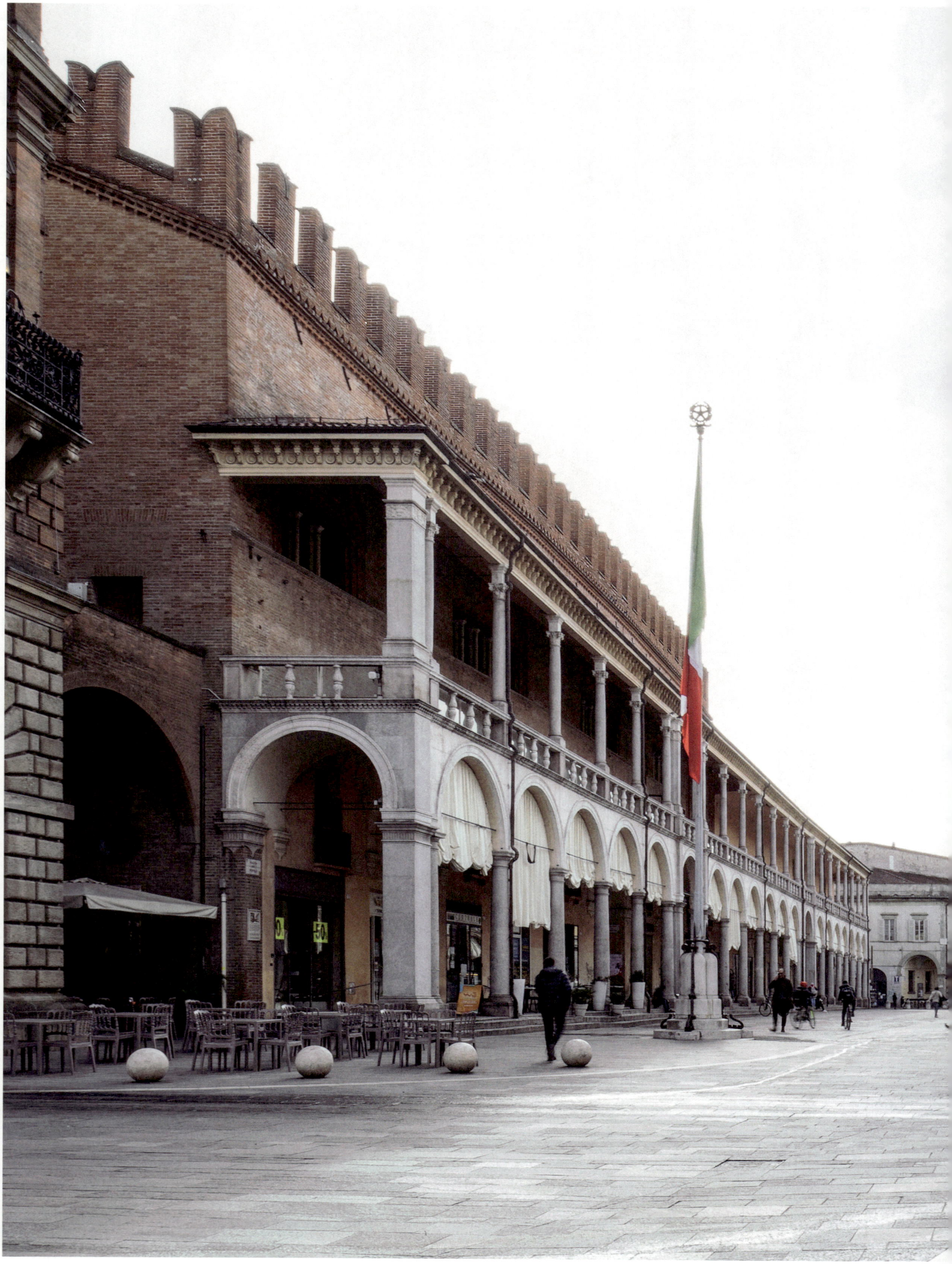

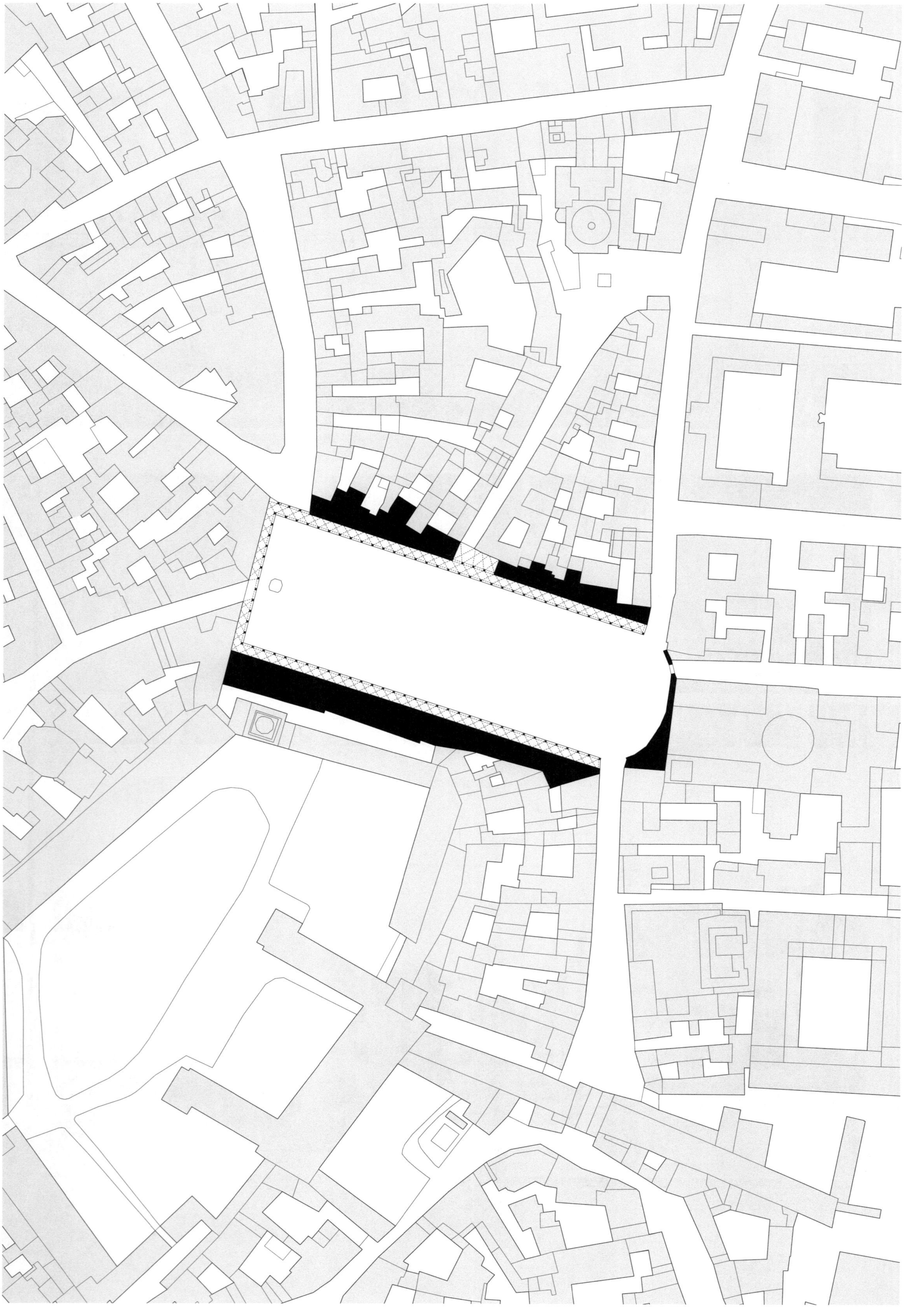

Piazza Ducale, Vigevano, 1492–1680   62–73

Commissioned by Lodovico il Moro starting in 1490, Piazza Ducale in Vigevano was envisioned as an antechamber and entrance court of the Visconti-Sforza Castle.

The piazza represents one of the first examples of unified architectural space built in coherence with Renaissance principles: there is a clear intention to counter the existing medieval urban fabric with the model of an abstract city based on rigorous tenets of geometry. The project, with its forceful humanistic character, was conceived as an "urban room." It is in fact a Renaissance interpretation of the type of the forum, with reference to a literary culture ranging from *De Architectura* by Vitruvius to the 15th-century treatises of Alberti and Filarete.

It can be supposed that the general idea of the piazza developed at the court of Ludovico il Moro in the discussions and suggestions of Bramante, while the construction was carried out by local craftsmen under the direction, according to a document from 1492, of the ducal engineer Ambrogio de Curtis.

The piazza was built by demolishing part of the medieval fabric to the south, where the castle stands, while reutilizing the buildings to the north and west, though aligning them thanks to the reconstruction of the façades. The Sforza-era project had the south side interrupted at the position of the tower by a large ramp connecting the piazza to the castle; the western and northern sides of the piazza were also interrupted in relation to intersections or the positions of streets entering the space.

The present configuration is the result of the project of 1680, ordered by the bishop Juan Caramuel y Lobkowitz, thanks to which the missing portion of the southern side was completed, where a flight of steps was inserted to replace the access ramp of the castle. Above all, the new façade of the cathedral was built: a concave façade, placed against the church like a theatrical wing, is on axis with the piazza rather than with the church that embraces and accommodates the facing space, reversing the original piazza-castle relationship and transforming the piazza into a churchyard.

The piazza has a length of about 135 meters and a width of 49 meters, and is defined on three sides by the homogeneous structure of the porticos, composed of a sequence of 84 columns with capitals of different types, and 85 round arches covered by groin vaults. The vaults are interrupted at the position of Via del Popolo, where for the space of two arches the wall frontage is free and the windows are painted. The depth of the porticoed space is 3.5 meters, matching the center-to-center distance between the two columns, while the keystones are at a height of 4.6 meters.

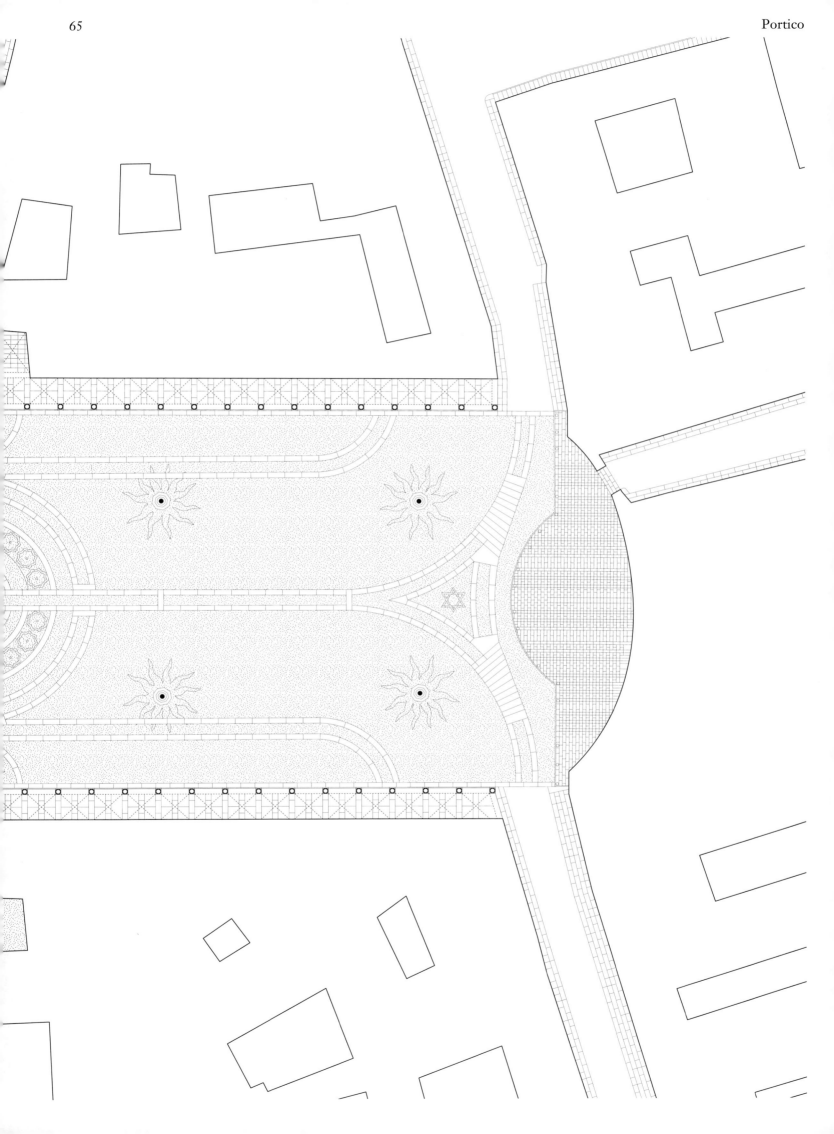

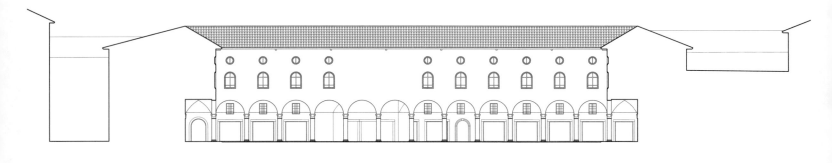

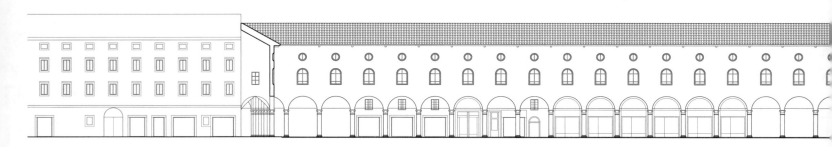

1:400

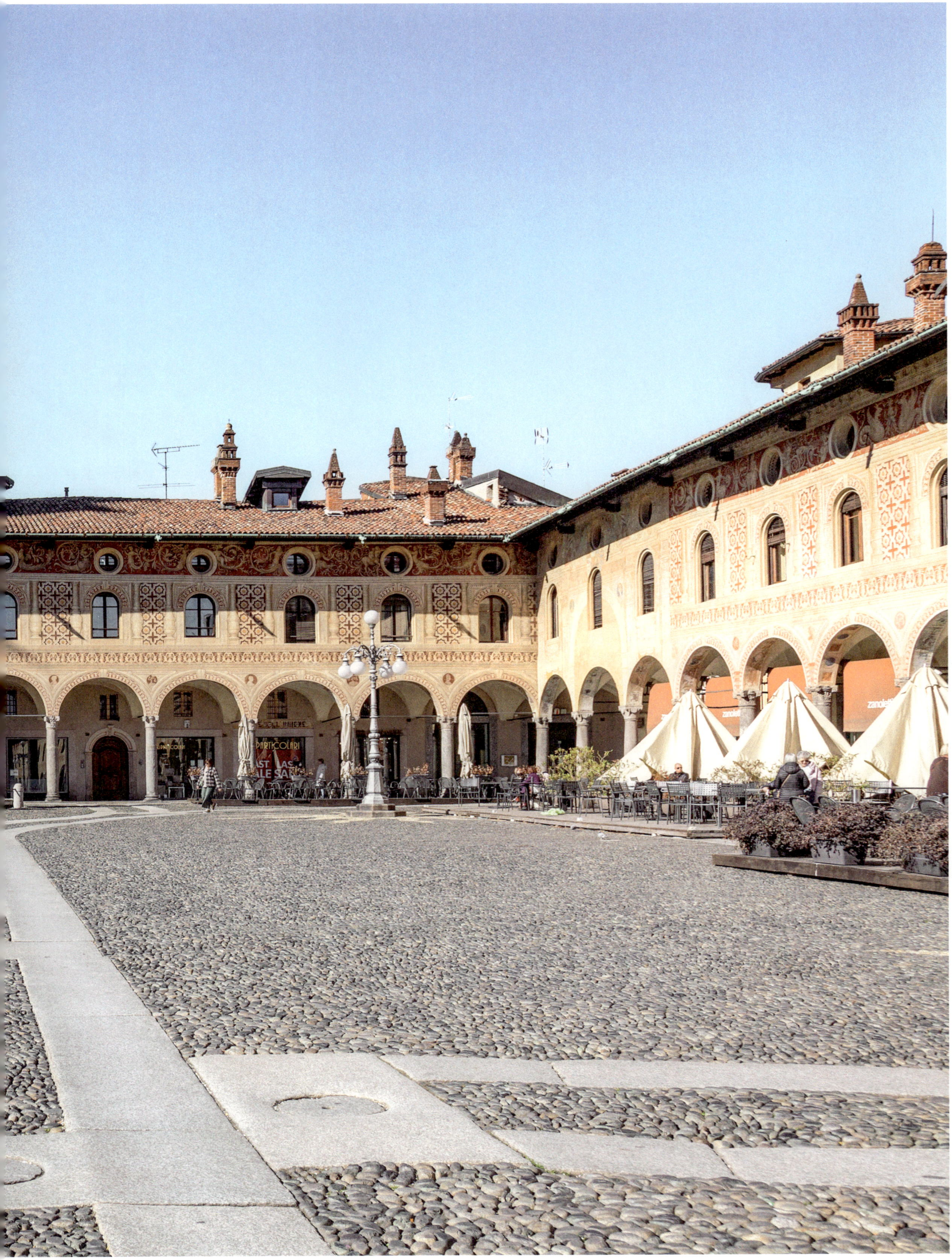

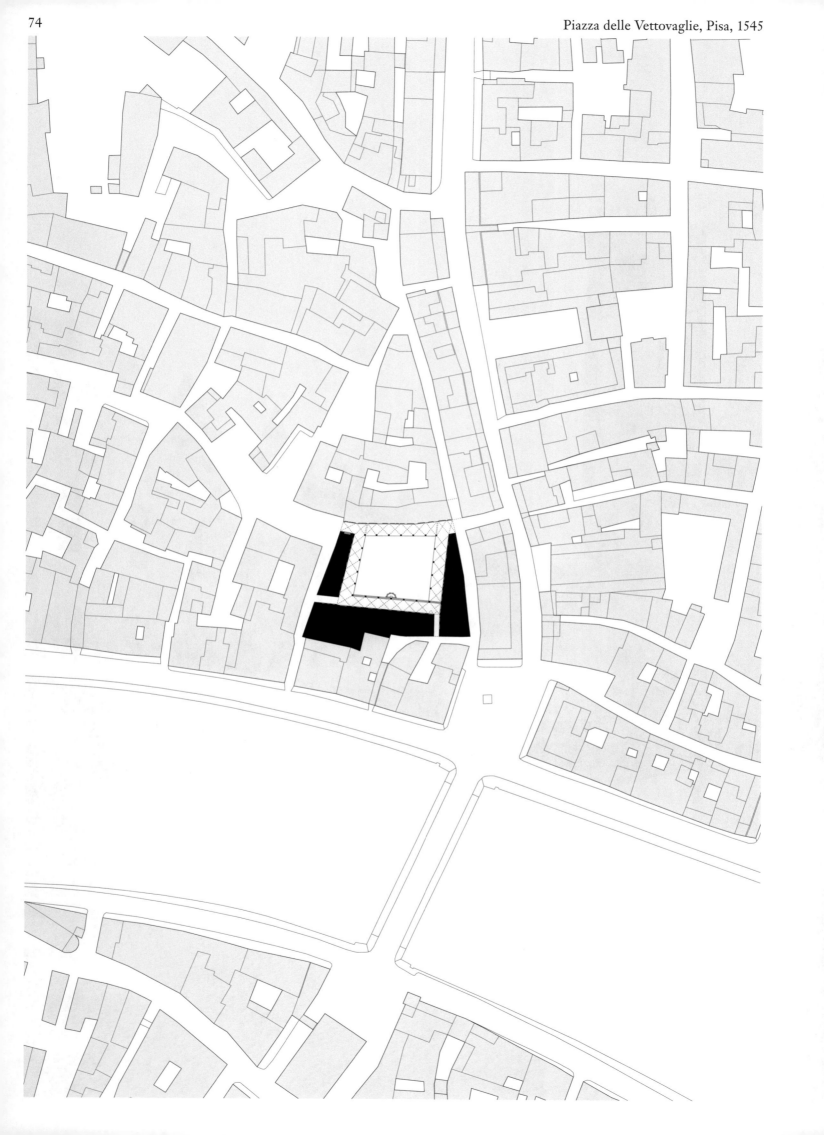

Piazza delle Vettovaglie, Pisa 1545   74–85

Referred to in the past as Piazza dei Porci or Piazza del Grano as it was the traditional location of the city's market, Piazza delle Vettovaglie took on its present name in 1771. These various names (meaning the square of "pigs," "grain" or "provisions") were derived from the site's function since the Middle Ages.

Constructed for commercial activities, the architectural structure of reference is clearly the 15th-century model of the monastic cloister, namely a place with a central character in functional and spatial terms, a gathering place. Though it has undergone many alterations and refurbishments over the centuries, Piazza delle Vettovaglie has never changed its original function and is still a market for traveling vendors of fruit and vegetables.

The unified character of the piazza is the result of a 16th-century project ordered by the Opera del Duomo (cathedral works commission), which starting in 1494 began to acquire some of the buildings existing in the zone, in the context of a series of urban renewal initiatives in the city. The start of the work, based on the first project designed by the Pisan architect Giovanni di Mariano, was postponed due to financial difficulties, and it was not until the rule of Cosimo I—from 1537 to 1574—that the project could be completed, with a design entrusted to Duccio and Matteo da Ponte a Signa and Stagio Stagi. The intervention called for extensive demolition and reconstruction of a portion of the medieval city to give form to the new market, composed of a double portico of columns of which only the ground floor remains visible.

At ground level the space is bordered by monolithic columns in *pietra serena* that support groin vaults in brick with stucco finish, while the upper level originally contained a loggia with slender columns to support the wooden framework of the roof. The ground floor was set aside for shops selling meat and grain, while the upper floor provided lodgings for the merchants. The architectural structure has an arrangement of six spans by five, for a total area of about 33 × 36 meters. Sustained by monolithic columns with Ionic capitals (often bearing a small shield with the seals of the Opera del Duomo or the Pisan coat of arms), the segmental groin vaults form a unified front with wide arches, about 4.75 meters in height, with spacing varying from 4.6 to 5.3 meters. On the four sides of the courtyard, over the arches, stand buildings of different forms and heights that take the place or the original second loggia order, from which vestiges remain of some small columns in sandstone, embedded in the masonry. The infill of the upper order took place in the 19th century, with the objective of transforming the balcony into residences, a choice that led to structural problems due to the excessive weight placed on the slender columns.

The structure, perfectly inserted in the surrounding medieval fabric, communicates with the neighboring streets through four vaulted passages.

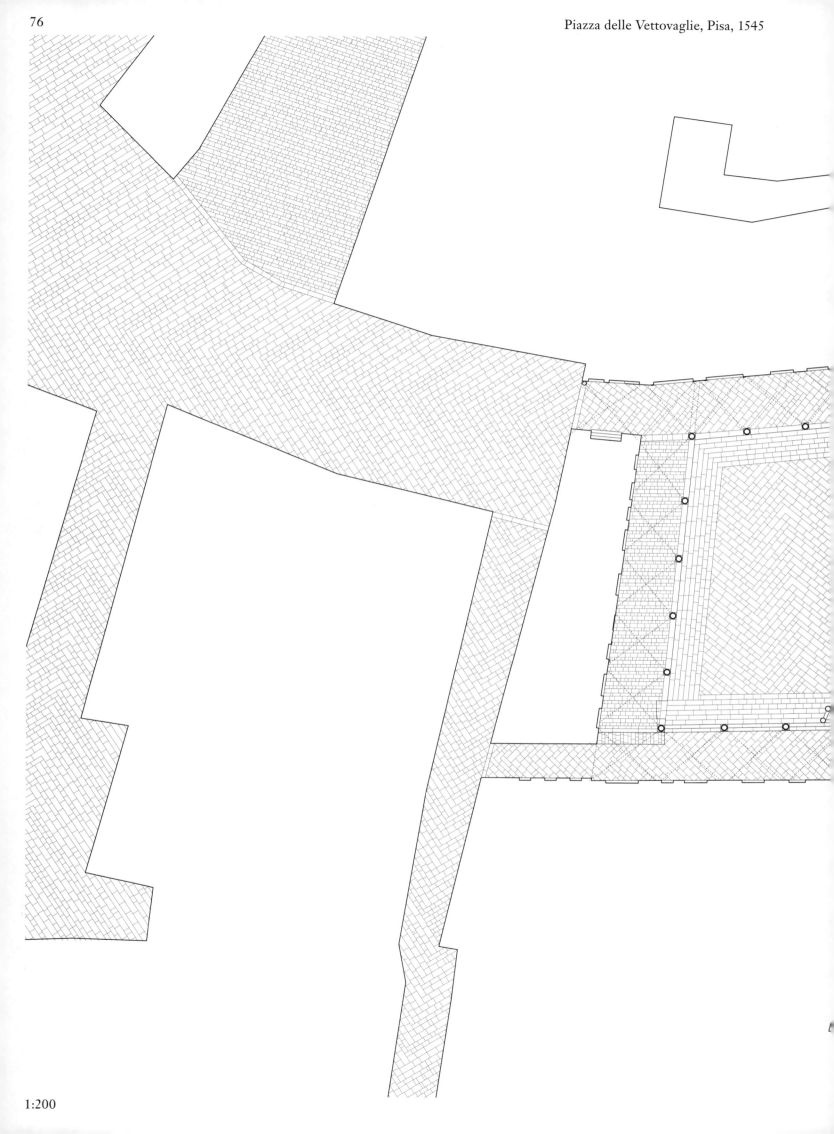

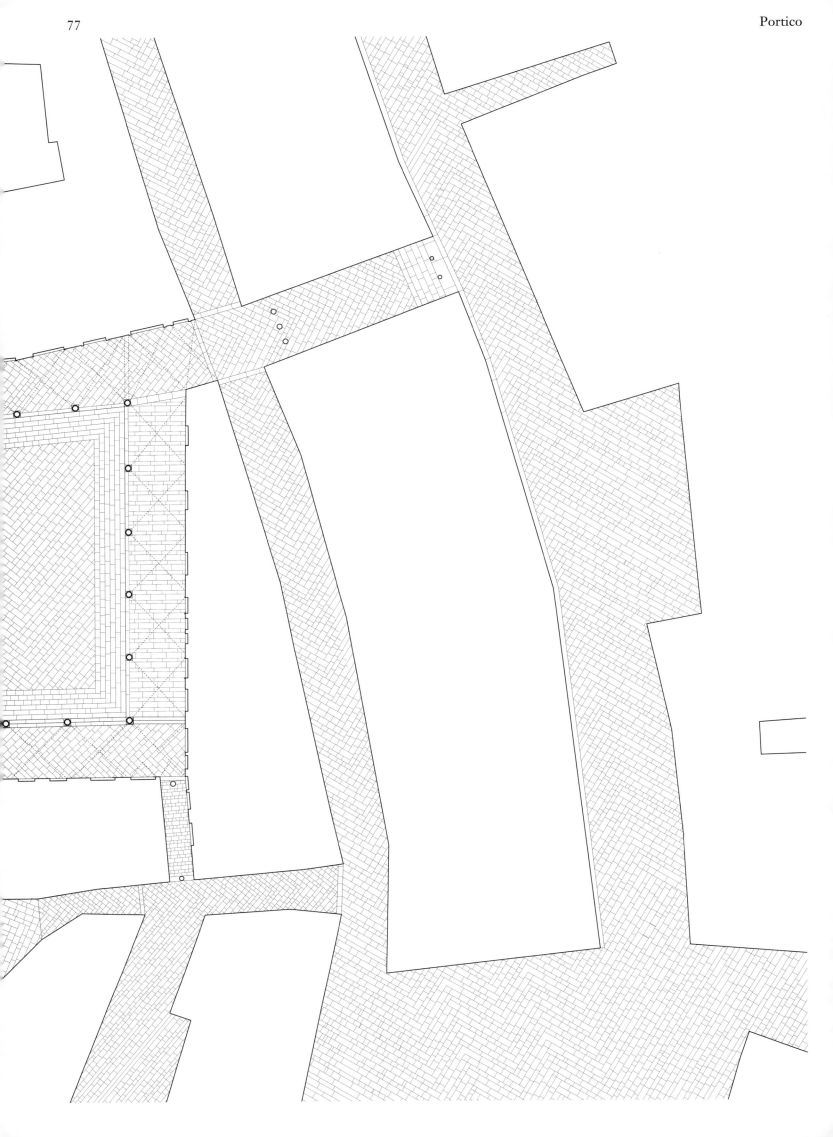

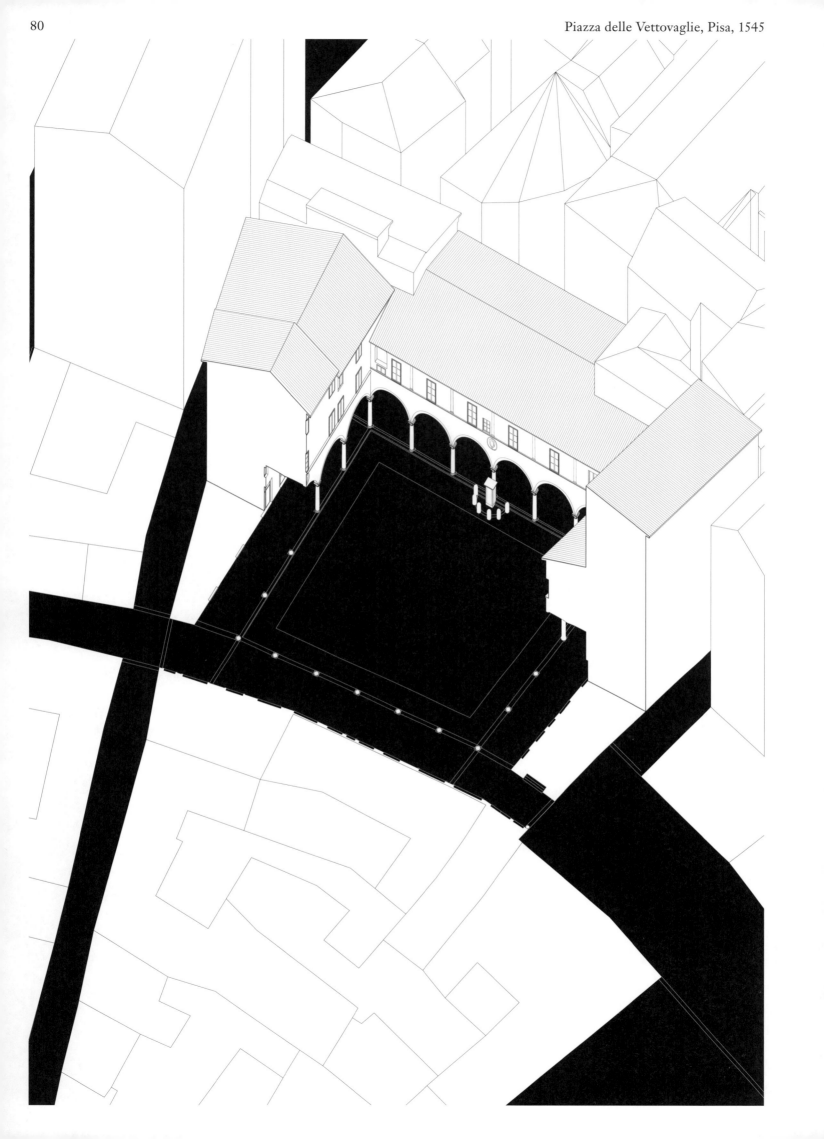

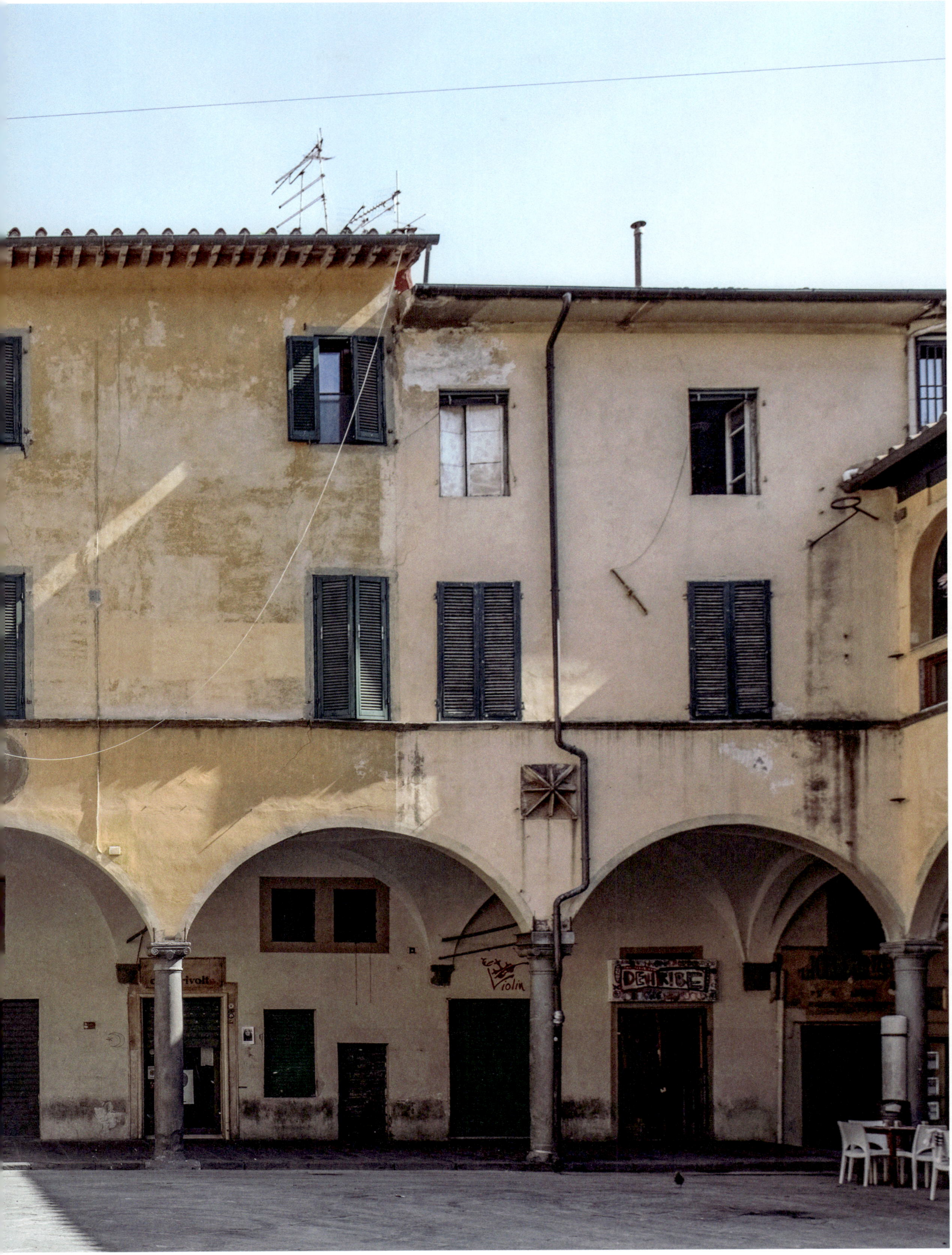

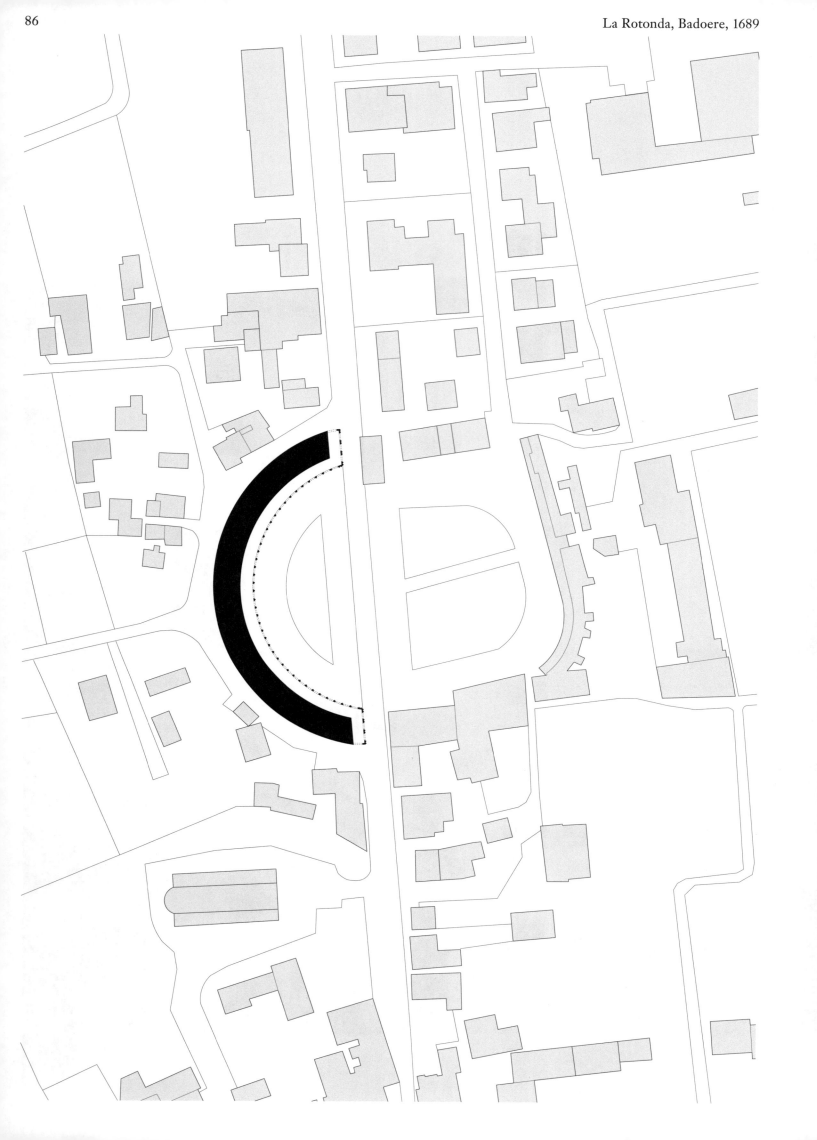

La Rotonda, Badoere, 1689   86–97

Commissioned by the Badoer family, a wealthy Venetian clan with vast land holdings in the province of Treviso from 1336, the Rotonda was built in the second half of the 17th century, based on a design probably by the school of Massari.

The architectural structure can be traced back to the *barchesse*, the rural service buildings typical of the architecture of the Venetian villa, set aside to contain workspaces. Usually having a portico structure with high round arches, with Palladio the *barchesse* took on greater architectural dignity, to the point of becoming an integral part of the design of villas.

Nevertheless, the Rotonda of Badoere, unlike the traditional *barchesse*, was made to host commercial functions, and therefore from the outset it had a public purpose connected with the territory, while also demonstrating the role and importance of the family, which already in 1556 had commissioned Palladio to design Villa Badoer at Fratta Polesine.

The piazza of Badoere is composed of two large independent structures—one of them semicircular, to the west, the other mixtilinear, to the east. The Badoer family built the two structures and the small church (1645) dedicated to St. Anthony of Padua with the aim of hosting the weekly market on Mondays authorized by the Venetian Republic in 1689 to the nobleman Angelo

Badoer. The market had become necessary due to increased agricultural and livestock breeding activities in the territory; in this sense, the structures differ from traditional *barchesse* because they are not closely tied in functional terms to the main family estate nearby—about 300 meters away—which was destroyed in 1920.

The plan of the western Rotonda has a semicircular form with a diameter of 120 meters; the portico, with a depth of four meters, is composed of 41 round arches, corresponding to the same number of vending stalls organized at ground level. Each arch is supported by pillars placed at a distance of 3.40 meters center to center. The arches measure 2.56 meters in diameter, while the keystones are at a height of 3 meters. The design called for each space to have an entrance from the Rotonda and a balcony opening upward with a showcase function. Under each arch of the western barchessa there was the shop of a craftsman or a merchant, while the more spartan eastern barchessa bordered the space of the market proper. The ceiling of the porticos is flat, with a single framework of wooden beams.

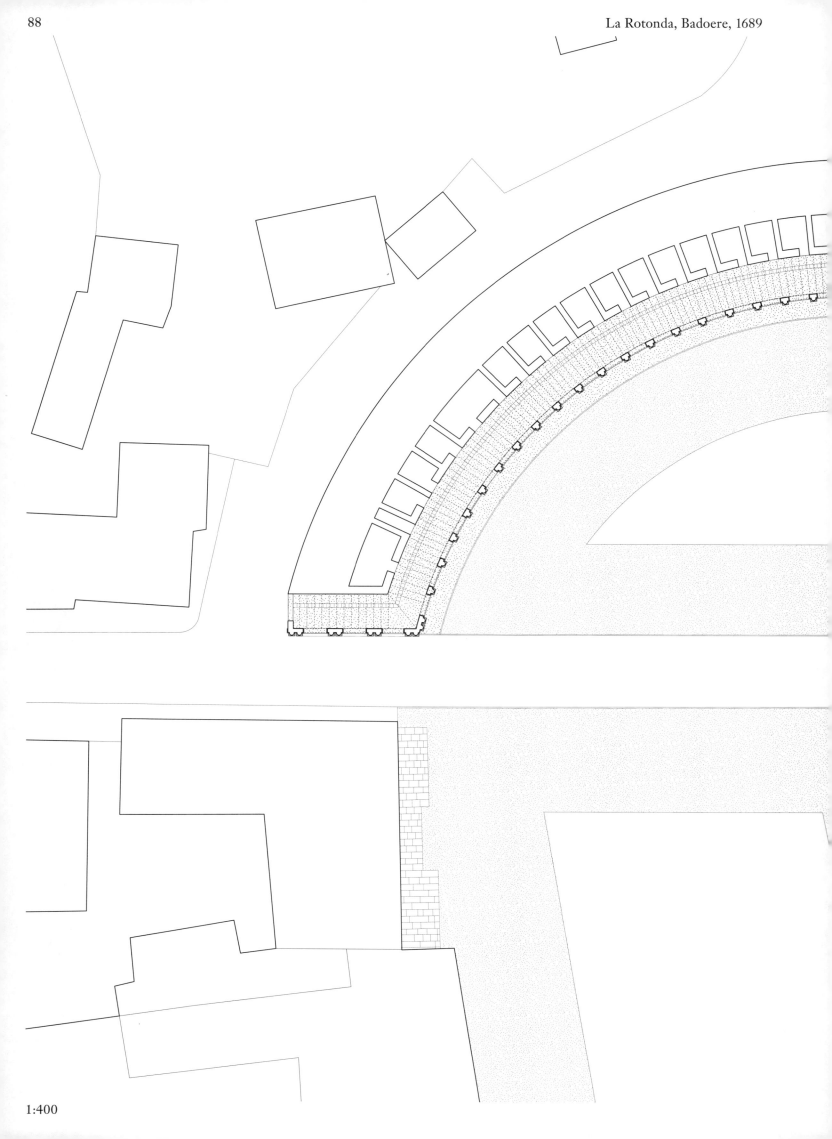

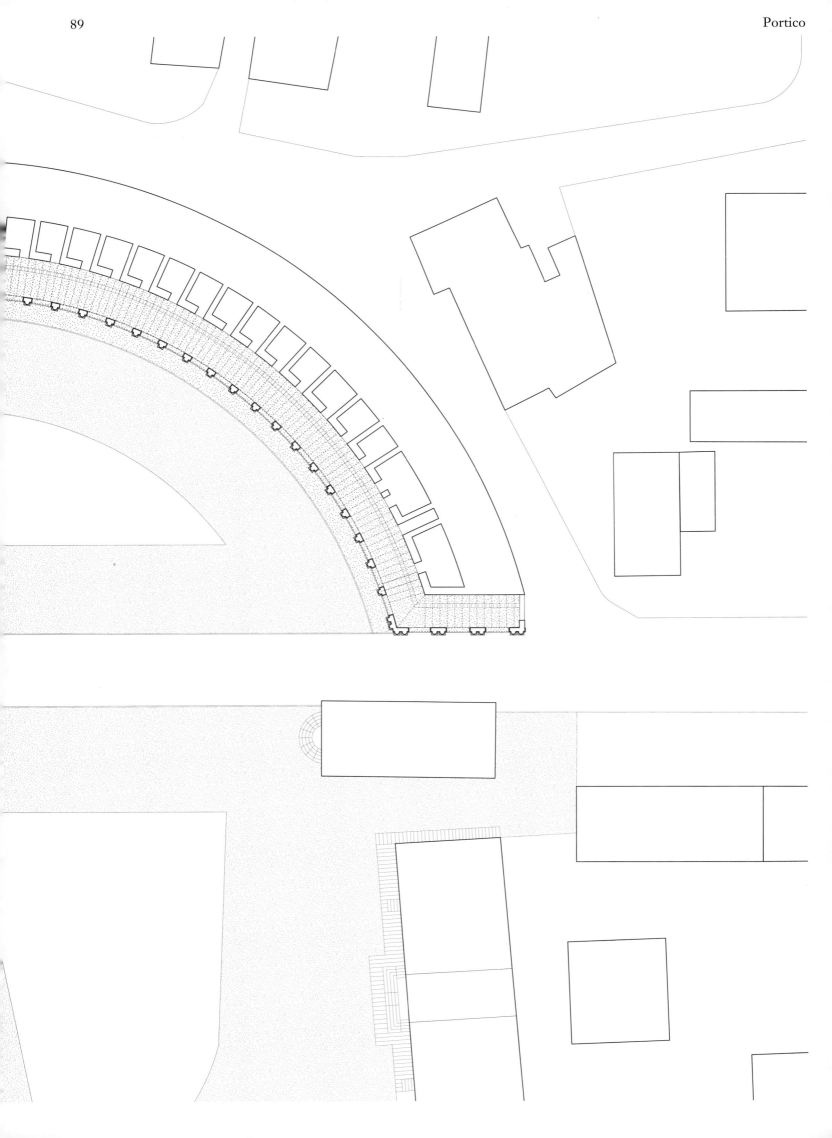

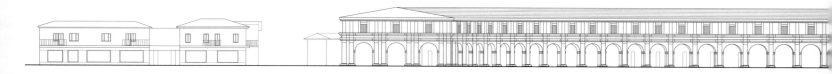

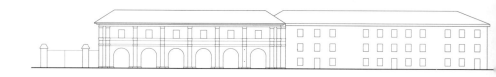

1:400

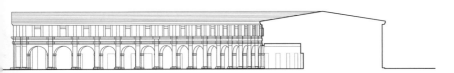

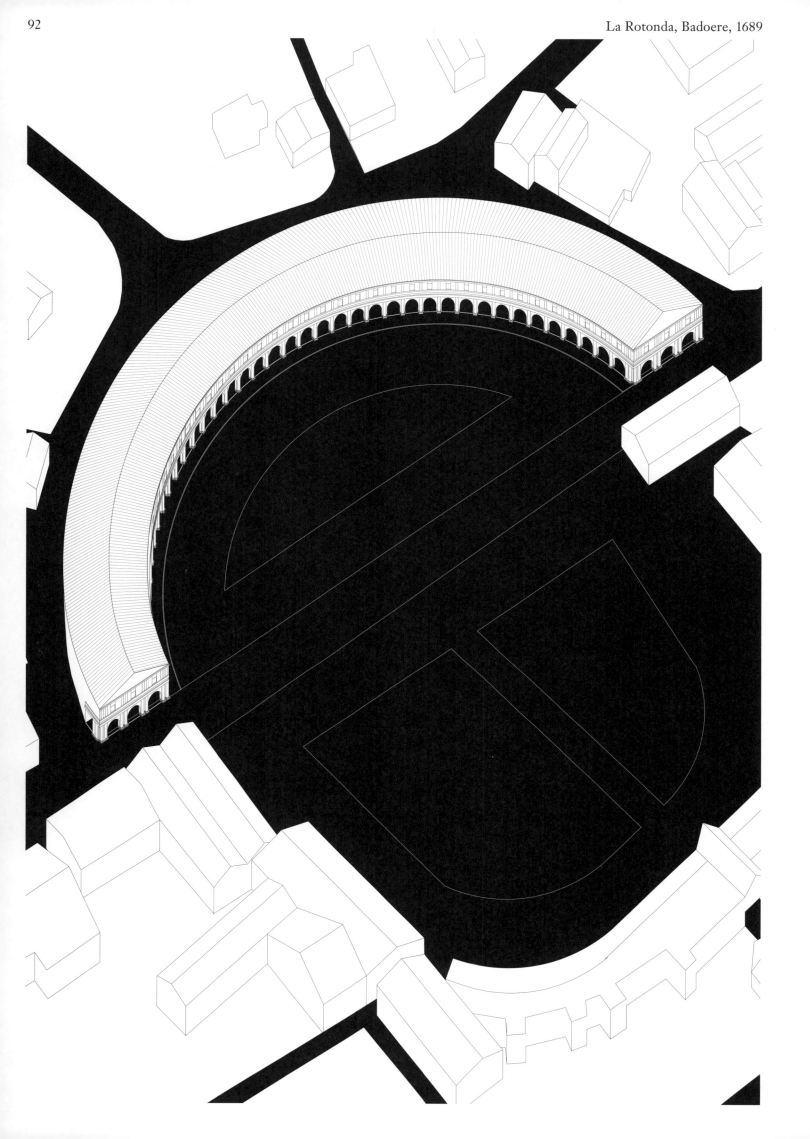

An architectural organism open on one or more sides, supported by pillars or columns, created to contain activities of a public nature: gatherings of citizens, administrative assemblies, mercantile activities.
In other words, when an architectural device forms a protected public space open to different uses and interpretations.

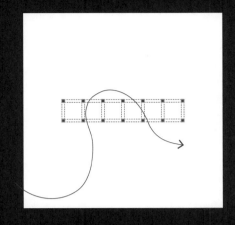

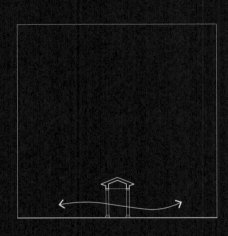

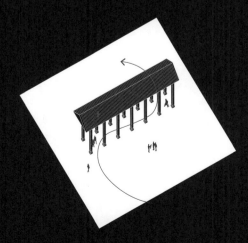

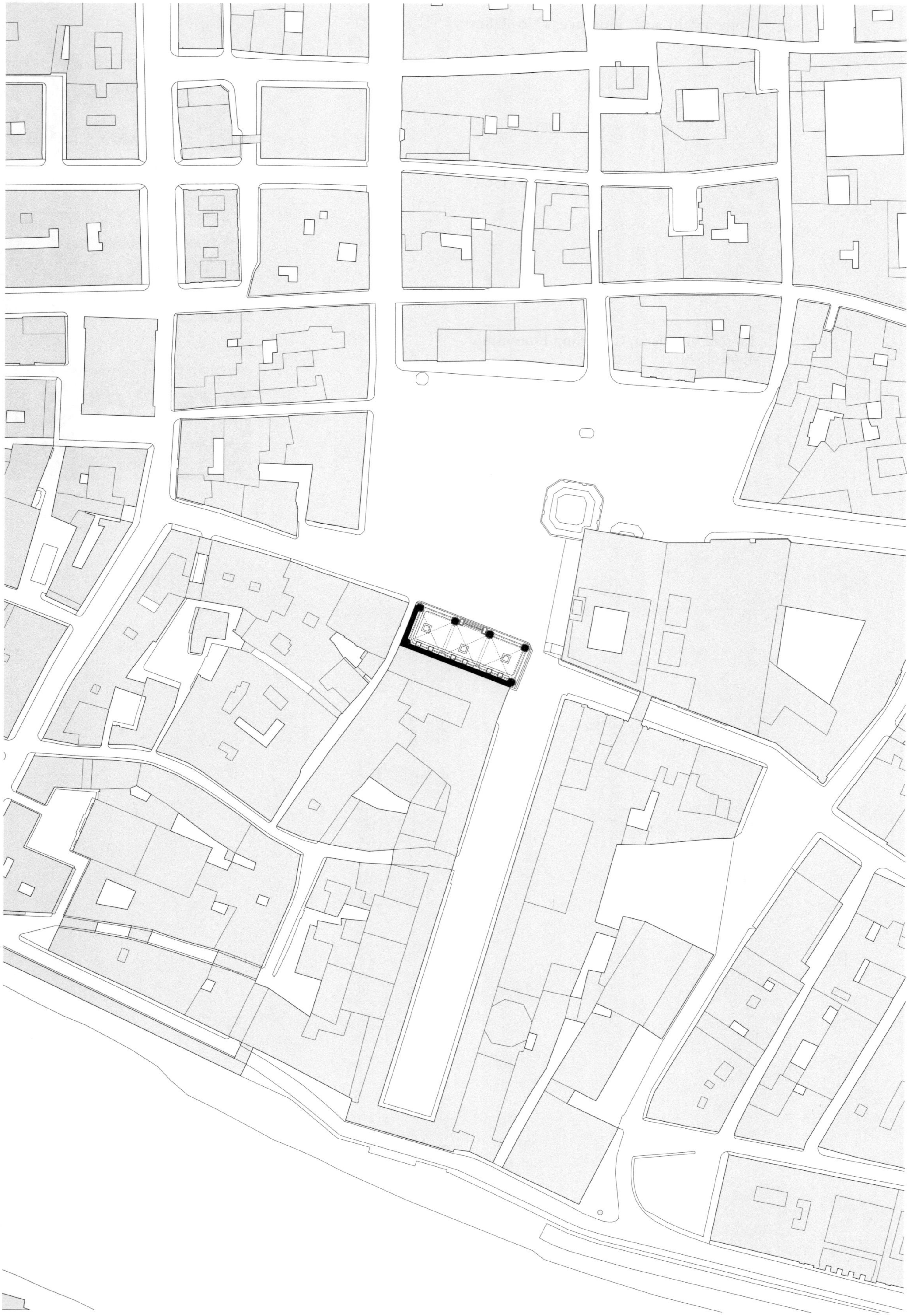

Loggia dei Lanzi, Florence, 1376–1382   102–113

Commissioned by the Florentine Republic in 1350 as a place for public assemblies and ceremonies, Loggia dei Lanzi was built from 1376 to 1382 on Piazza della Signoria in Florence. Later, by order of the Medici, it was utilized to display a remarkable collection of sculptures.

The architectural structure is based on the model of the medieval loggia, a typology developed in the 11th and 12th centuries, during the passage from a feudal society to the Communal period, to host gatherings of citizens or business activities. The scale and proportions of the space and its position at the entrance of the Uffizi have made it a monumental and highly symbolic presence for the city of Florence over the years.

Its construction began in 1376, under the supervision of Benci di Cione and Simone Talenti. Various interpretations exist regarding the name Loggia dei Lanzi: it could refer to the fact that the Grand Duke Cosimo I's guards, the German mercenary pikemen known as *landsknechts* (*Lanzichenecchi*, in Italian), were housed there, or it might be derived from the term for lances (*lanze*).

With the fall of the Republic in 1532 and its transformation into the Duchy of the Medici—within the Grand Duchy of Tuscany—the original function of the loggia was revised. The Medici did not use the place to involve the townspeople in choices regarding the city, and the republican institutions were definitively suppressed. Given the monumental size of the loggia and its crucial location on Piazza della Signoria, Cosimo I made it into a sculpture gallery, one of the first exhibition spaces in the world. The choice of the sculptures and their arrangement in the space was not based on purely aesthetic criteria, but also on clear intentions of a political character. In 1583 Bernardo Buontalenti, after the completion of the work on the Uffizi, created a terrace at the top of the loggia from which to watch ceremonies and performances.

Though it was built in the late Gothic period, Loggia dei Lanzi foreshadows several typical features of Renaissance architecture: it has a regular sequence of round arches, three on the long side for a total length of about 36 meters, and one on the short side for a depth of about 12 meters. The polygonal pillars support a system of three groin vaults whose keystones are at a height of 16 meters from the inner pavement of the loggia. This inner pavement is 1.2 meters higher than the level of the piazza. The polylobate panels resemble those utilized shortly thereafter in the Spedale degli Innocenti.

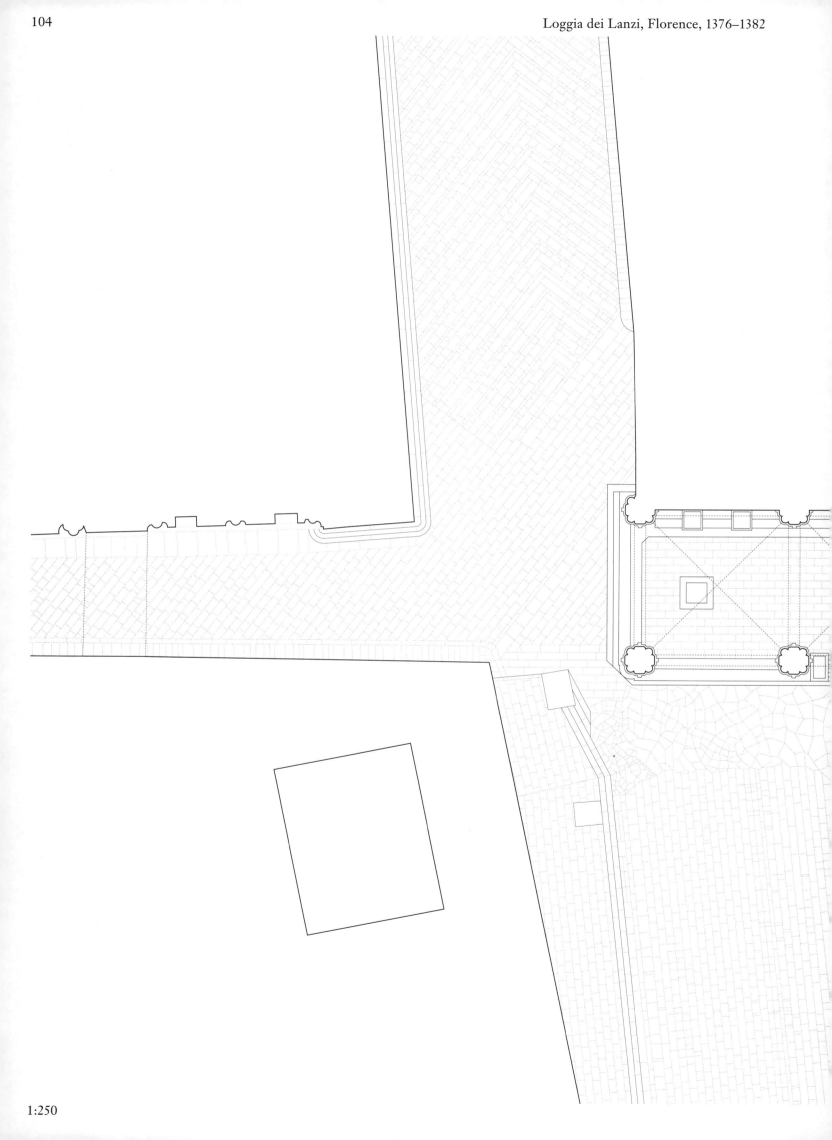

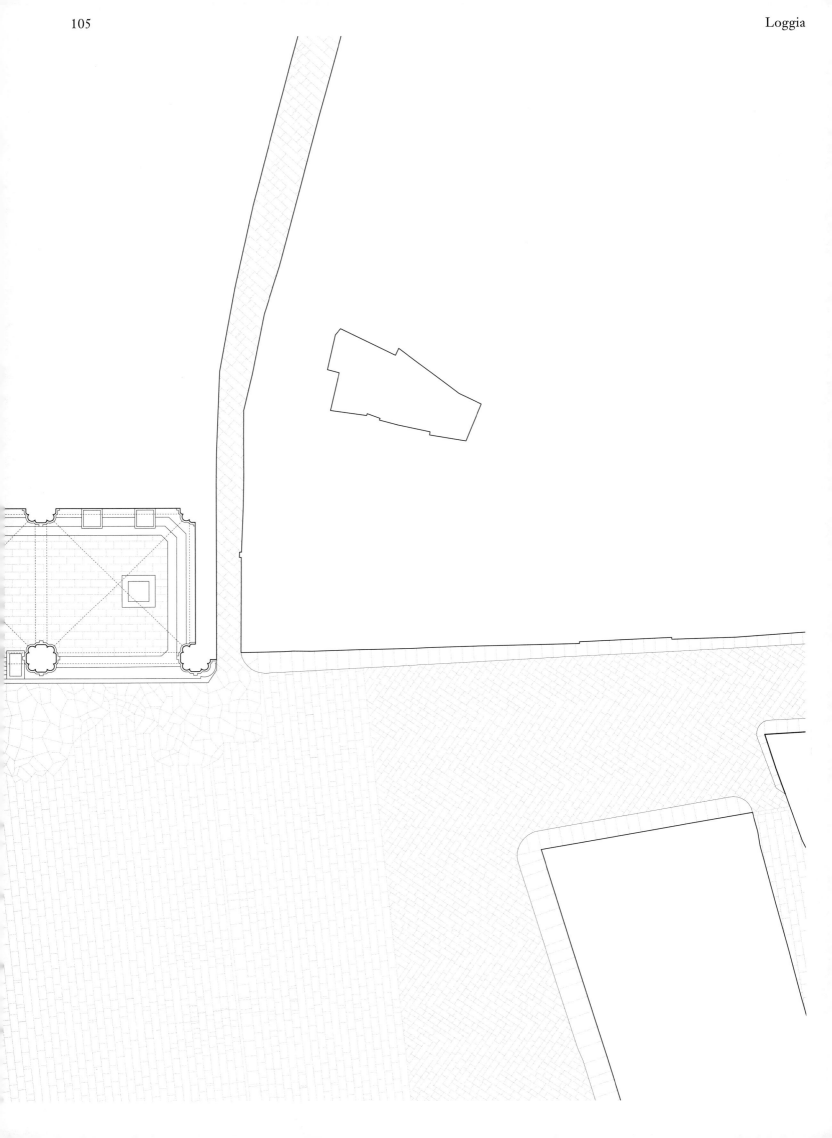

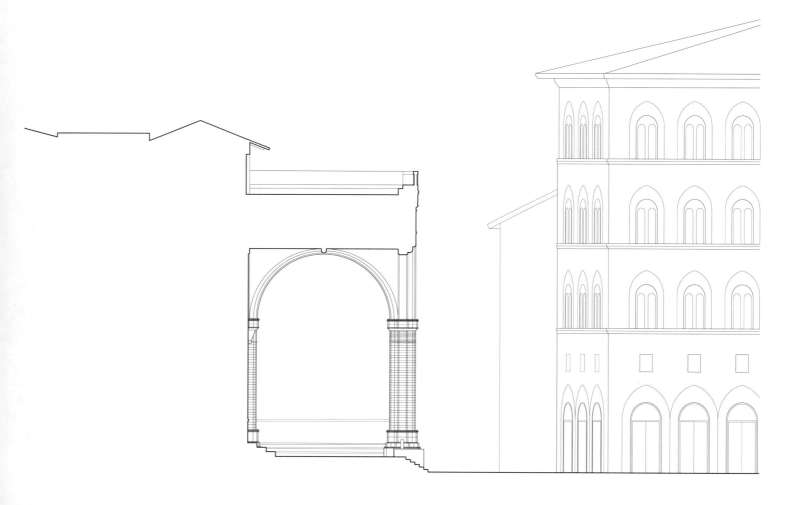

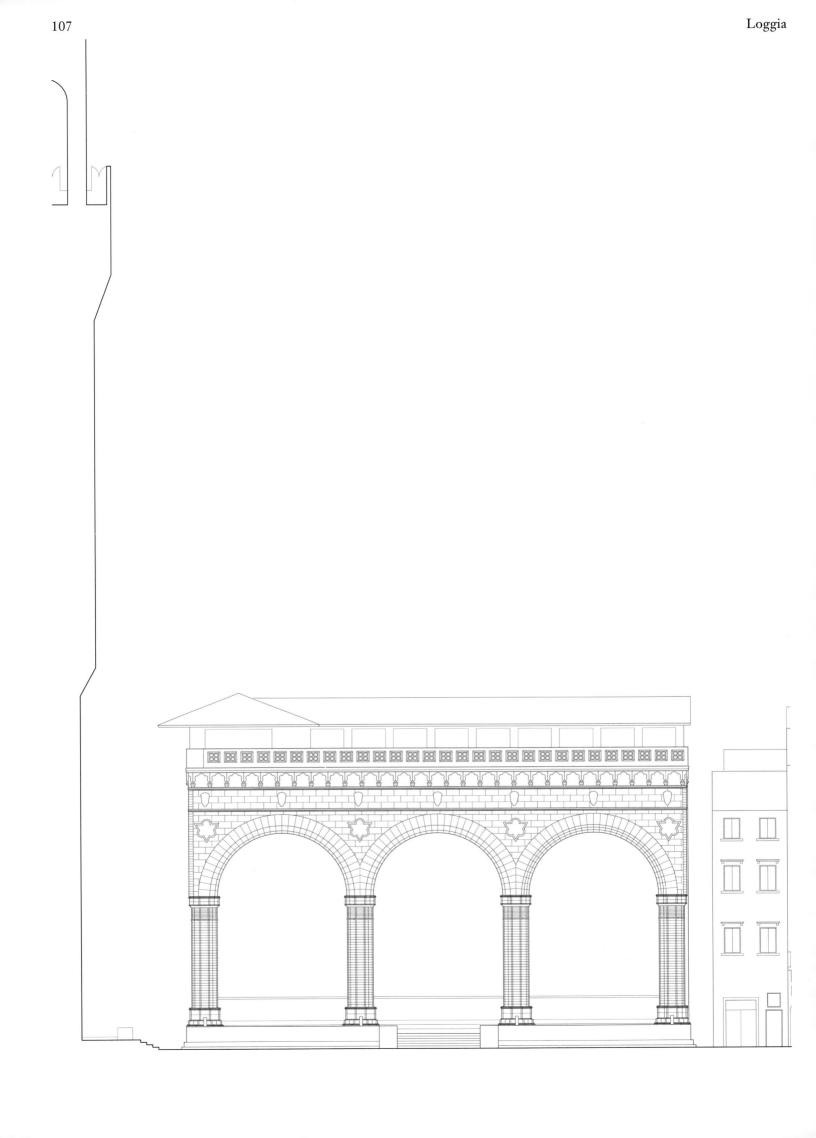

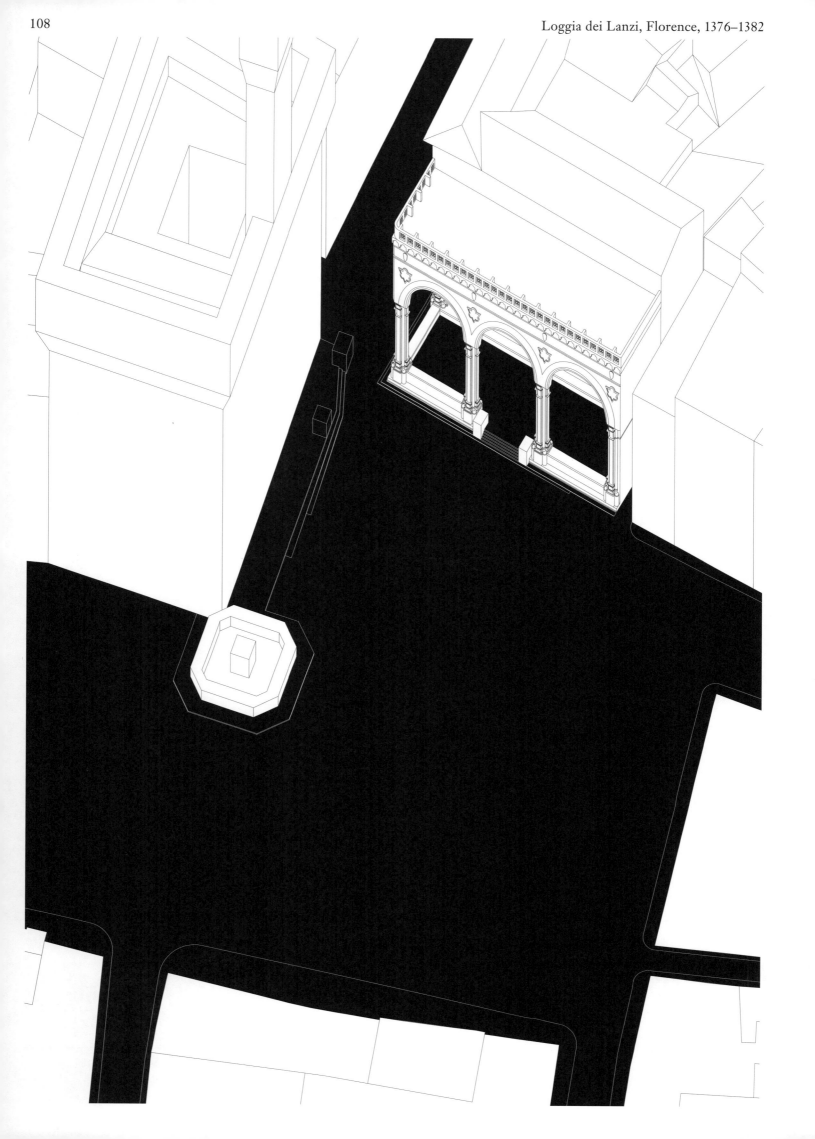

Loggia del Pesce, Florence, 1568–1569 114–125

Commissioned by Cosimo I, the Loggia del Pesce, based on a design by Giorgio Vasari, was built from August 1568 to September 1569 to shelter the fishmongers who had previously been located near Ponte Vecchio on the banks of the Arno.

The Loggia del Pesce is an emblematic case of an isolated loggia; it is a small structure designed and built for purposes of trade. The lightness of the structure, its oblong proportions and graceful appearance, make this loggia—a forerunner of modern canopies—a structure capable of acting as a gathering place for inhabitants of the city.

The Loggia del Pesce has had a troubled history: in 1699 the structure was expanded by one bay on each side by order of Cosimo III, an addition financed by the Magistrato della Grascia, which supervised the sale of victuals in Florence. In 1889, during the period of the so-called *risanamento* of Florence, the loggia was dismantled and moved from its original location, the former Piazza del Mercato Vecchio, now known as Piazza della Repubblica. The parts of the structure in good condition (crests, tondi with fish, capitals, etc.) were stored in the warehouse of the Museum of San Marco, thanks to the intervention of Guido Carrocci. It was not until 1955 that the city's aesthetics advisory committee, with funds from the Cassa di Risparmio di Firenze, decided to reconstruct it under the supervision of the engineer Giulio Cesare Lensi Orlandi Cardini, in what is known today as Piazza dei Ciompi.

The loggia has an oblong rectangular form—30 × 5 meters—and is composed of nine single bays covered by Bohemian vaults, topped by a small attic and a wooden pitched roof. On the front the round arches have a diameter of 3.1 meters, with keystones at a height of 6.7 meters above the piazza level. The arches are supported by square pillars—the first corner pair and the central—alternating with columns of the Tuscan order in *pietra serena*. The inner pavement of the loggia is reached by means of three steps placed along the entire perimeter, leading to the level of one meter. The facades are decorated with tondi depicting various fish species, placed in the spandrels of the arches; eight medallions on each side present reminders of the sea, fishing, and related activities, in tune with the original function of the loggia.

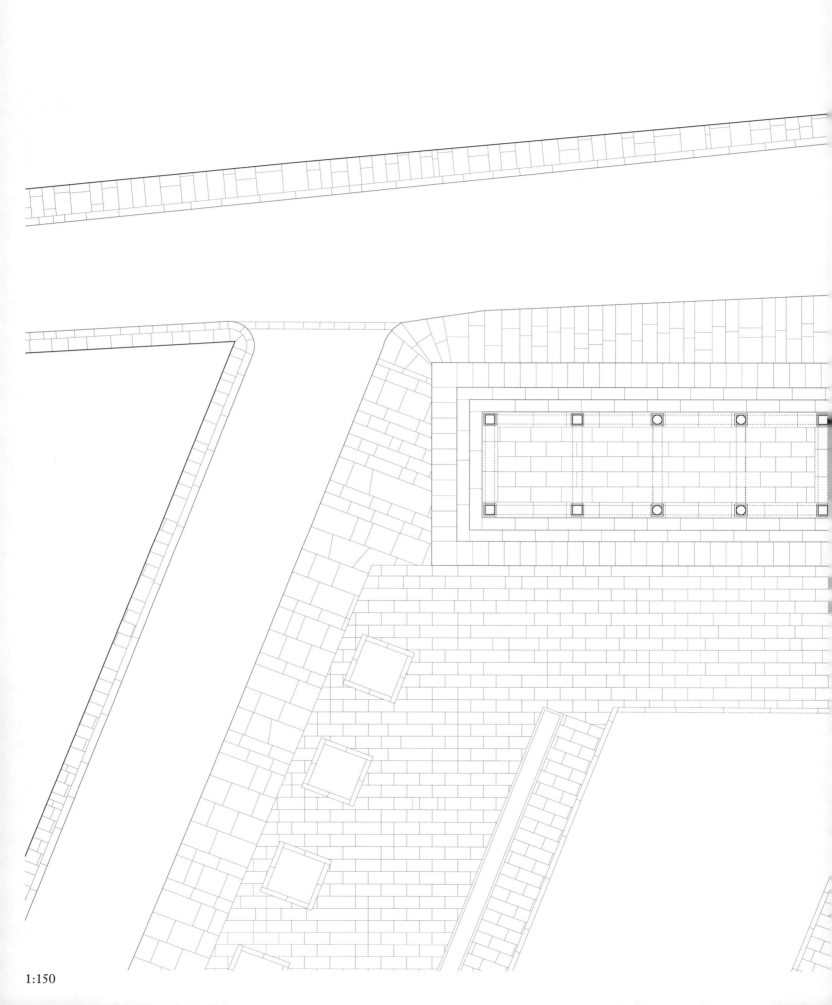

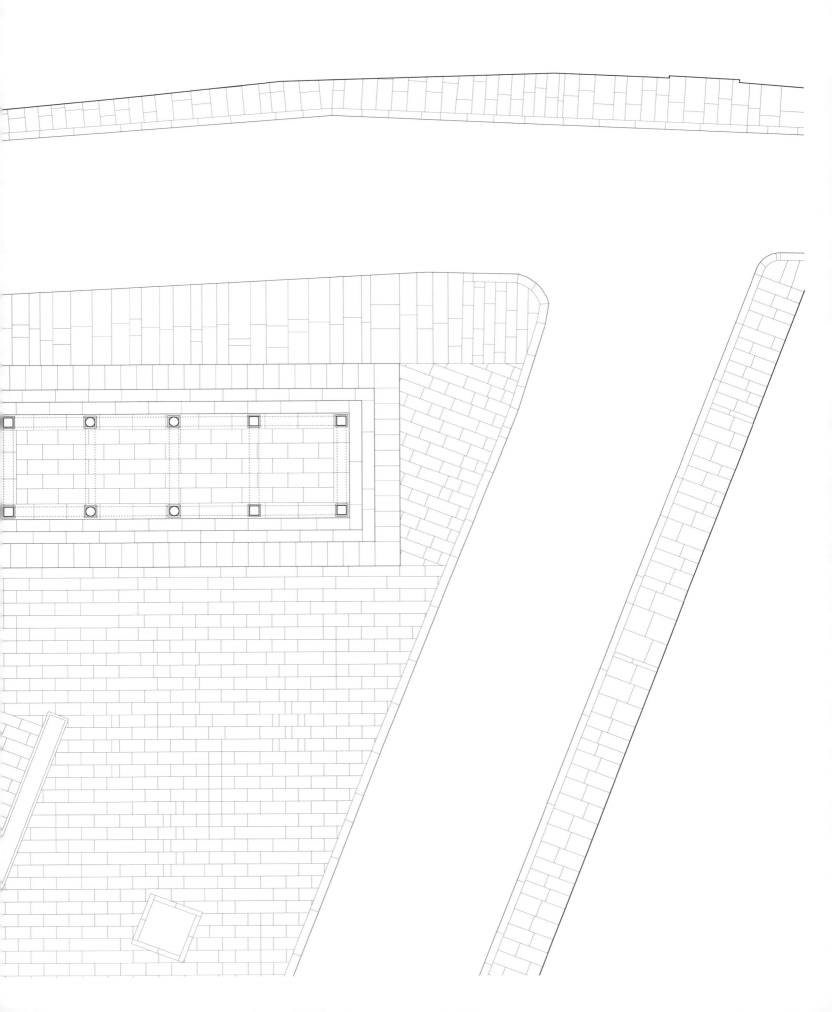

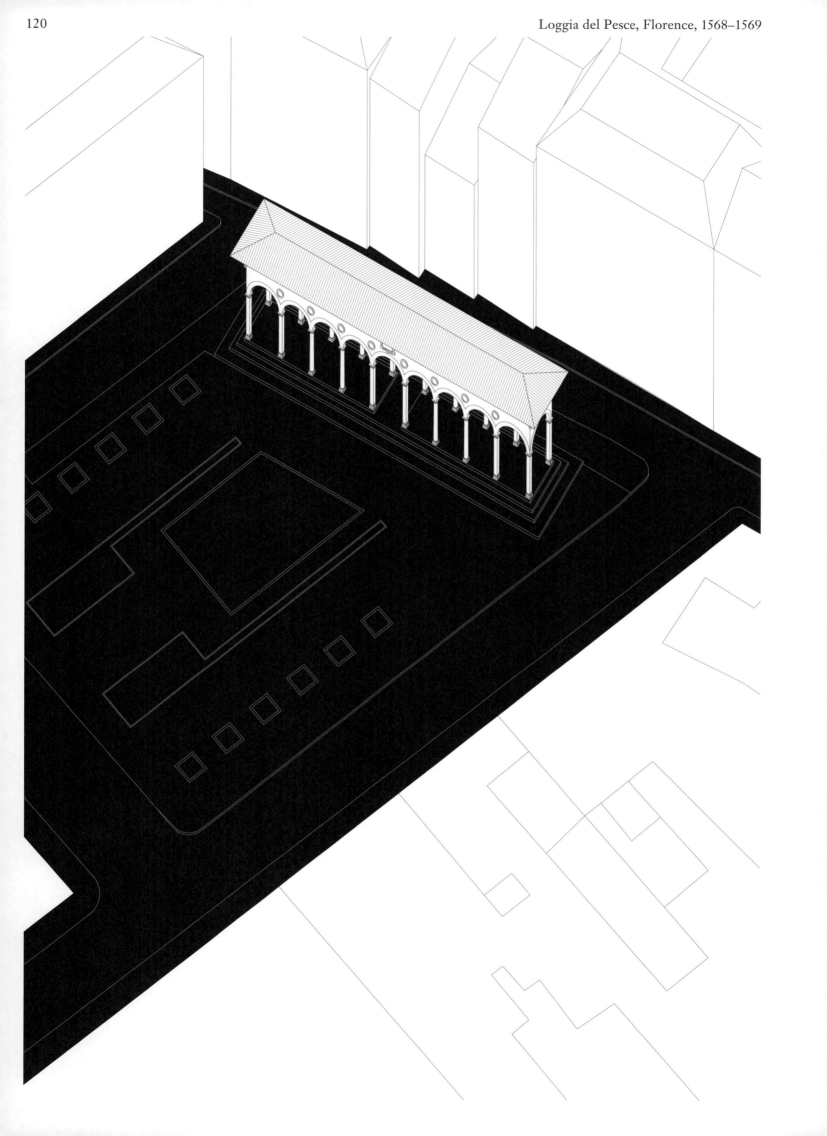

Loggia Vasariana, Castiglion Fiorentino, 126–137
1560–1570

The loggia on Piazza del Municipio in its present form is attributed to Giorgio Vasari, who from 1560 to 1570 supervised the restoration and partial reconstruction of an existing structure, by order of Cosimo I.

The loggia of Castiglion Fiorentino, unlike those created for purely mercantile purposes, reflects the need perceived in many cities of central-northern Italy, toward the end of the 15th and start of the 16th centuries, to construct one or more large squares enhanced by the presence of porticos, in compliance with the indications contained in Alberti's *De re aedificatoria* calling for "the ornament of the forum or piazza by the presence of an elegant portico below which the elders can walk, sit, take a siesta and attend to each other's burdens."

It is probable that the Piazza del Municipio of Castiglion Fiorentino already contained a public loggia in wood, built for activities of commerce; but it was not until 1513 that a masonry structure was created by Bernardo del Ghirba and Filippo di Bellinzona with the aim of embellishing the town's central piazza. The loggia, positioned in front of the Palazzo Comunale, acted as a filter between the historic Piazza del Pietrone (presently Piazza del Municipio) and the opening towards Val di Chio.

Halfway through the 16th century the loggia and the structures below it were already in poor condition; in 1558 the Tizi family offered to reconstruct the church of San Sebastiano and the loggia itself, under the supervision of the architect of reference of Grand Duke Cosimo I, Giorgio Vasari.

The rectangular loggia has a length of 34 meters and a depth of 6.5 meters. Towards the piazza, the structure is paced by a series of nine arches on pillars placed at a distance of 3.8 meters from each other. The round arches have a diameter of 3.3 meters and an overall height of 5.3 meters. The vertical structures and the moldings of the barrel vaults in local stone stand out against a stucco background, in keeping with the Florentine tradition. Towards the valley three arches, with the same geometry, open the space of the loggia and the piazza to the landscape. The back wall displays the coats of arms of commissioners and magistrates in stone or terracotta, and a historic fresco depicting the Annunciation. The roof of the loggia is supported by wooden trusses.

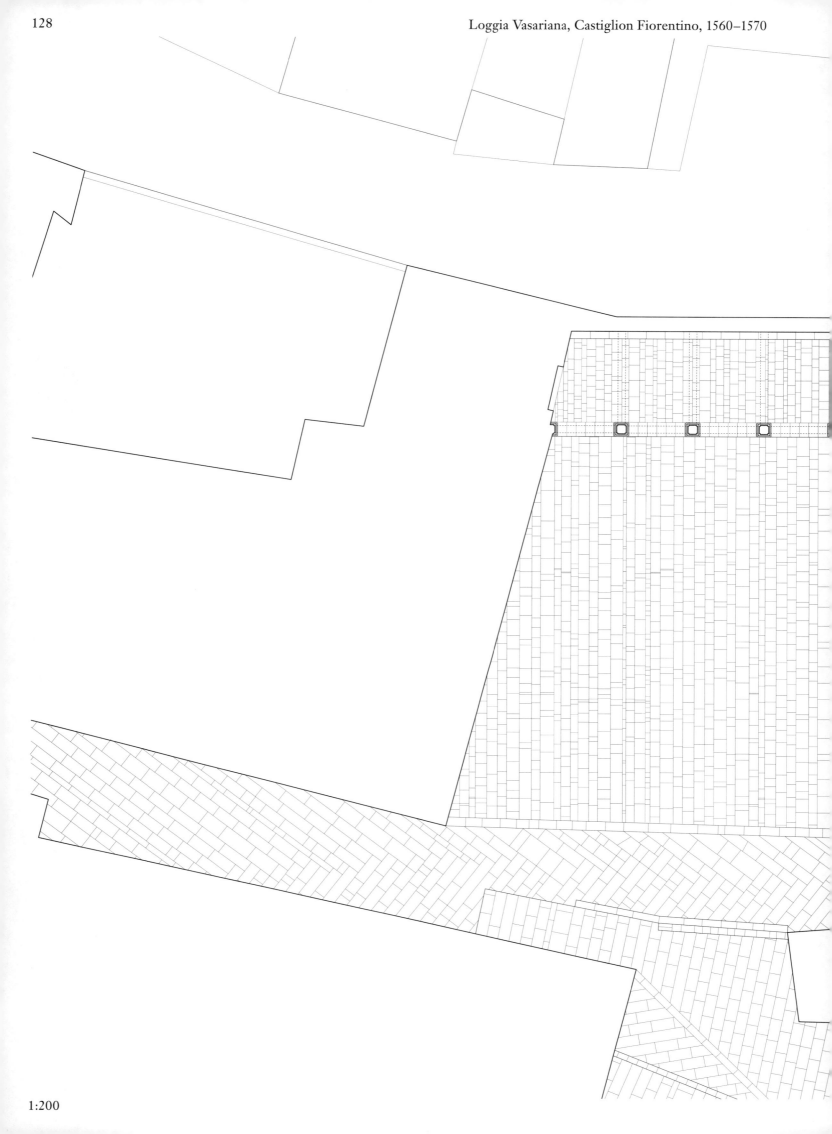

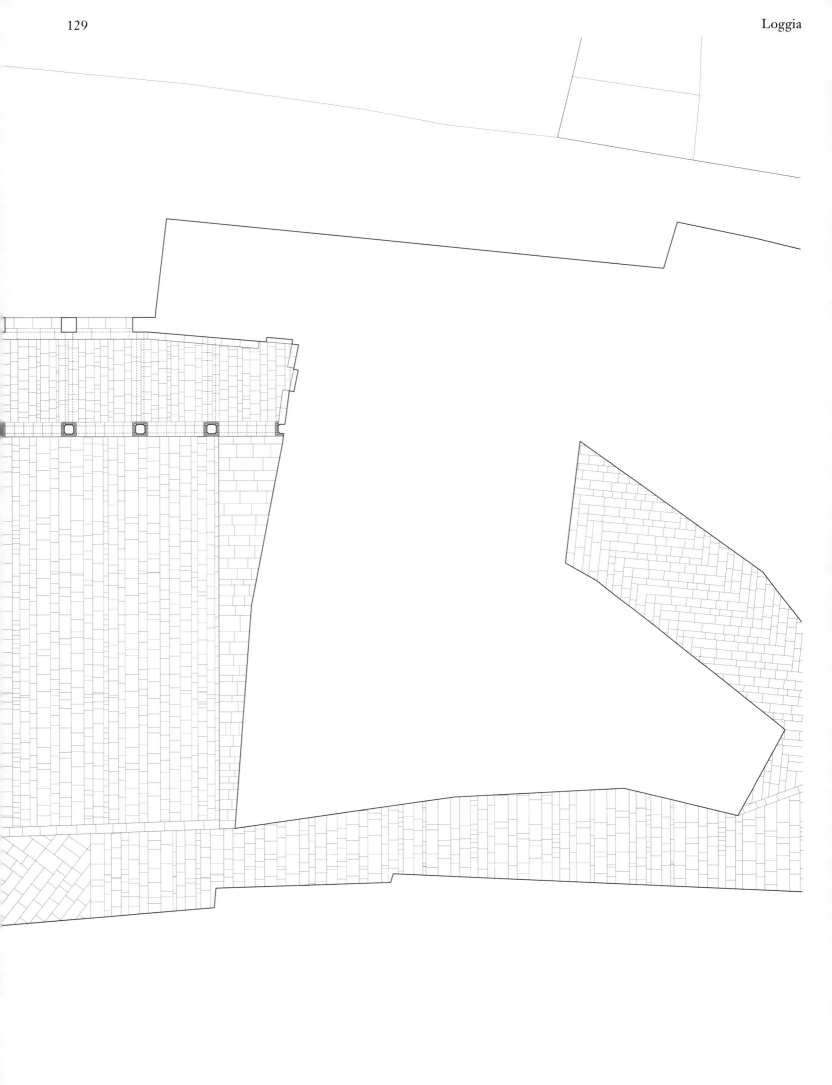

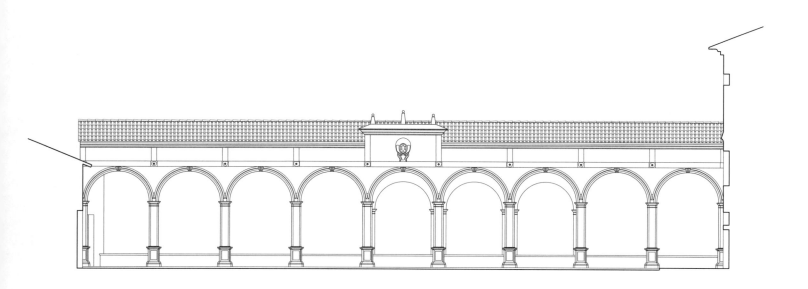

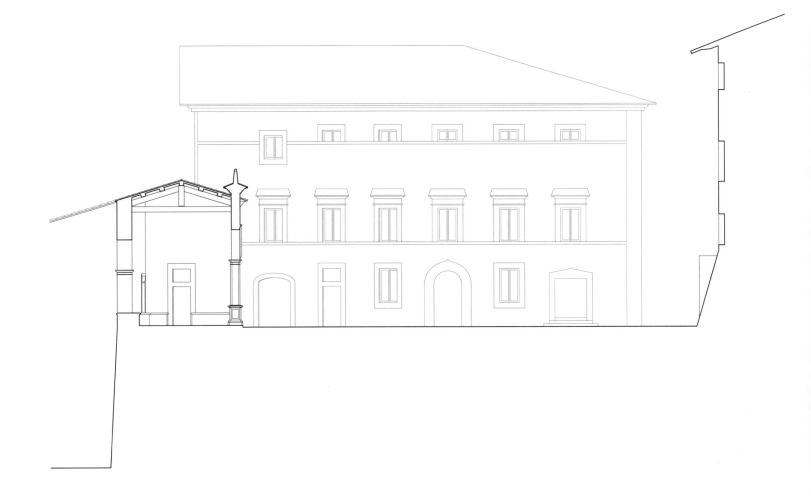

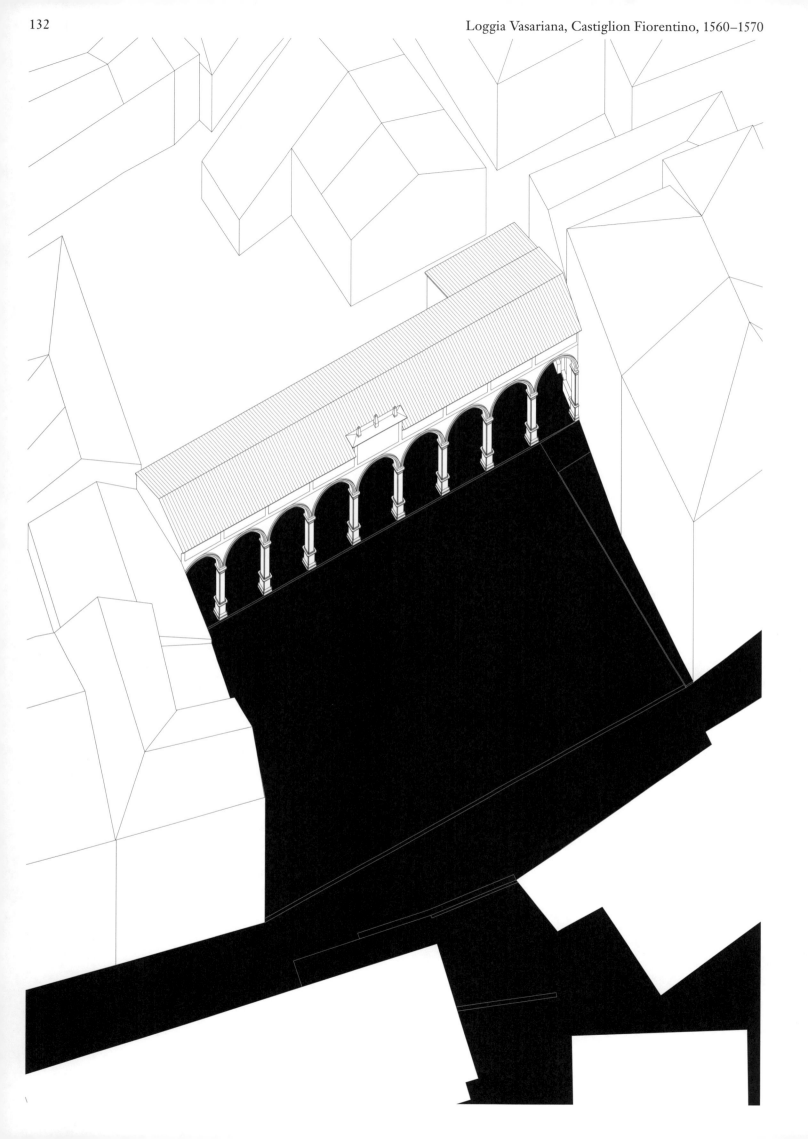

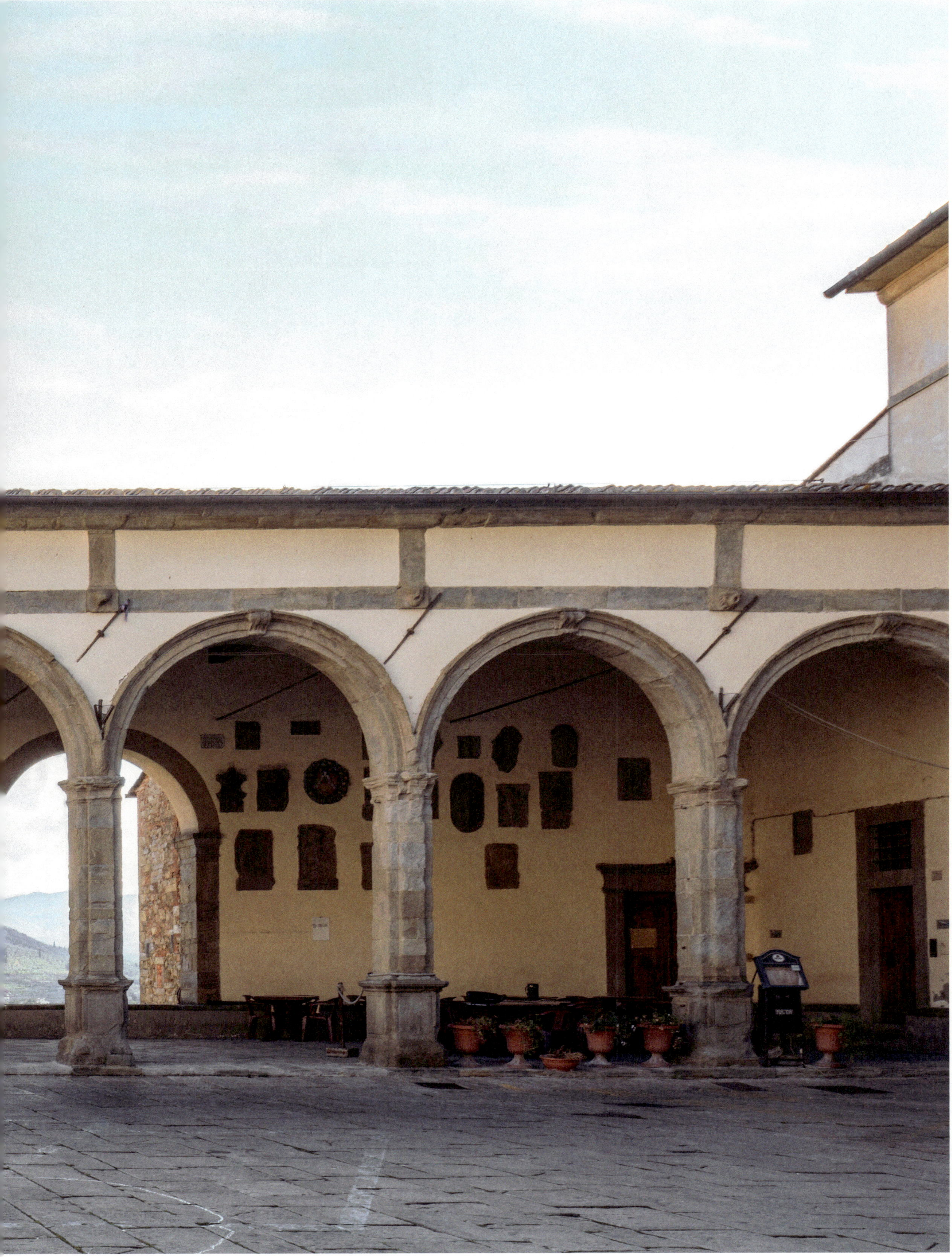

A space at ground level open on multiple sides, supported by pillars or columns, over which rises a building whose purpose is functionally connected to the space.

In other words, when a building is raised off the ground, entirely or in part, in such a way as to avoid interrupting the continuity of the surrounding urban space, while creating a new sheltered public space.

Covered Square

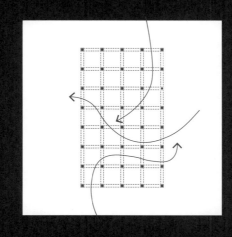

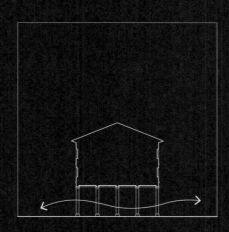

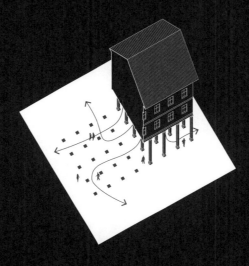

Covered Square

Palazzo della Loggia, Brescia, 1492–1574   142–153

The outcome of a rather complicated history, Palazzo della Loggia in Brescia is presently the seat of the municipal government, as was envisioned when it was built towards the end of the 15th century.

Palazzo della Loggia was first created as a civic building for the municipal administration, representing the new Venetian rule (1426). The complex, besides acting as a facility for the hearings of the Podestà, was to contain the Consiglio Cittadino and the Collegio dei Notai, demonstrating its central status in the life of the city in both geographical and political terms. For this reason, the building corresponds to the typological theme of the loggia palace typical of the communal era, featuring an open space on the ground floor for gatherings of citizens, topped by a large hall for governmental functions.

Under the rule of the Serenissima Republic many cities, including Brescia, underwent major urban interventions with the aim of creating new complexes or transforming old civic centers into new facilities for the Venetian administration. In Brescia the civic center once represented by the Palazzo del Broletto, a vestige of the communal period, was moved towards the new square later known as Piazza della Loggia, where various public buildings were constructed to house the government and the economic administration of the city. The construction of the palazzo had a complex history, and was the result of various contributions: the first design, illustrated with a wooden model by Tomaso Formenton in 1489, was probably very different from the complex that was eventually built. Some sources attribute the latter project to Bramante or architects of his school, while others point to Vincenzo Foppa. In any case, construction began in 1492 during the Venetian rule, as the headquarters of the "special council" of the city's aristocracy. At the end of the 1400s the lower order was to be completed, but the work was interrupted in 1512 by wartime events.

Resumed in 1549 by order of the city council and after consultations in 1550 with Andrea Palladio, in 1554 the civic administration of Brescia commissioned Jacopo Sansovino to complete the work. Therefore we can attribute to Sansovino the design of the second level, set back from the ground floor, and of the top with a balustrade adorned by sculptures. The wooden model of the roof with the form of an overturned ship's hull, built by Ludovico Beretta, director of works and superintendent of civic construction, dates back to 1556. After destruction by fire in 1575, the roof was not reconstructed until 1769, by Luigi Vanvitelli, who also designed the large octagonal hall that still exists, and an attic that was later removed.

The overall footprint of the building in the plan measures 46 meters on the long side and 29 meters on the short side; a portion of 27 × 29 meters is occupied by the loggia. In the lower part, the building is open to the city on three sides, through nine round arches with diameters of 6 meters, arranged in keeping with precise geometric ratios, supported by composite pillars and framed by semi-columns in relief. The nine openings provide access to the covered square that occupies a large part of the ground level: a space sheltered by groin vaults and composed of three aisles with three bays each, supported in the central part by four columns arranged in a modular scheme of squares measuring 8 meters, for the positioning of the structural elements of the loggia and the façade.

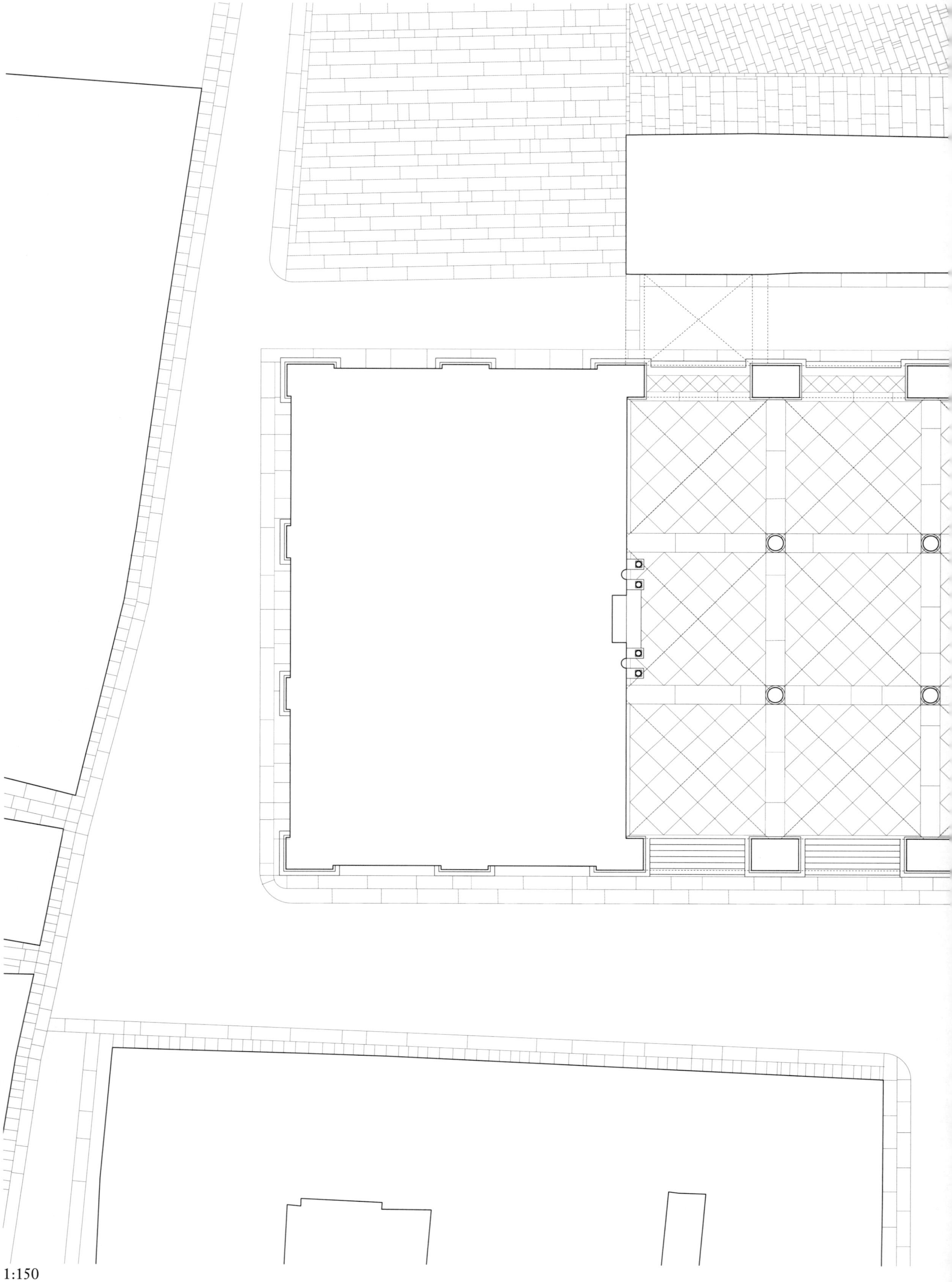

1:150

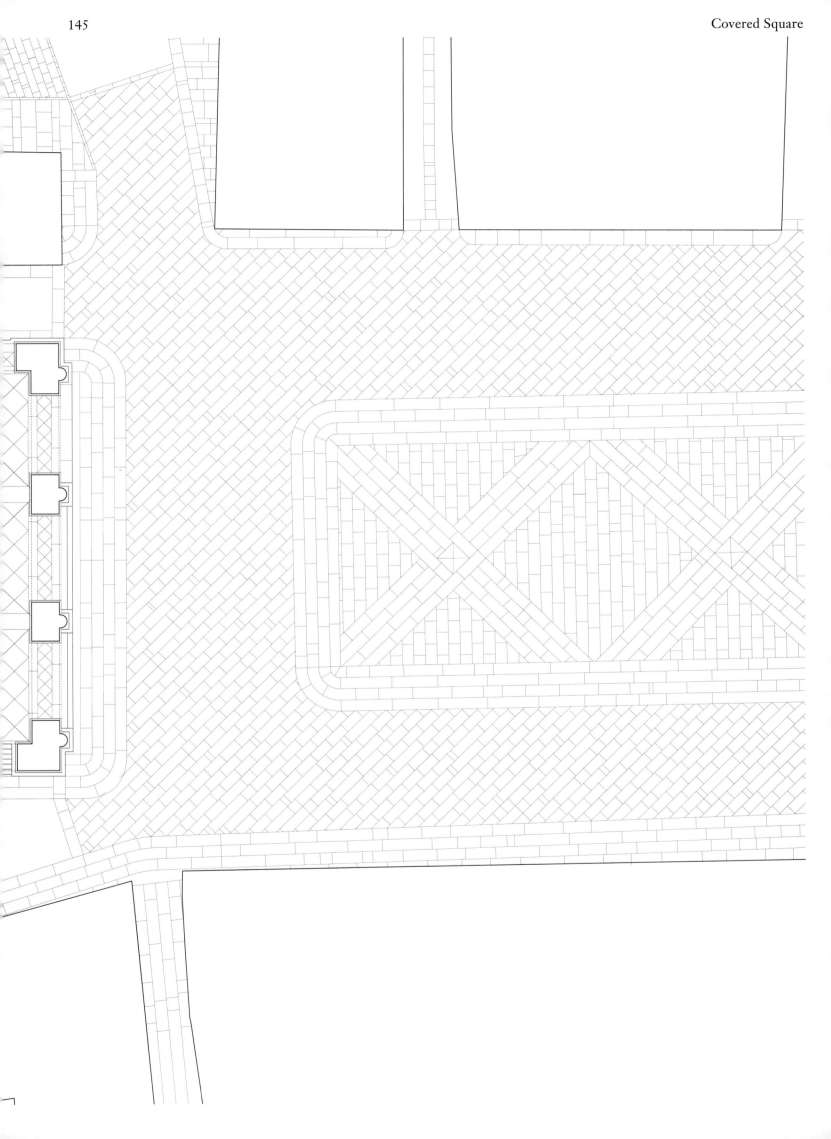

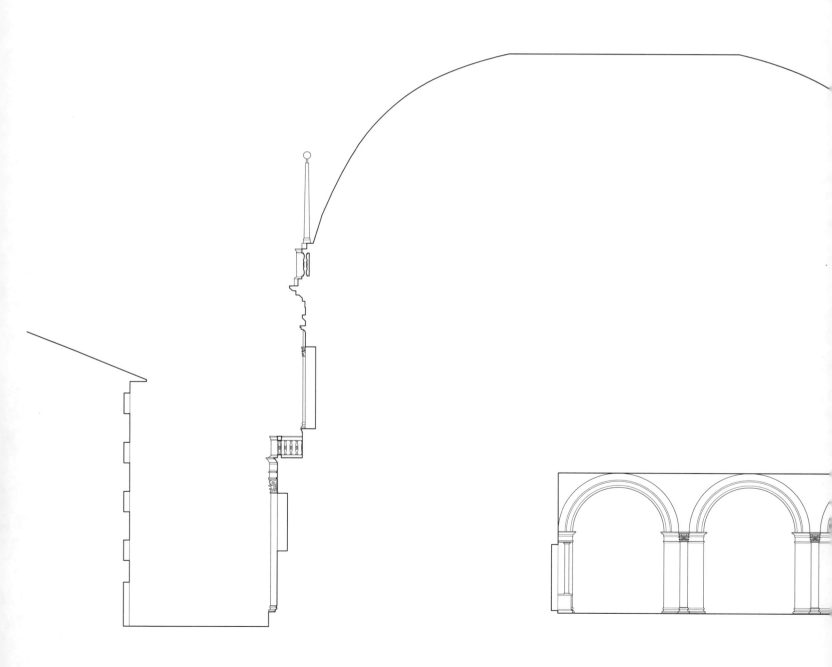

1:150

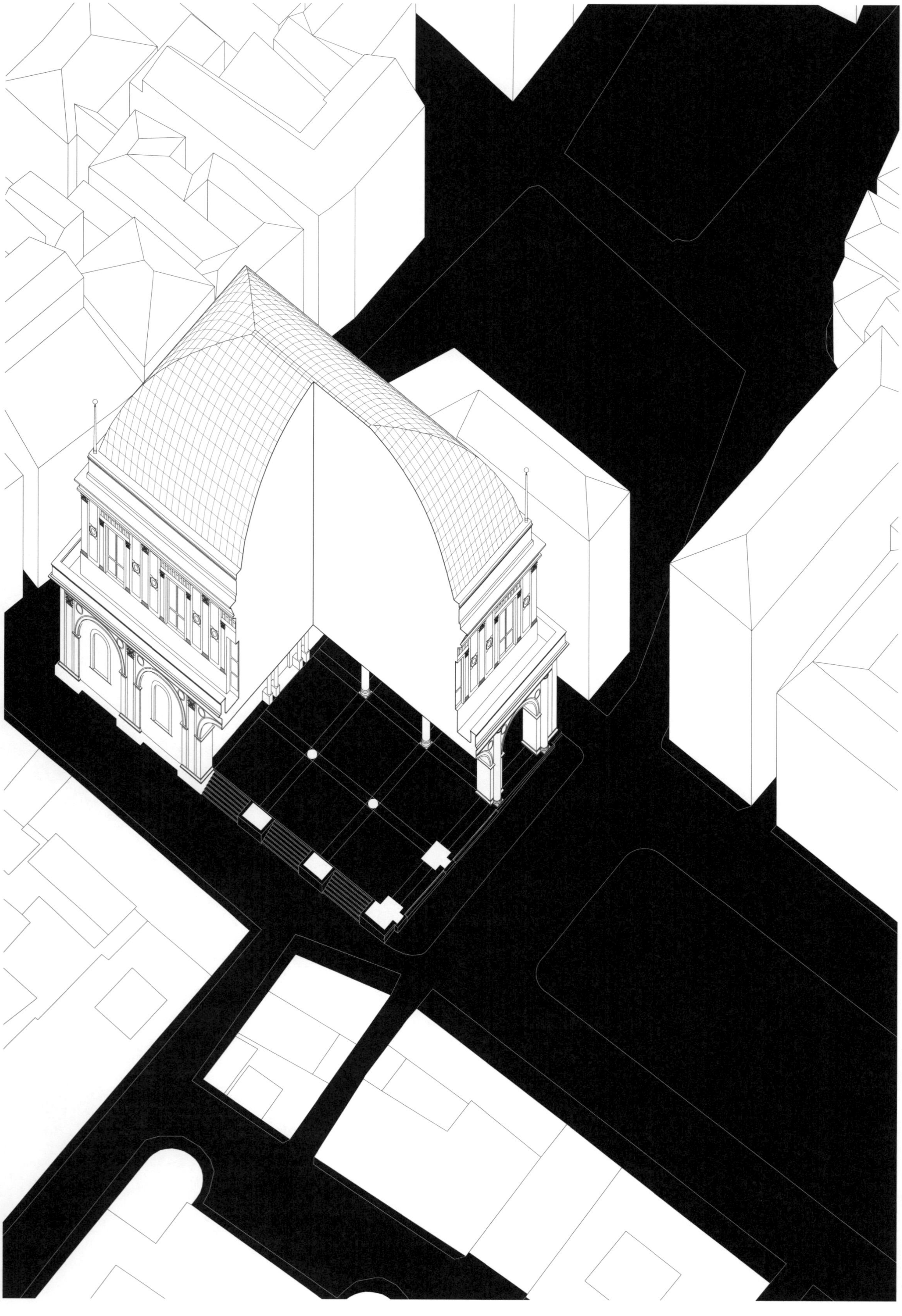

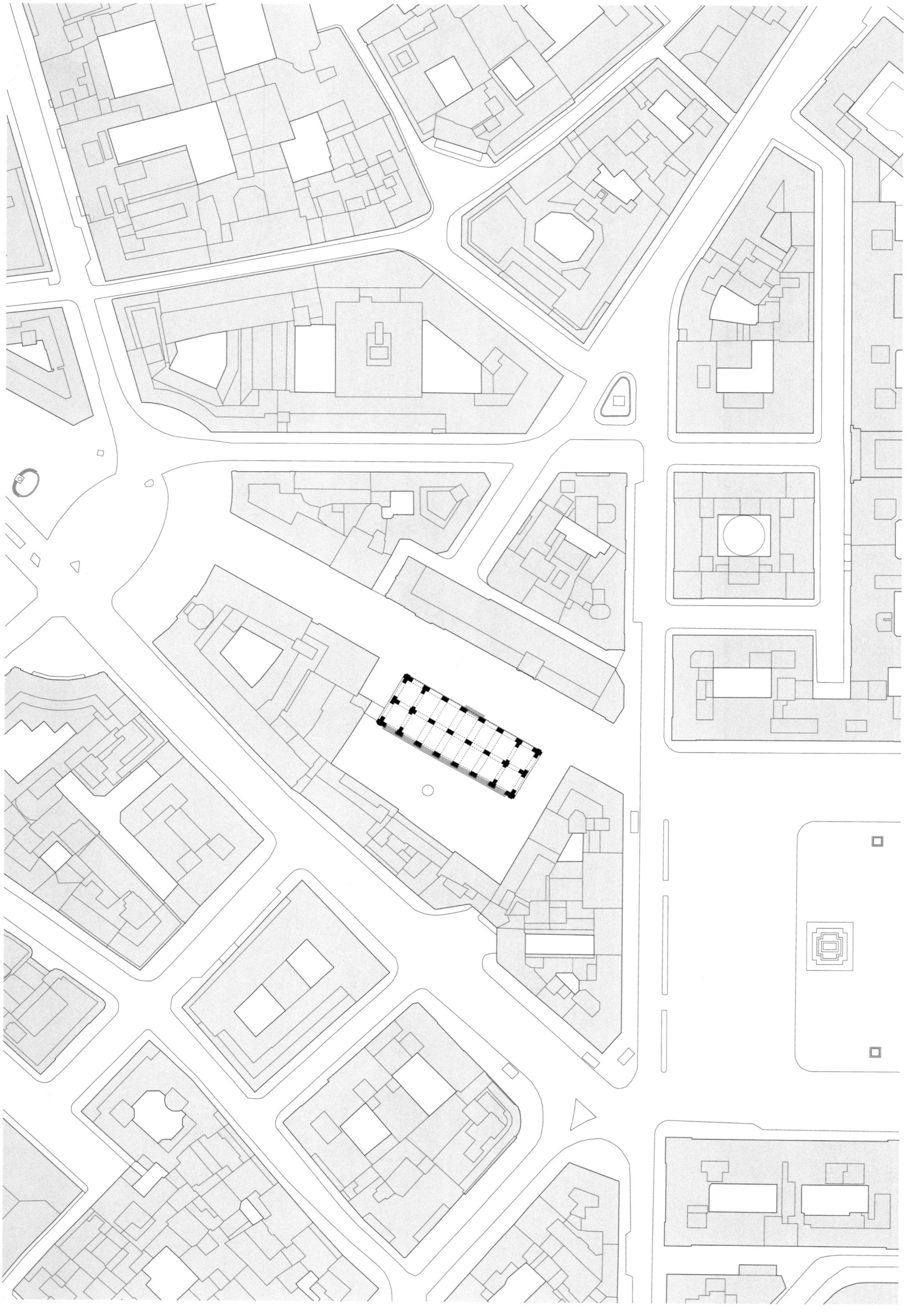

Palazzo della Ragione, Milan, 1228–1251   154–165

Palazzo della Ragione, which was the seat of the municipal government from 1251—the year of its completion—to 1786, stands on Piazza dei Mercanti, in front of the Loggia degli Osii in Milan.

The architectural structure links back to the typology of the town hall, as formulated in the 13th century at the time of the passage from a feudal society to that of the communes, reflecting growing self-awareness on the part of the citizenry and the desire to embody it in symbolic buildings. The large space on the ground level was the seat of the Consiglio dei Novecento, the representative assembly of the city, which was simultaneously its parliament and its court.

The history of the building is inseparable from that of the square around it, Piazza dei Mercanti, the city's political center from the medieval communal period to the 18th century. The Broletto Nuovo, i.e., Palazzo della Ragione, stood at the center of a space completely bordered by buildings, a sort of little citadel of power, in which only six passages were opened to correspond to the six subdivisions of the city. The construction of the square was deliberated in the year 1228—under the authority of Aliprando Fara da Brescia—by the communal rectors, who decided to construct a new town hall to replace the old one that stood in the area later occupied by the Palazzo di Corte (now Palazzo Reale). Initially envisioned as a double portico of a single level for assemblies, legal proceedings, and ordinances, it was raised thanks to a decree in 1233 of the podestà Oldrado da Tresseno di Lodi in order to create a large hall for the most important occasions. The building had an impact on the definition of the space around it, gradually attracting the main administrative institutions of the city into its proximity. The work on the square, where commercial activities spread over time, and on the surrounding buildings came to a conclusion roughly in 1251. The building remained unchanged until 1773, when Maria Theresa of Austria ordered the architect Francesco Croce to add another story, adapting the building for the use of the Notarial Archives.

The space of the ground floor—with a length of 50 meters and a depth of 19 meters—is composed of two aisles with seven bays each, and enclosed on the perimeter by round arches with a diameter of 4.7 meters. The arches become pointed in the spans at the extremities of the nave, and their width is reduced to 3.7 meters. The vaults in brick and marble blocks were built in 1771–1773 in place of the wooden structure, and cover a span of 7 meters, the width of the two aisles, while the large pillars are in stone. The façades in exposed brick present three-mullioned windows corresponding to the arches of the portico. The portico is raised from street level by five steps. They occupy a single span towards Via dei Mercanti, while towards Piazza del Broletto they extend for the entire length of the building.

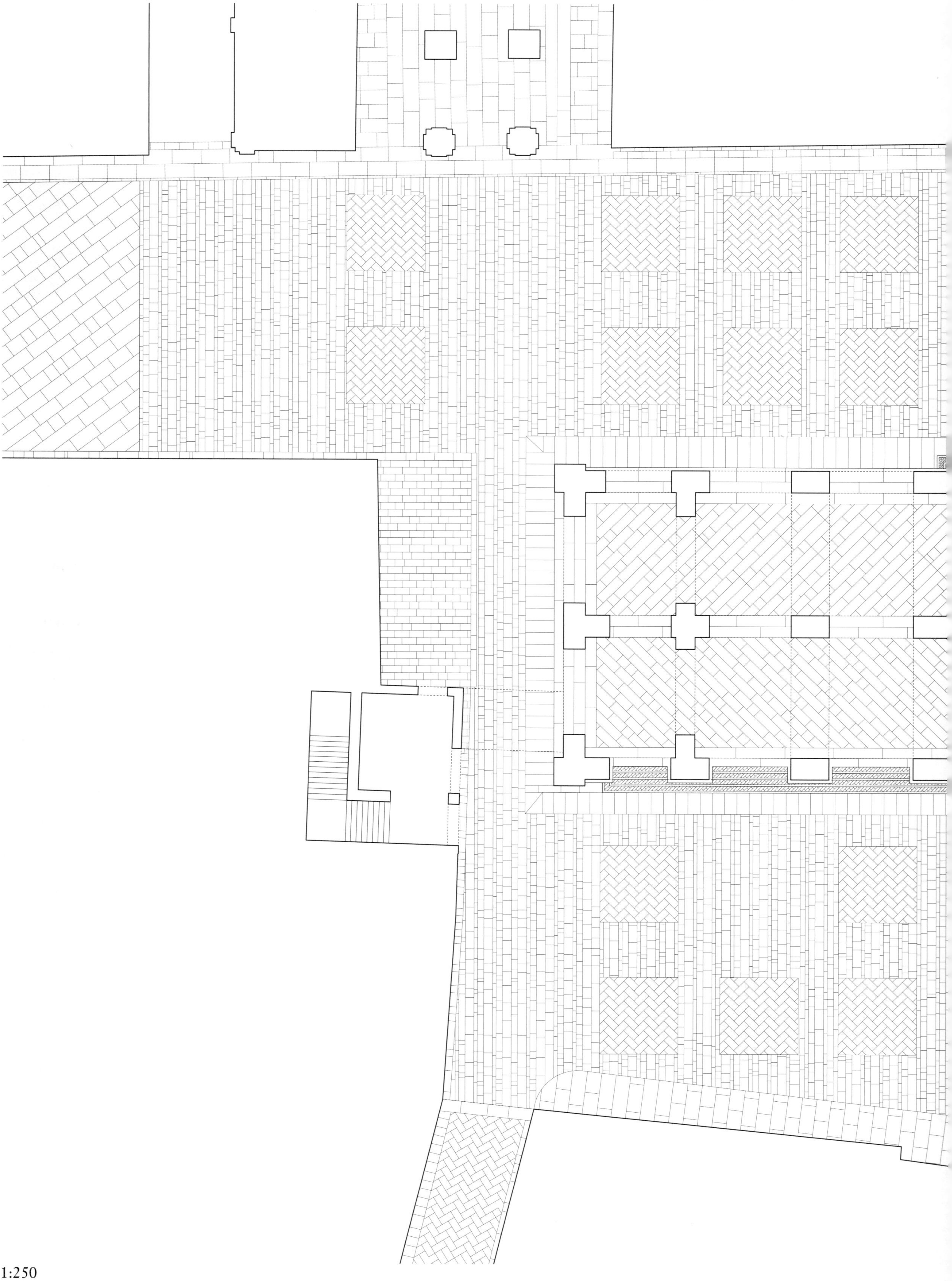

1:250

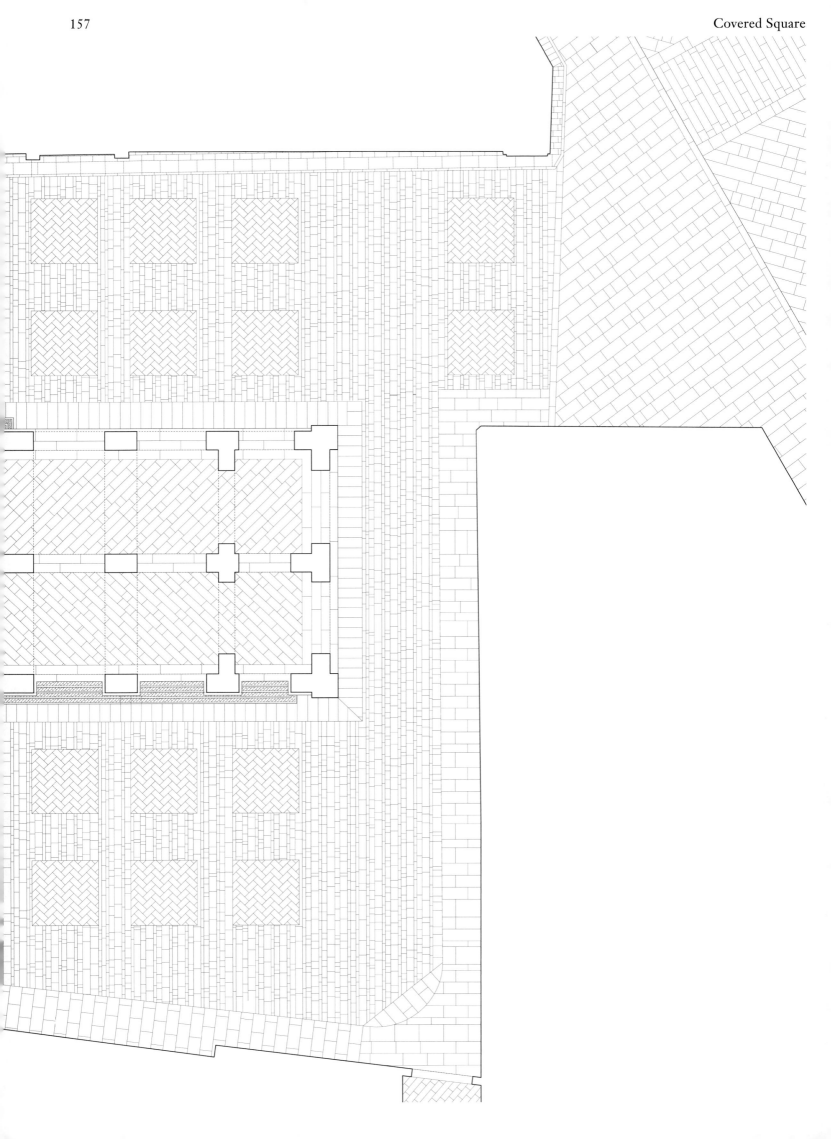

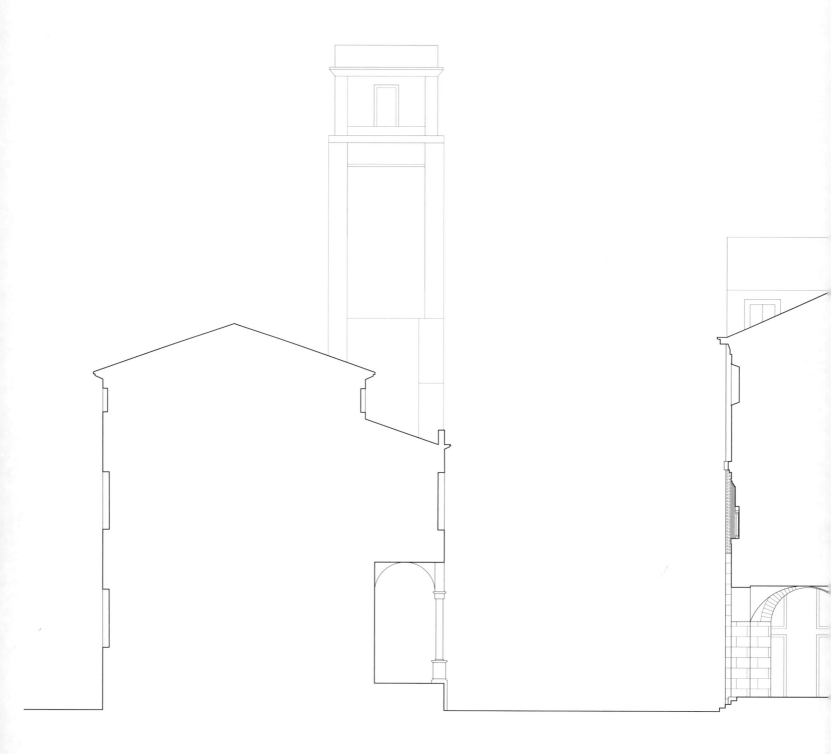

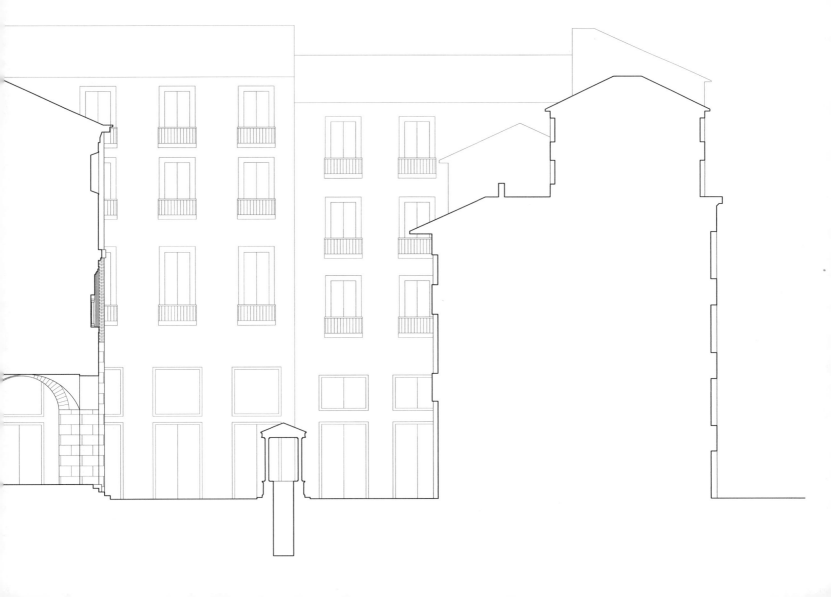

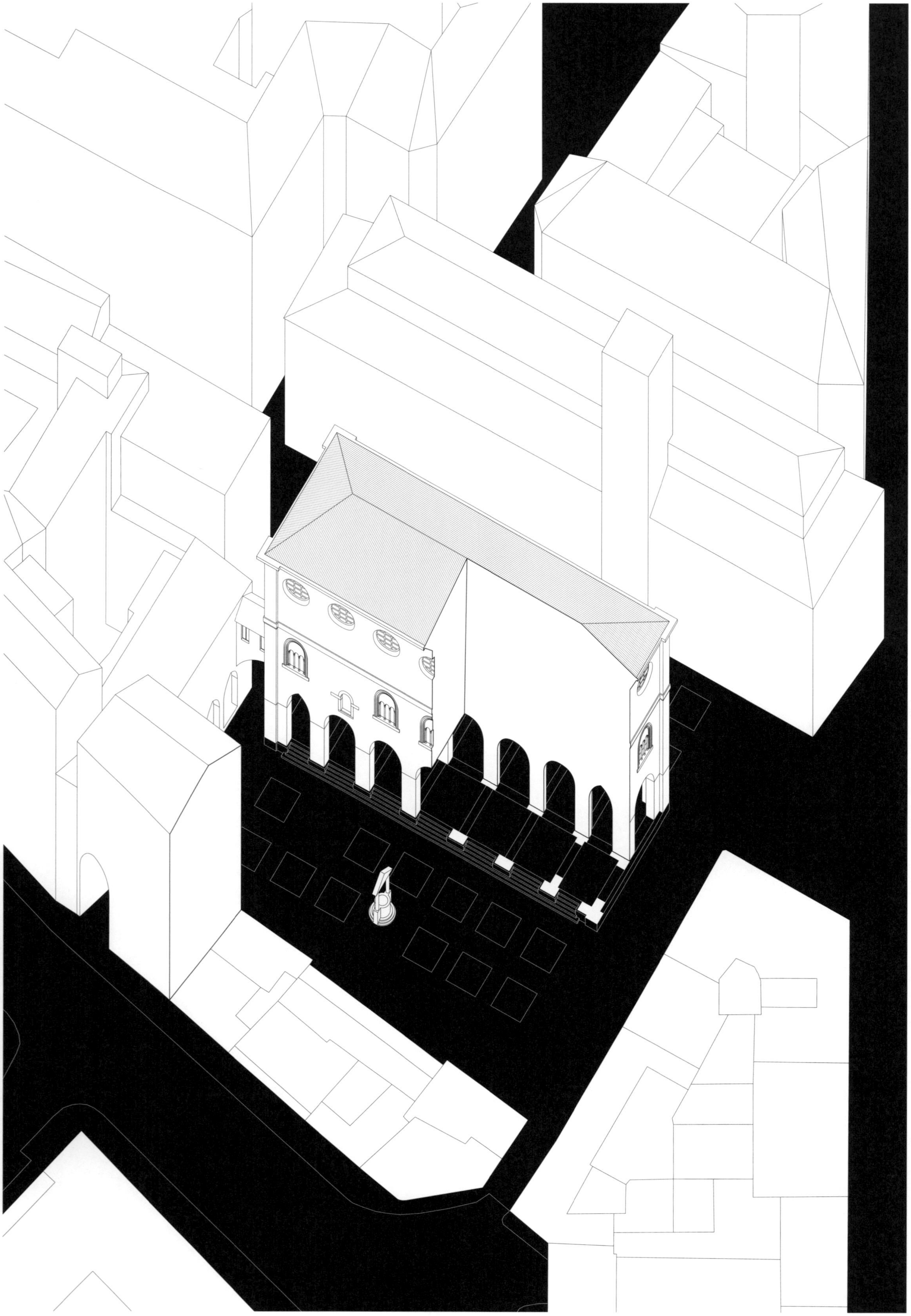

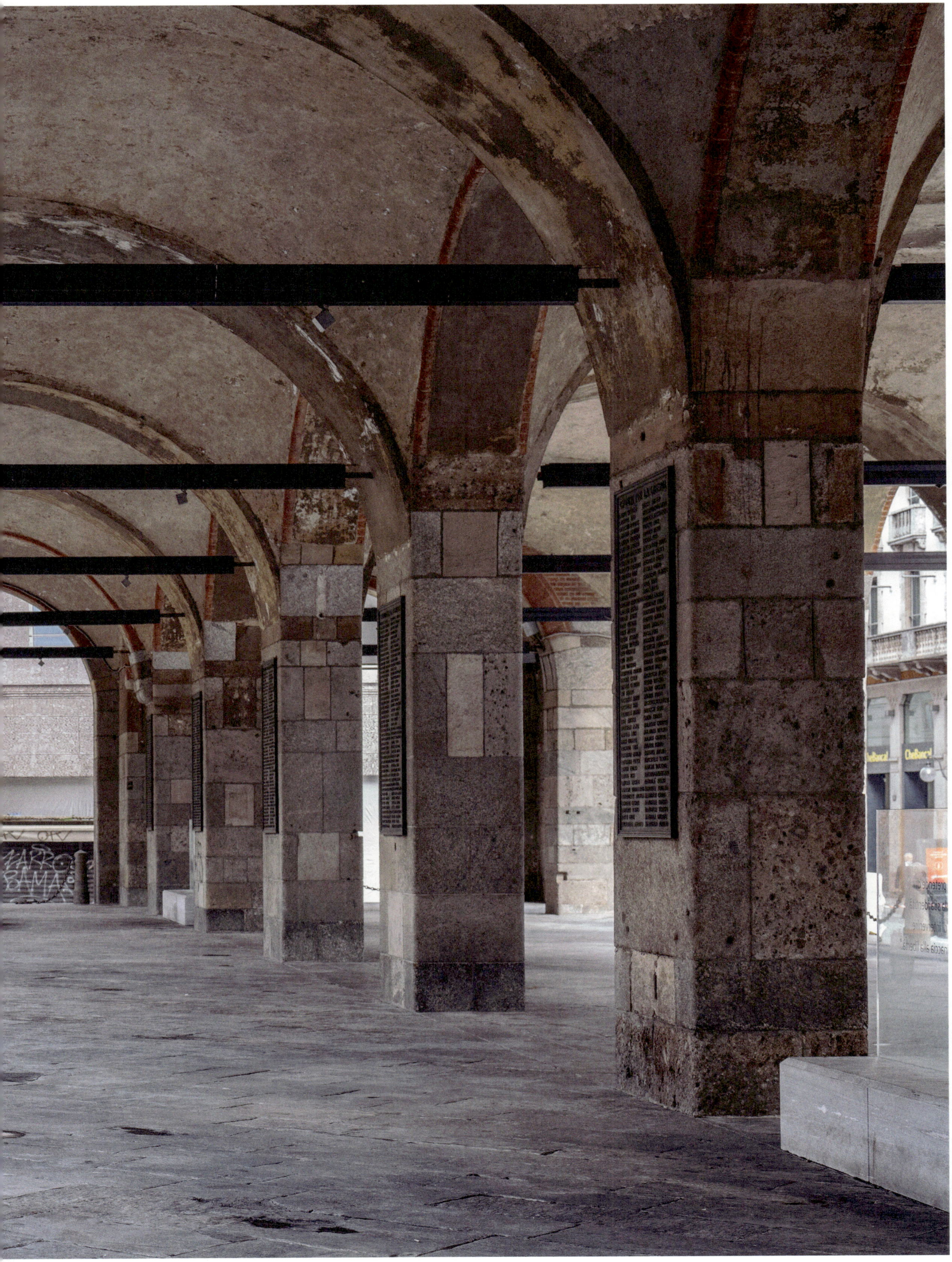

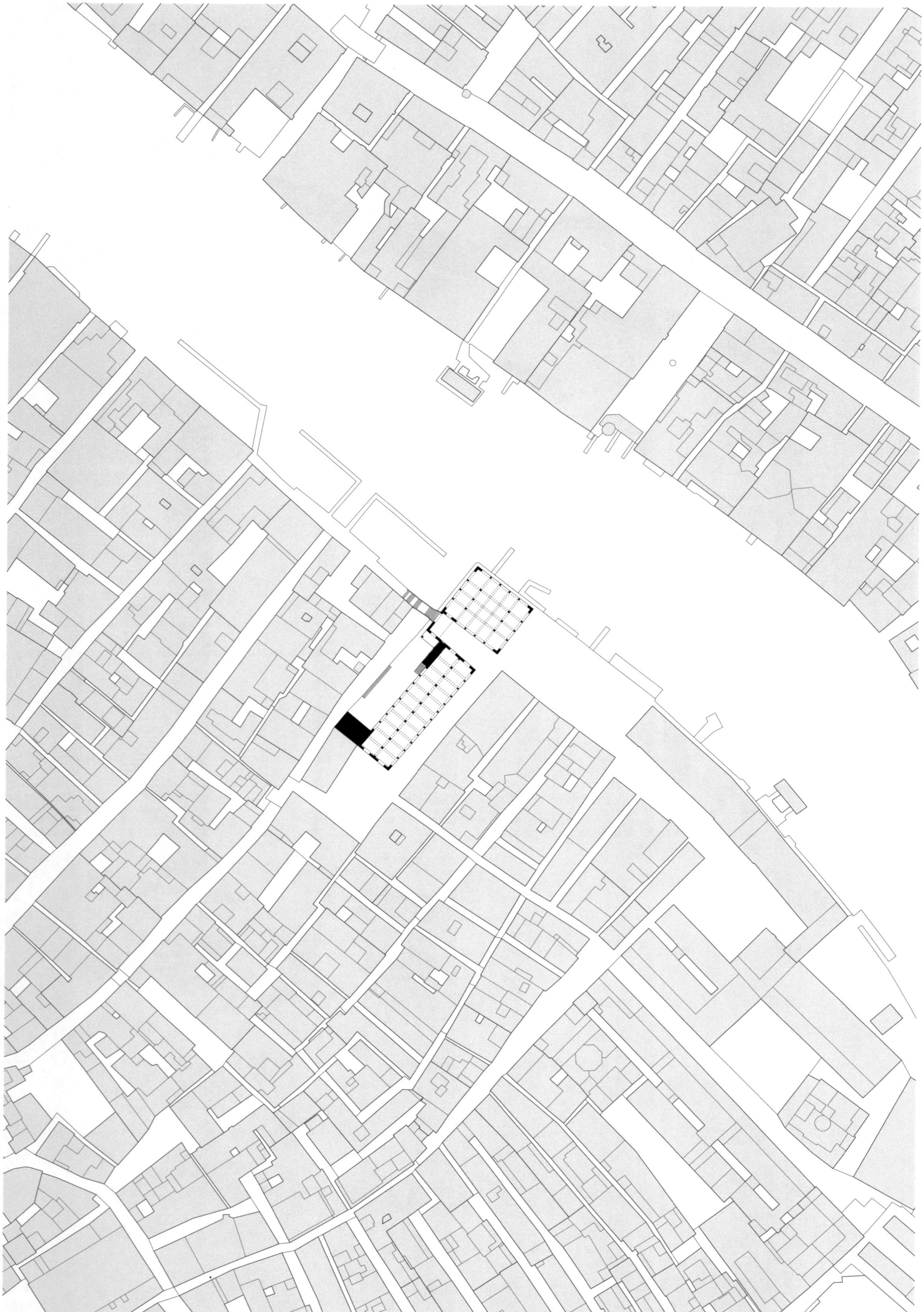

Mercato del Pesce di Rialto, Venice, 1907   166–177

The Rialto Fish Market is composed of two buildings connected by an elevated walkway: the 14th-century sheltered market of the Stalon dei Querini, and the Pescària, the neo-Gothic building constructed in 1907.

This complex is of interest not only for the architecture of the individual buildings, but also for the urban character of the whole and the ability to form an articulated system of open spaces in continuity with the surrounding urban fabric; a junction of commercial activities and a place for socializing.

Rialto is one of the oldest areas of settlement in Venice, together with the districts of San Marco and San Polo. The name comes from the Latin *rivus altus*, or "deep canal" in reference to today's Canal Grande, of which the islands of Rialto formed the banks. Already prior to 1097, the year of the market's relocation, the Rialto zone had always been a place of trade, a vocation that has continued into the present. Over the centuries the market has expanded, for both retail and wholesale trade, thanks to the construction of warehouses and storage facilities. In the 1500s a vast campaign of construction was begun, which would redesign the areas of the market in their present form: in 1525 construction began on the Palazzo dei Camerlenghi and the Fabbriche Vecchie, while the Fabbriche Nuove, designed by Jacopo Sansovino, are only slightly more recent (1553), like Palazzo dei Dieci Savi. In 1551 a competition was announced which led in 1591 to the opening of the present Ponte di Rialto. Inside this long process of development, the Pescària, one of the two buildings that form the fish market, was not built until 1907, based on a project by the architect Domenico Rupolo and the painter Cesare Laurenti.

The Pescària, organized on a quadrangular plan of 18 × 21 meters, has a completely open ground level bordered by wide pointed arches that permit free access from the outside. The arches are supported by stone columns placed at a distance of 3.6 meters, and brick pillars at the four corners of the building. The first floor is faced in brick with three-mullion windows and a large loggia facing the Grand Canal. The Pescària is connected by an elevated walkway to the Stalon, a previously existing structure for which the new building constitutes the continuation towards the Grand Canal.

The Stalon, whose architectural language is replicated by the Pescària, was a slaughterhouse in the 1300s, then transformed into a market whose present configuration is the result of major reconstruction carried out at the end of the 19th century. The space on the ground floor is organized as a large hall with a rectangular form of 12 × 41 meters, subdivided into two spans by a central row of 12 free columns with a height of about 6 meters, supporting a wooden deck. The building opens outward through a series of pointed arches, 12 on the long side and 8 on the short side.

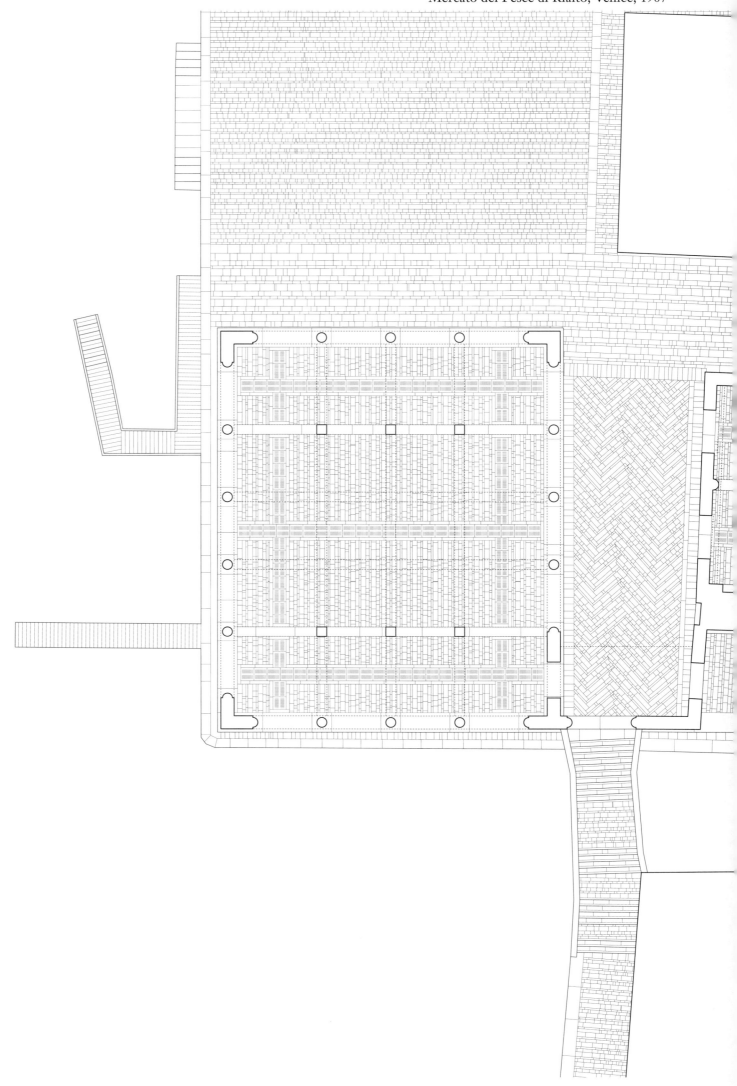

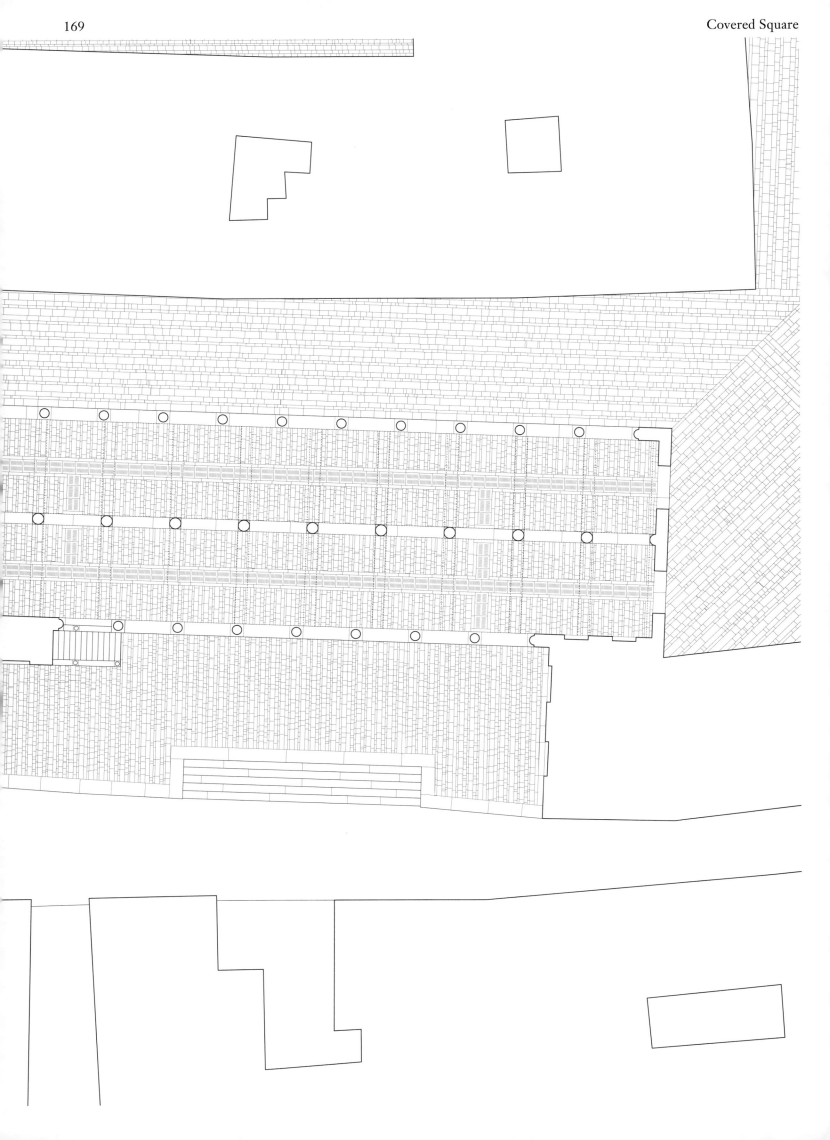

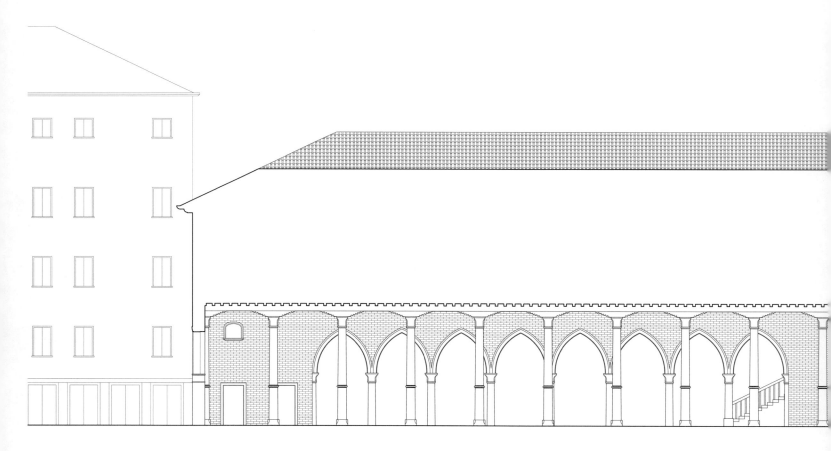

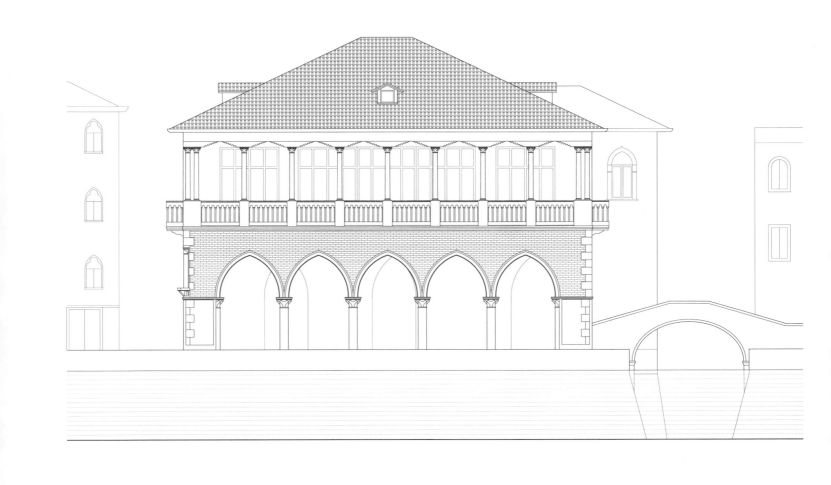

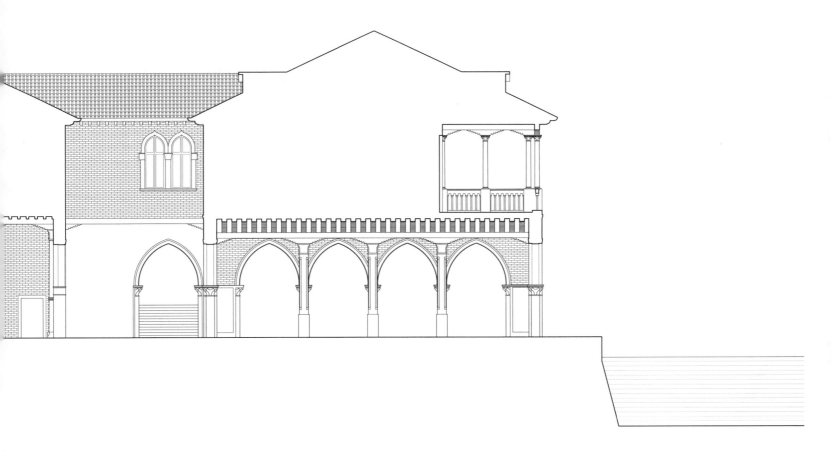

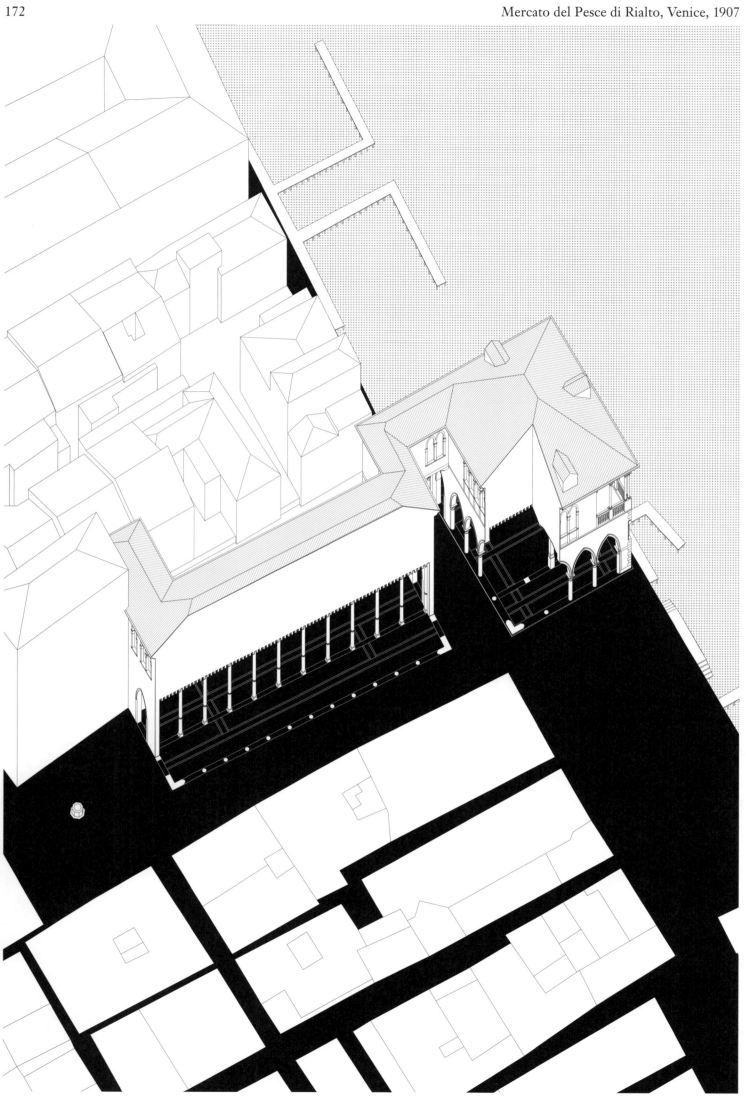

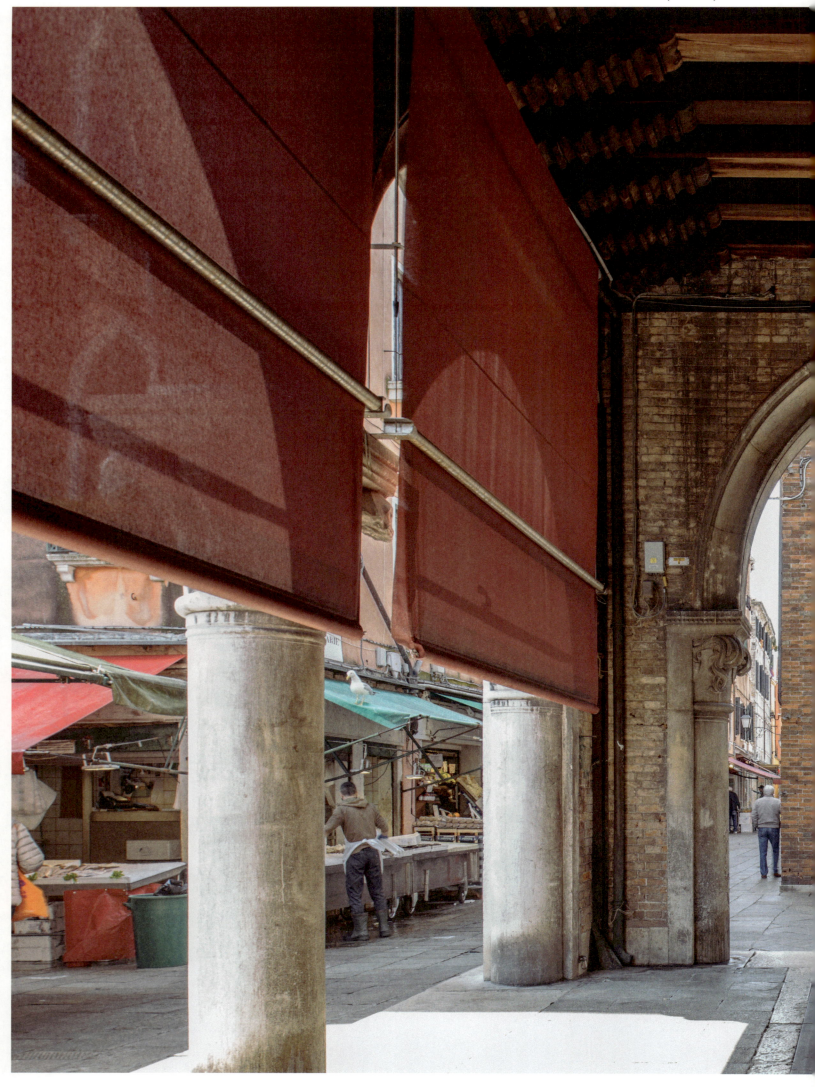

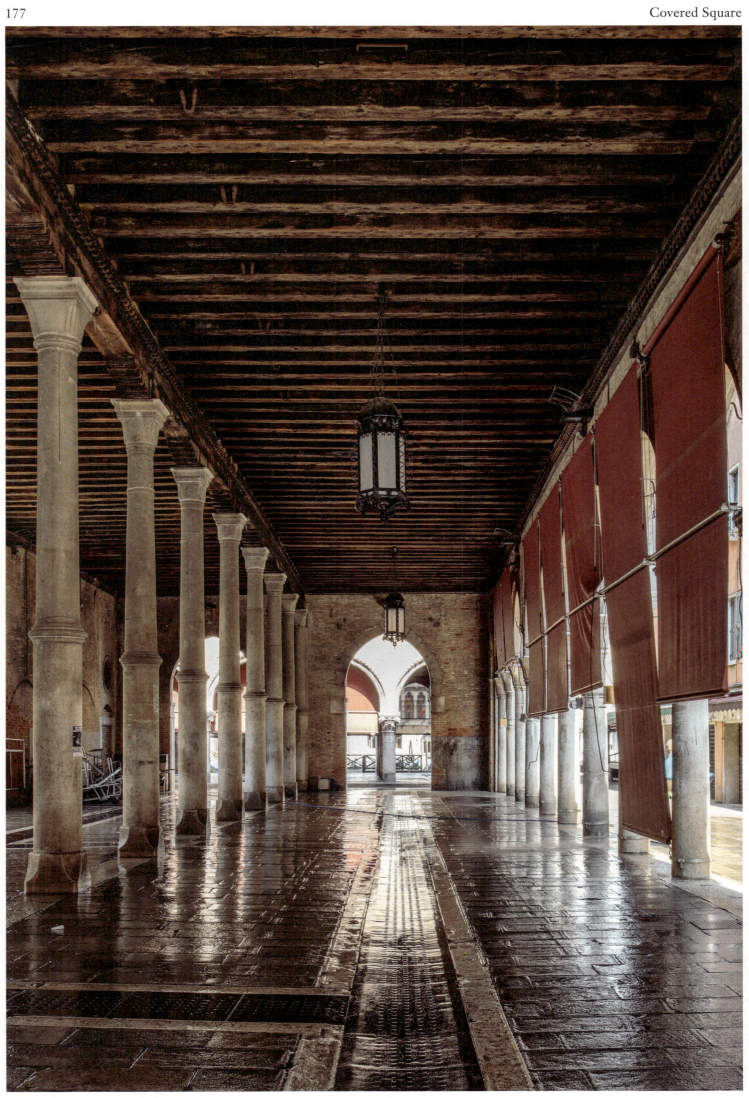

A portion of open space between the volumes of a building that brings air and light to its interiors, available for public use on the part of persons and vehicles.

In other words, when the private courtyard of a building is opened to the outside, become part of the public space.

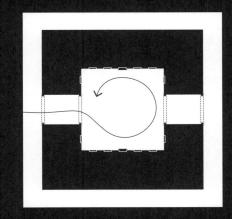

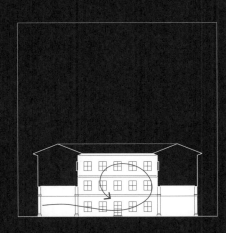

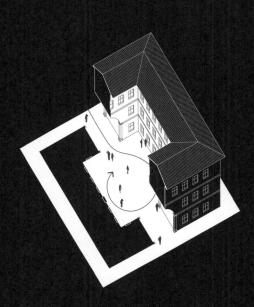

Urban Courtyard

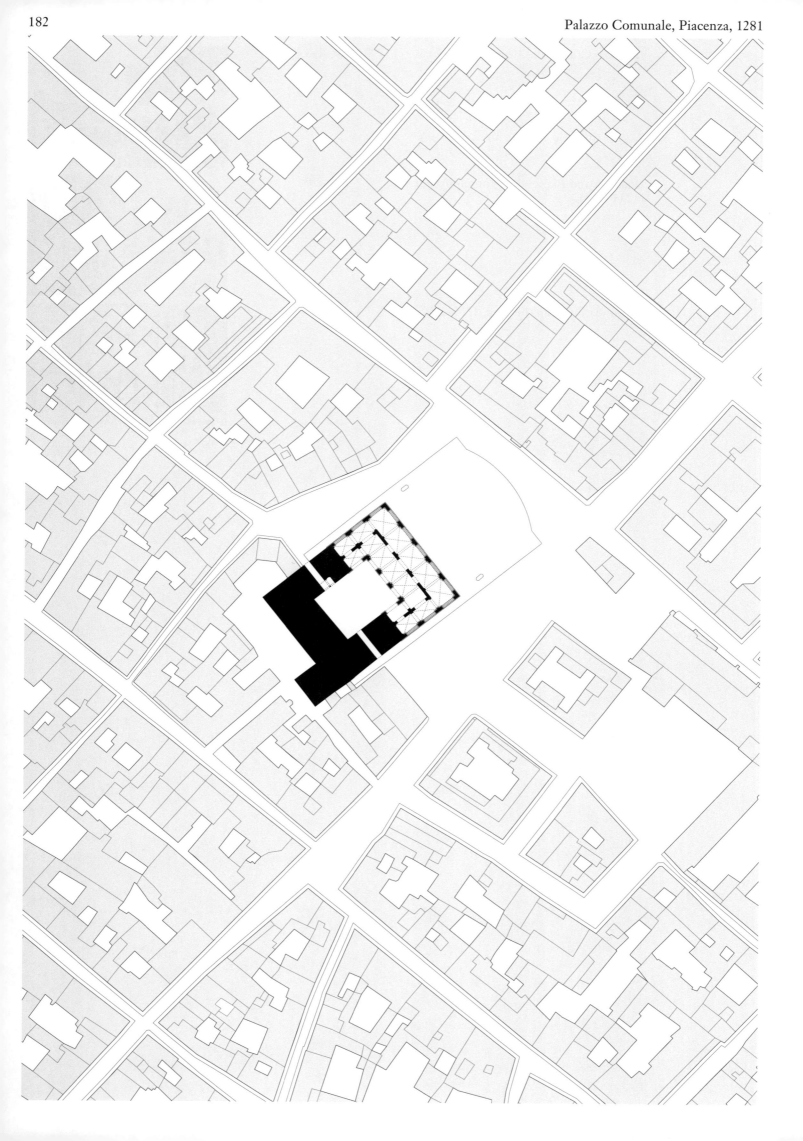

Palazzo Comunale, Piacenza, 1281   182–193

Palazzo Comunale, known as *il Gotico* due to its clear Lombard Gothic style, stands in the center of the city of Piacenza, on Piazza dei Cavalli.

The Palazzo has ties to the tradition of the Lombard *broletto*, the seat of the municipal government and courts; with respect to the medieval model—marked by a compact body with a large loggia on the ground floor—the Palazzo Comunale has a hybrid scheme that combines the courtyard type with that of the *loggiato*: the result is an original, open, porous layout in which the public spaces at ground level permeates the entire complex.

Its construction began in 1281 by order of Alberto Scotti, a nobleman and politician from Piacenza. The work was overseen by four local architects: Pietro da Cagnano, Negro de Negri, Gherardo Campanaro, and Pietro da Borghetto. As a result of an economic crisis caused by a plague outbreak, from the original design only the northern side towards the piazza was built, responding to the municipality's need for the rapid availability of a council chamber for meetings of the city's government, becoming the true symbolic heart of the city. The U-shaped portion towards the back is the result of a series of additions and adaptations over time. Nevertheless, the complex has preserved the quadrangular courtyard scheme already visible in the initial project. In the 16th and 17th centuries the palazzo underwent many modifications, including an added balcony on the side overlooking Piazza Cavalli. These modifications were then eliminated in the many renovations conducted in the late 19th and early 20th centuries, which triggered debate regarding the various approaches to architectural restoration. In 1884, based on a project by the architect Angelo Colla, the restoration of the palazzo began with the aim of a return to its original appearance. Among other measures, the medieval turret at the northeastern corner, which had been walled up during the 16th century, was brought back to

light. The terminal portion of the monument was also reconstructed, all the way to the crenellations at the top.

The building measures 46 × 50 meters, while the inner courtyard measures 25 × 20 meters. The loggia on the ground level is covered by cross vaults supported by pillars placed at a distance of 8.5 meters. Along the central spine the width of the arches is reduced from 5.5 to 3 meters, modifying the geometry of the arches. The elevations of the main volume have a base clad in white and pink Verona marble, paced by a row of five pointed arches that are 10 meters high in the main elevation, and three arches of the same height on the lateral elevations. The base forms a strong contrast with the upper part, featuring a red cotto finish with large decorated multiple windows, framed by round arches. One significant feature, besides the overhanging cornice, is the top composed of Ghibelline swallow-tail merlons placed at a height of 24 meters, and turrets that reach a full height of 30 meters.

Three steps mark the entrance to the palazzo from the piazza. Two round arch openings on the long sides of the U-shaped portion of the building constitute further crosswise connections between the courtyard and the exterior.

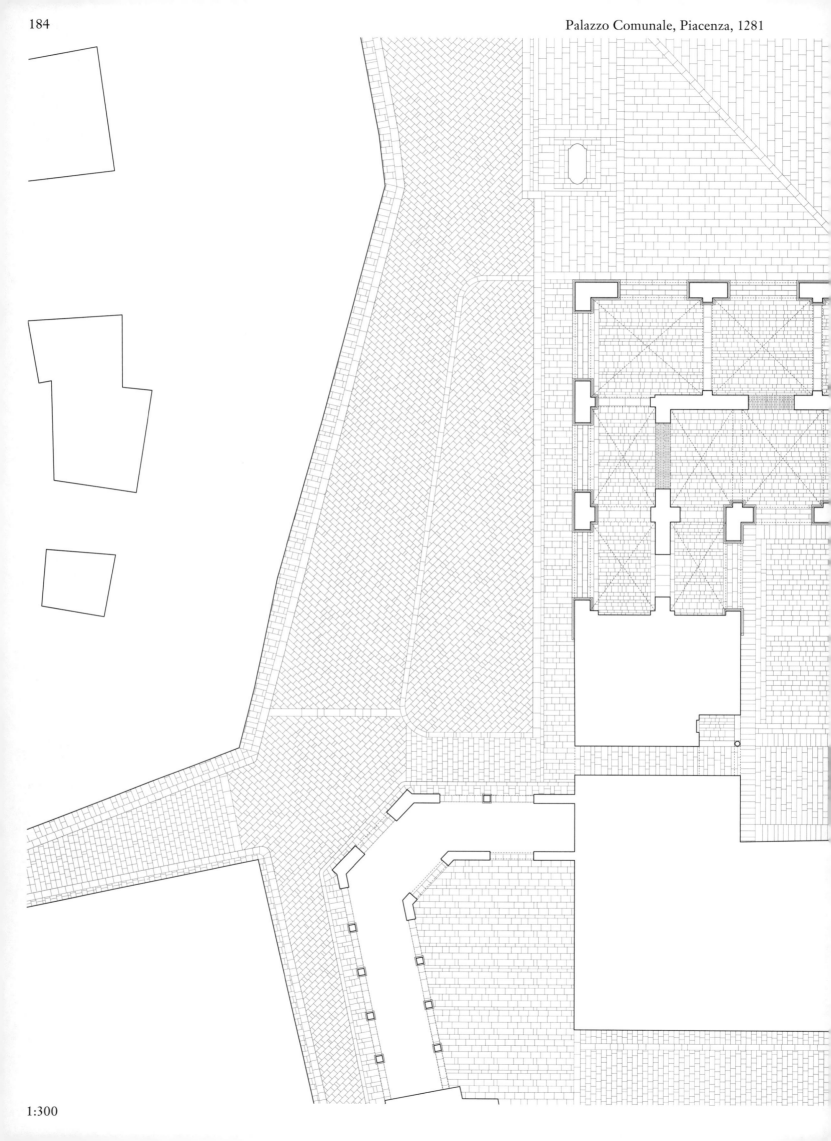

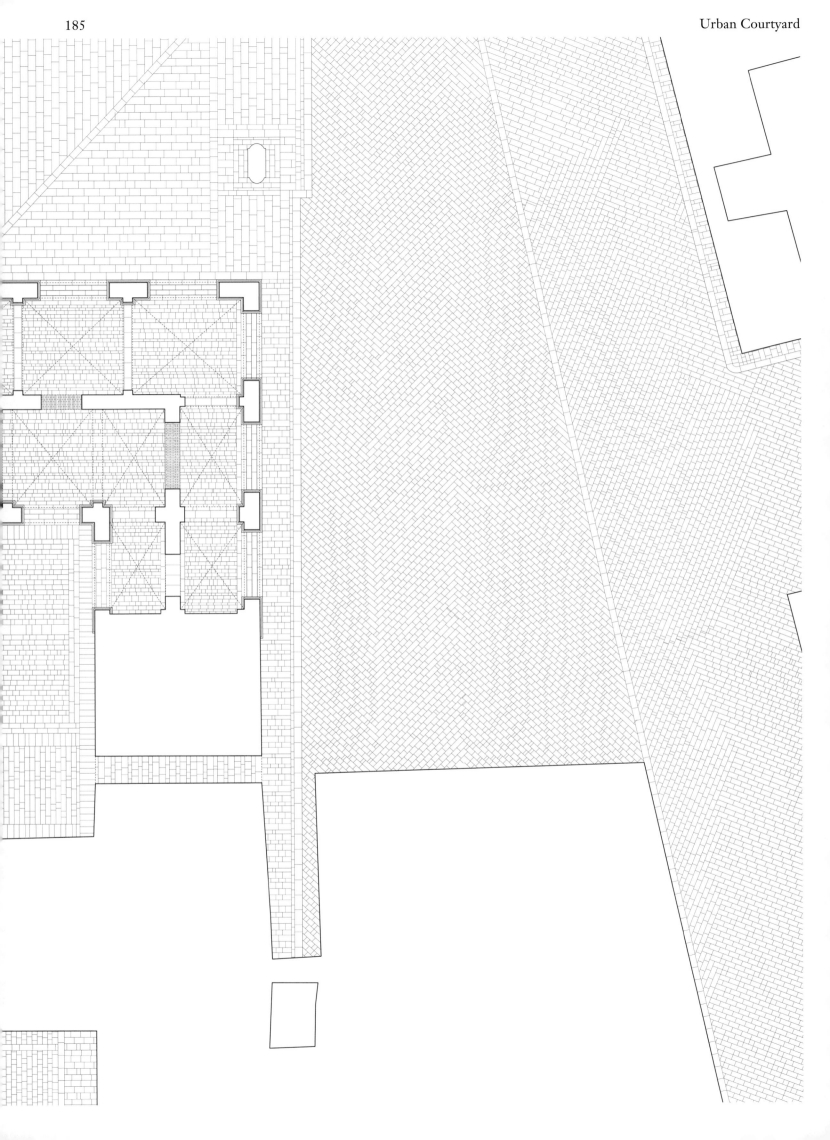

A few meters from the Este Castle, facing the large marble façade of the cathedral, stands the Palazzo Municipale of Ferrara, a ducal residence of the House of Este until the 16th century. A heterogeneous gathering of buildings constructed in successive phases forms a quadrangular urban courtyard of great breadth.

The interesting aspect of this structure does not lie in the specific, individual episodes that give rise to the complex, but in the quality and proportions of the open space, which becomes an element of aggregation between the various buildings and a junction of urban crossing. Through the three passages positioned on three of the four sides of the quad, the courtyard of the palazzo opens to the city, becoming a place of convergence of various flows.

The construction of the palazzo began in 1245 with the erecting of the "L" that faces Via Corso dei Martiri and Via Cortevecchia, recognizable thanks to the high merlons of the Torre della Vittoria. This block, the historic location of the ducal palace, is now a remake done in 1924 in Neo-Gothic style. The courtyard layout visible today took form starting in 1450, with several projects that were part of a systematic program of works ordered by Ercole I d'Este. They include the buildings that enclose the quadrangle to the northwest, the Giardino delle Duchesse and the walkway known as Via Coperta—a protected pathway at the *piano nobile* of the palazzo, supported by five arcades—which joins the northern wing to the Este Castle of Ferrara.

The main entrance to the piazza, known as *Volto del cavallo*, is a coffered atrium bordered by two large slightly depressed arches, on squat pilasters made in masonry; towards the cathedral, this access is flanked by an elegant Renaissance arch attributed to Leon Battista Alberti, and by a column with a sumptuous capital.

Inside the courtyard, measuring about 43 × 52 meters, the four sides speak very different languages in terms of height, form and number of the windows, and the arrangement of the ground level, clues to the formation of the complex over time. The southeastern side, divided into two halves by the entrance arch, has an impressive flight of steps on one side—designed by Pietro Benvenuto degli Ordini in 1481, with a vaulted roof and cupola supported by five arches on six columns in composite order—and by three arches on marble columns, on the other side, enclosed by filler elements in approximately 1375. The southwestern side features large entrances for the shops on the ground floor, with arches having a very limited rise, topped by three orders of windows with a slightly different rhythm than the openings on the ground floor. Along the northwestern side, eight segmental arches, of which one has been closed, on low columns and with a composite capital of simple form, are topped by an equal number of biforate windows. Finally, on the last side to the northeast, we again find entrances to shops, topped by a double order of windows that create a rhythm interrupted by the portal of the former court chapel, built in 1476. This heterogeneous set of elements is held together by the large paved surface, entirely covered in brick: in a rectangle measuring 34 × 40 meters, indicated by a double row of rectangular granite blocks, squared panels of brick are laid in a herringbone pattern, following different orientations.

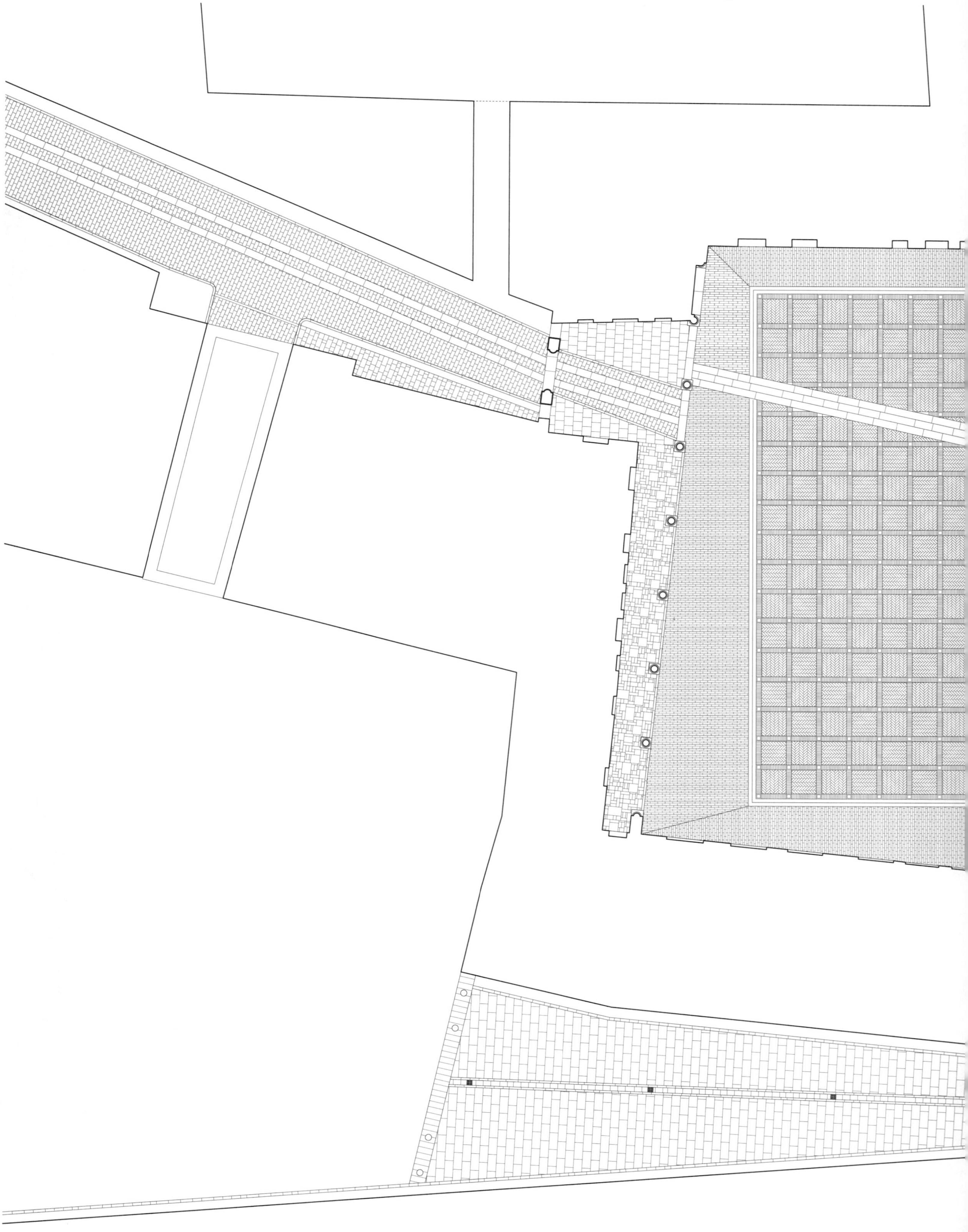

1:300

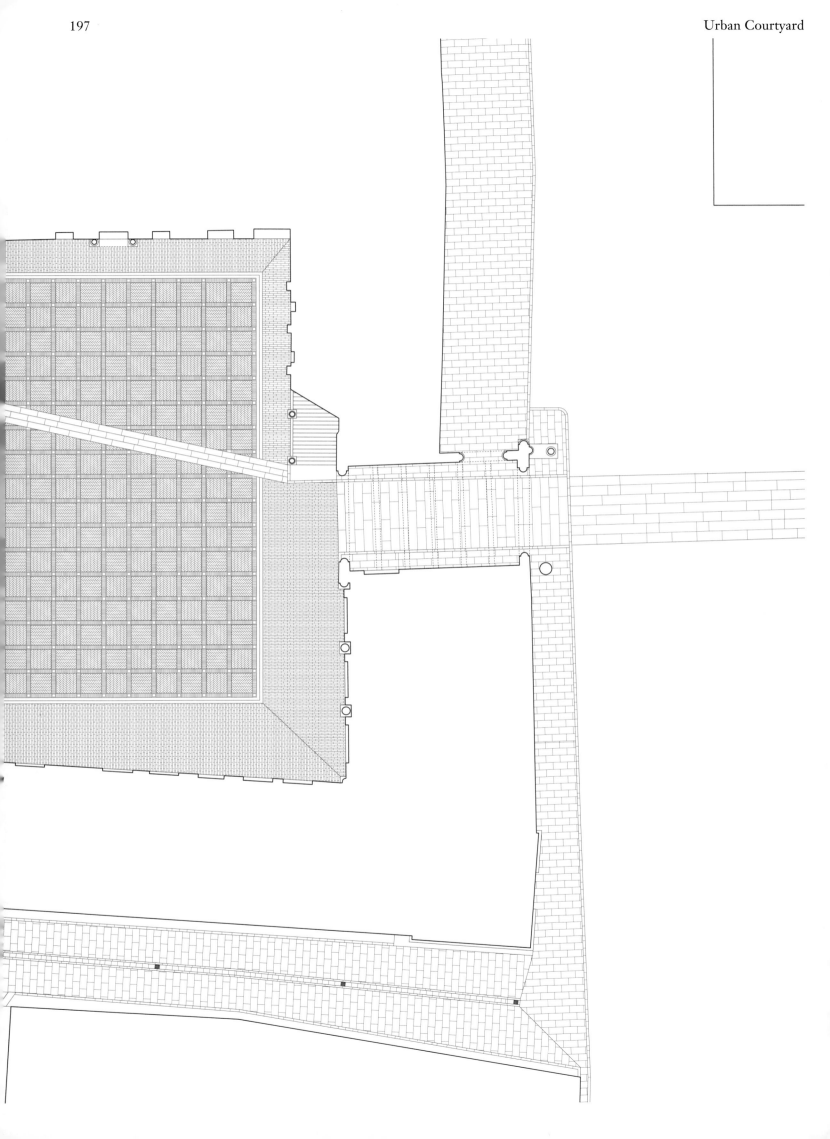

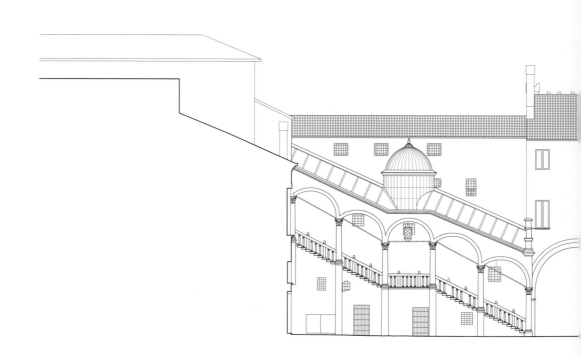

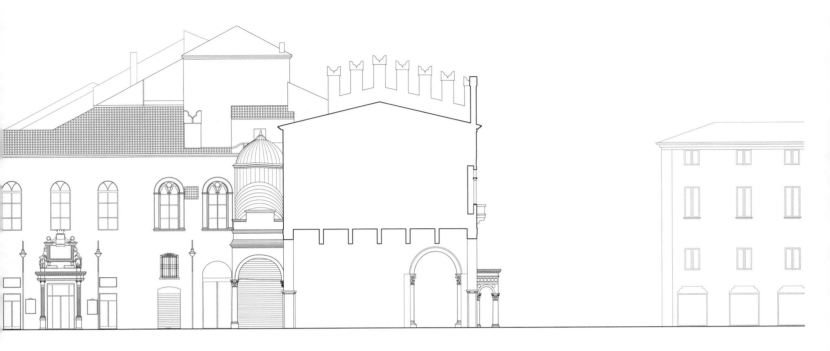

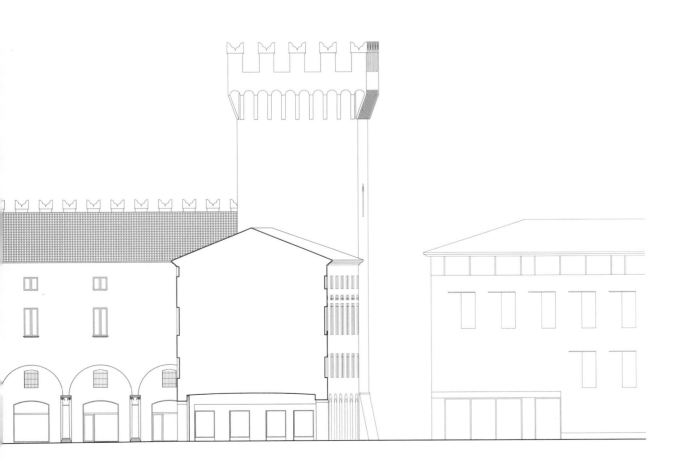

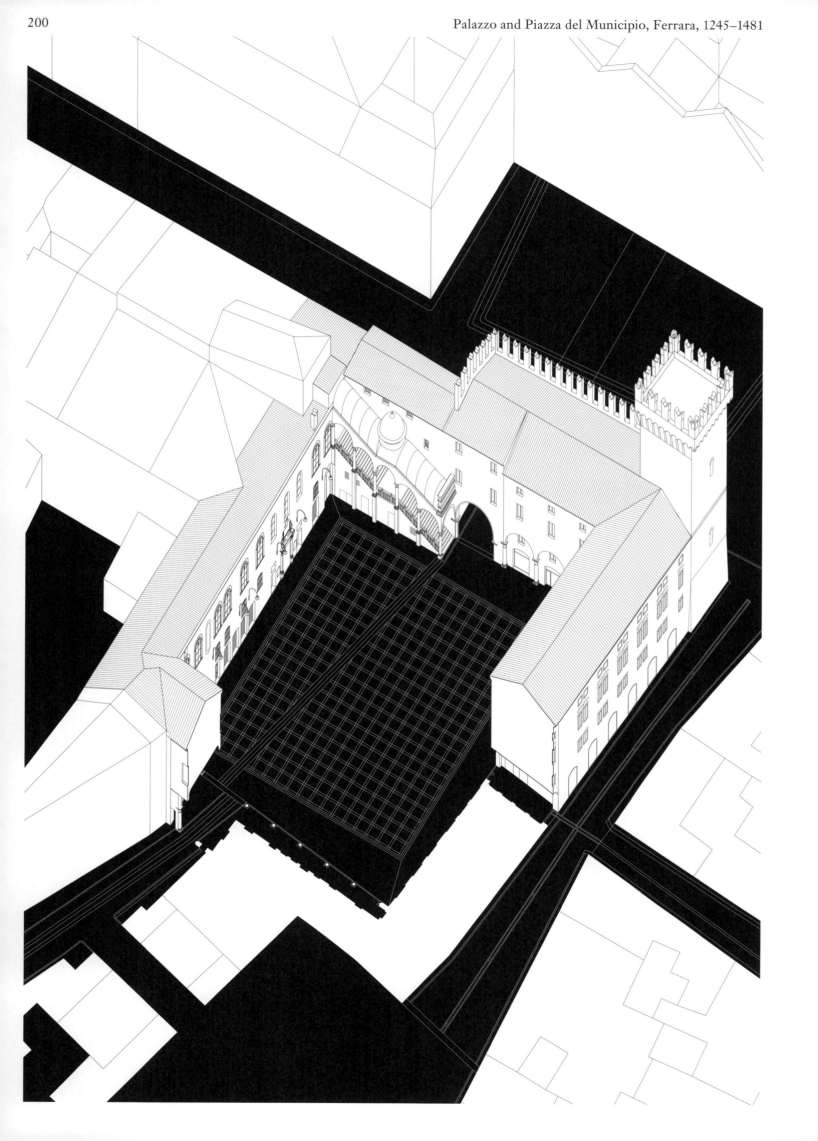

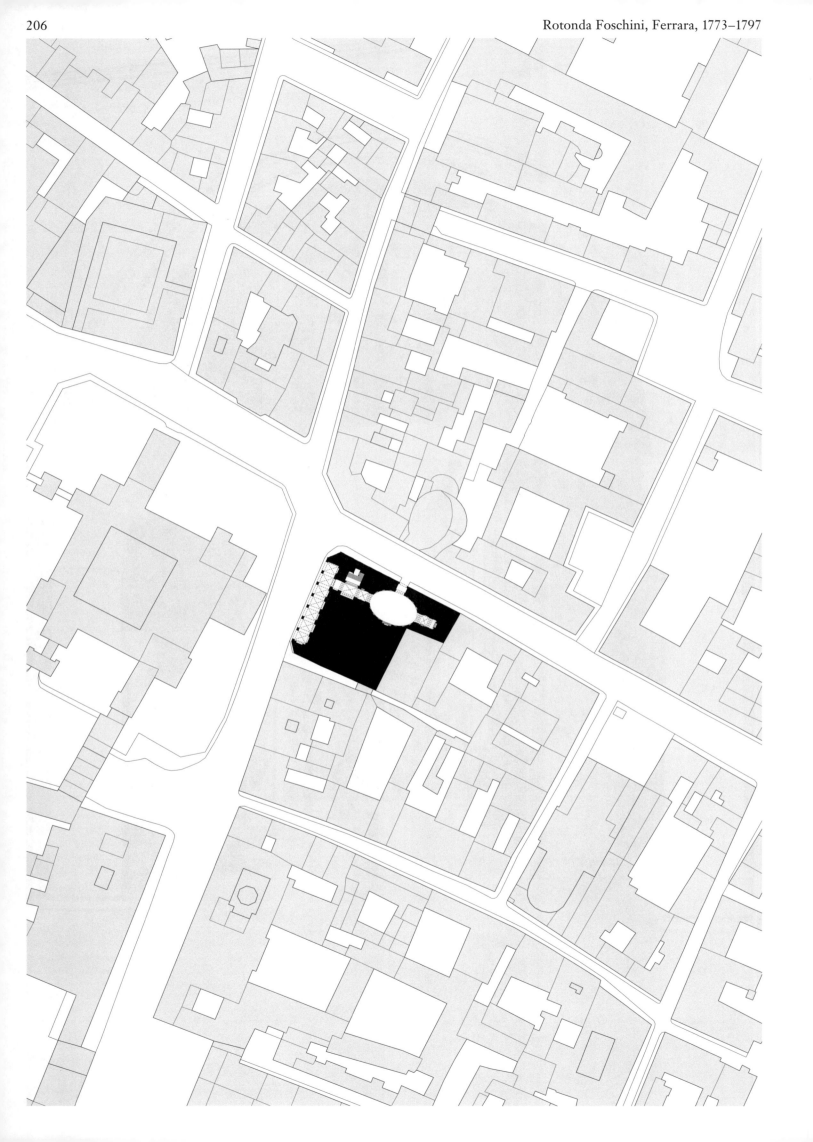

Rotonda Foschini, Ferrara, 1773–1797   206–217

An integral part of the architecture of the Teatro
Comunale of Ferrara, Rotonda Foschini is a
small oval courtyard connected to the city by two
different covered passageways.

     In spite of its closed and apparently not
very visible geometry, this intimate location
full of charm belongs to the public space of the city,
thanks to the two vaulted accessways on the main
façade of the theater, on Corso Martiri della Libertà
and Corso della Giovecca.

     The history of the Rotonda is inseparably
linked to that of the Teatro Comunale: at the
end of the 1700s, with the rise of the bourgeoisie,
the necessity emerged to create a new theater
of adequate size, in spite of the fact that the city of
Ferrara already contained various facilities for
the performing arts. In 1773 the cardinal legate
Scipione Borghese commissioned Antonio Foschini
and Cosimo Morelli to design the new theater, to
be built on an already identified area in front
of the Este Castle. The construction, after many
interruptions and revisions, was completed in 1793.

     The space of the Rotonda was initially
designed for the transit and parking of carriages,
offering direct access to the theater from Corso
Martiri della Libertà and Corso della Giovecca.
Today the Rotonda, dedicated to the engineer
Antonio Foschini, one of the two designers of the
structure but not directly of the Rotonda,
which was designed by Cosimo Morelli, is utilized
as a pedestrian passage.

     The space of the Rotonda, with its oval
form, measures 18 meters in length and 12 meters in
width, developing vertically with four orders of
windows to reach the eaves of the roof at a height
of 16 meters.

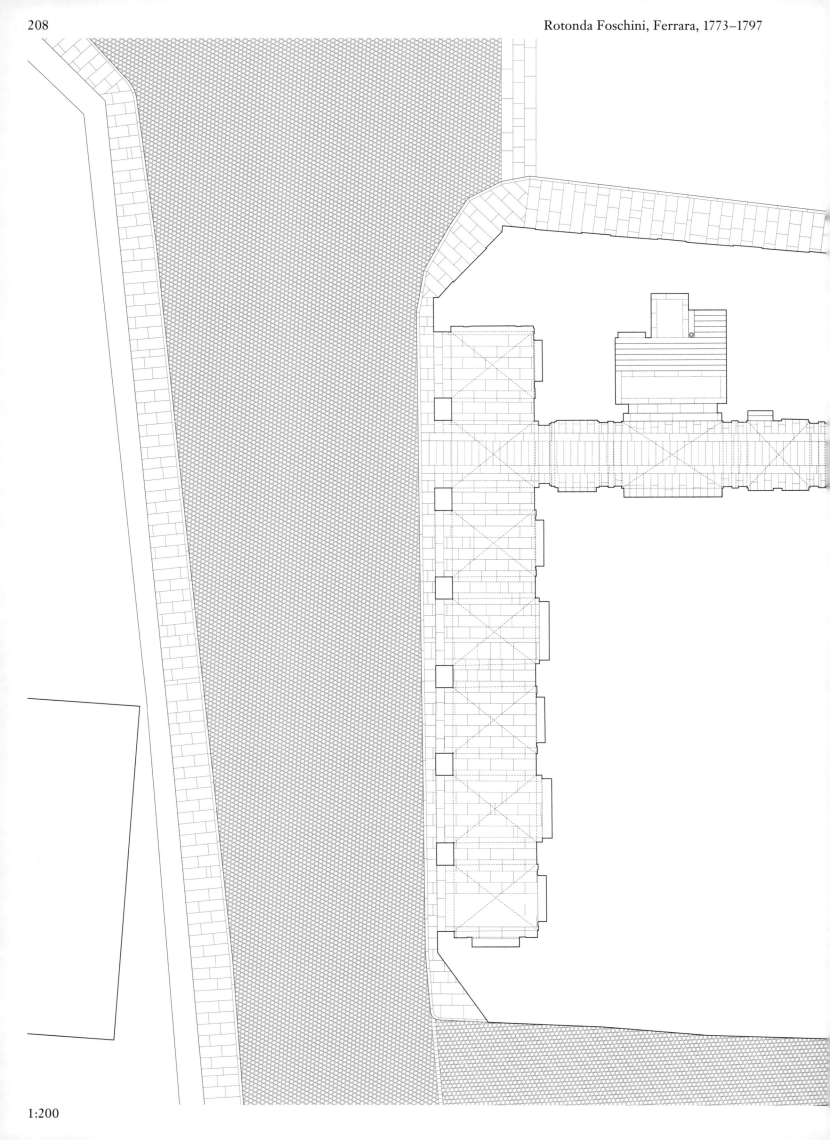

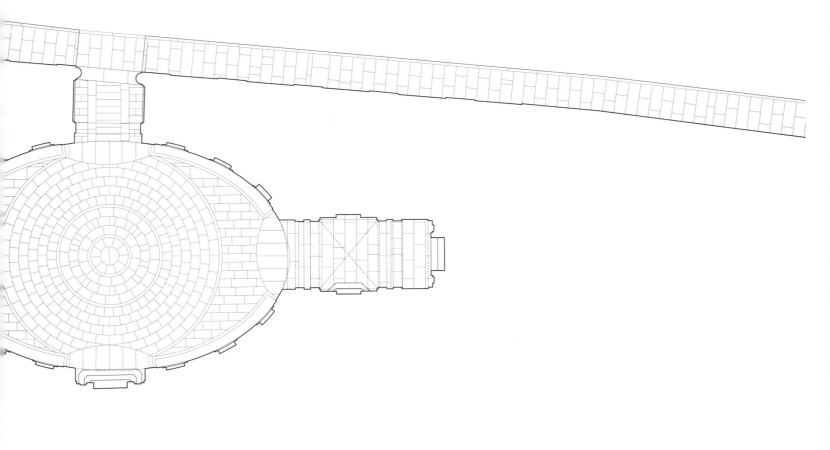

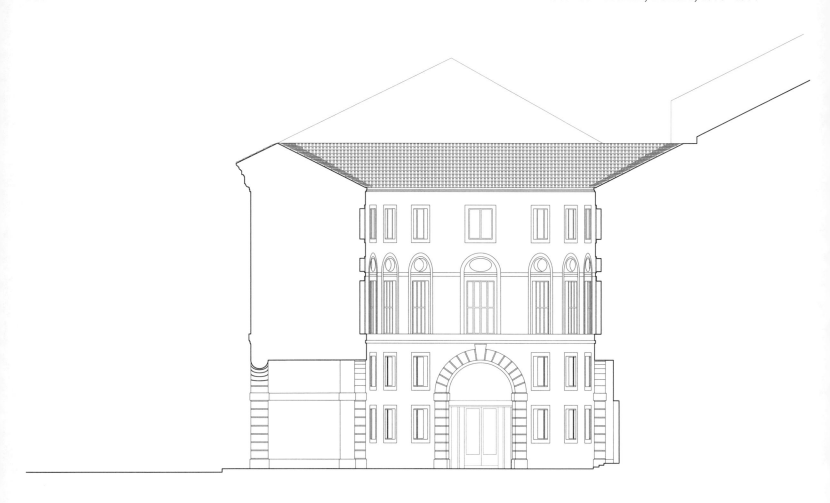

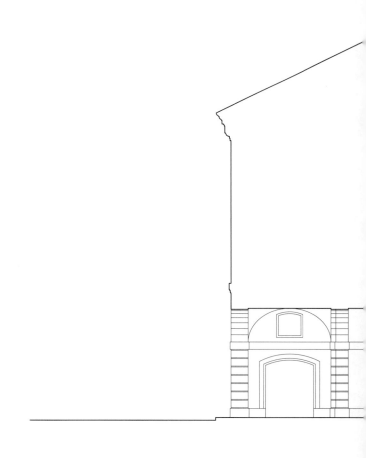

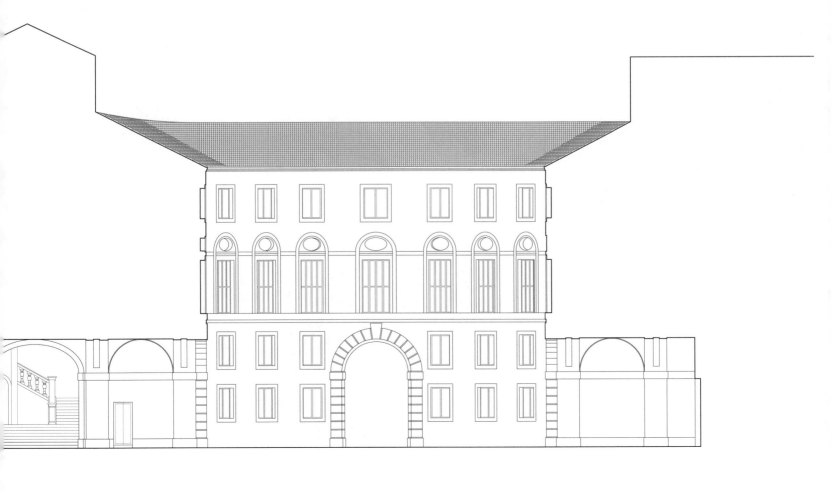

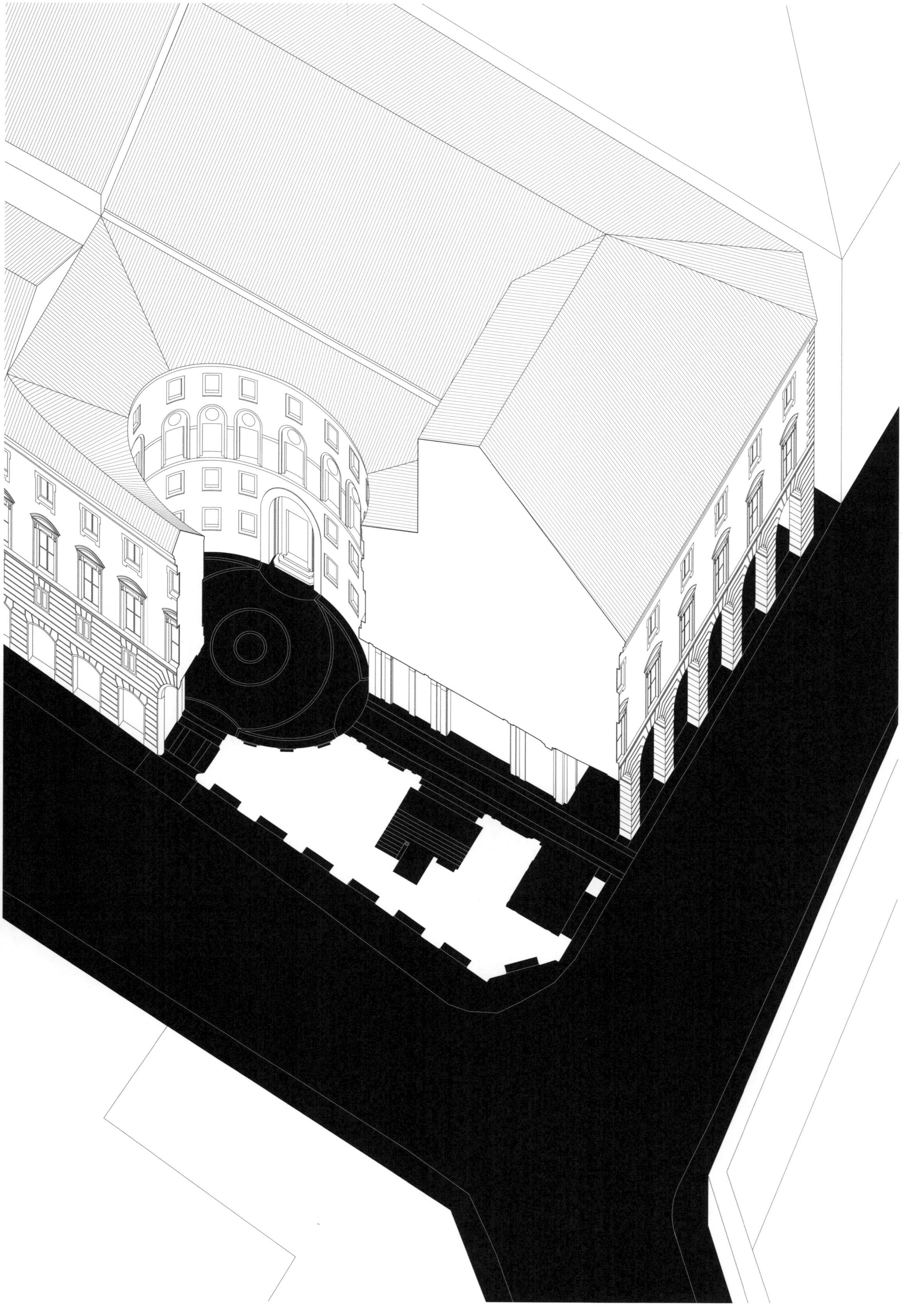

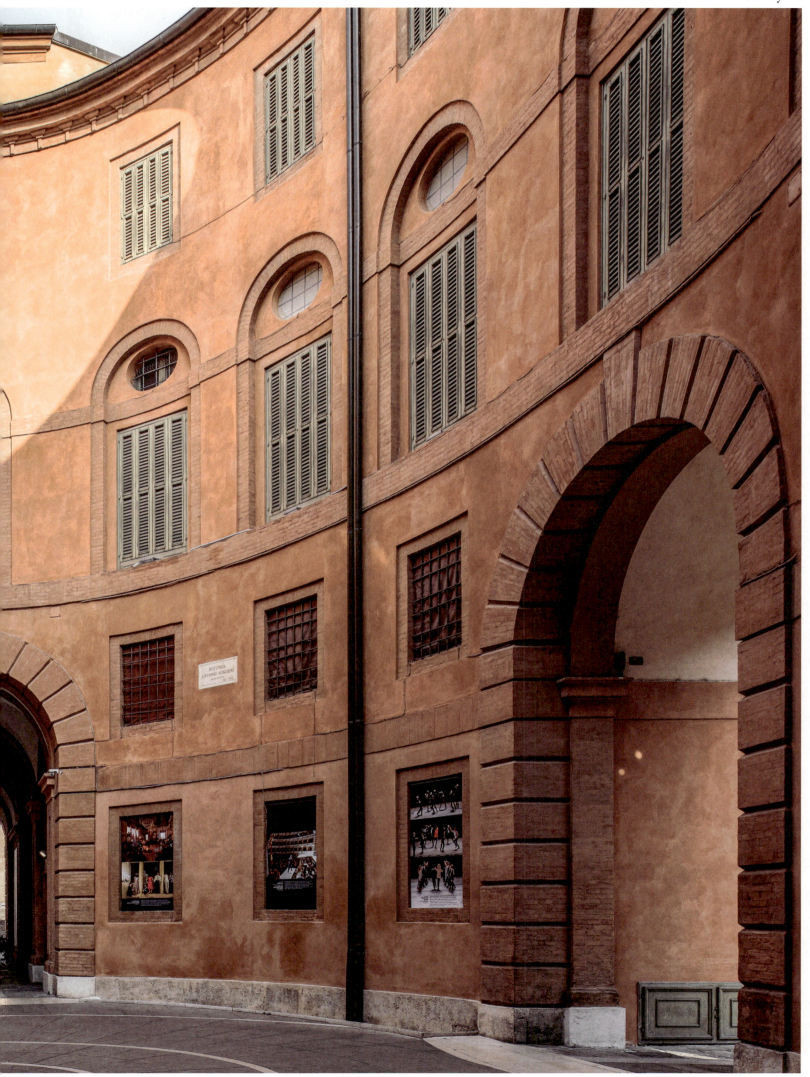

An oblong space created inside large buildings or by covering a segment of a public street to act as a center of urban life containing cultural activities, food and beverage facilities, or shops.

In other words, when a building or group of buildings incorporates the urban condition of the street and the square inside itself, producing an inversion between interior and exterior, private and public.

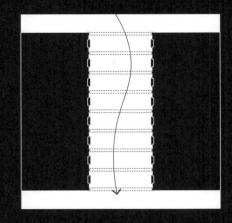

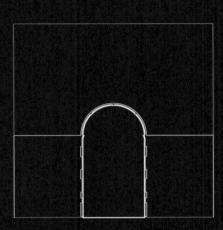

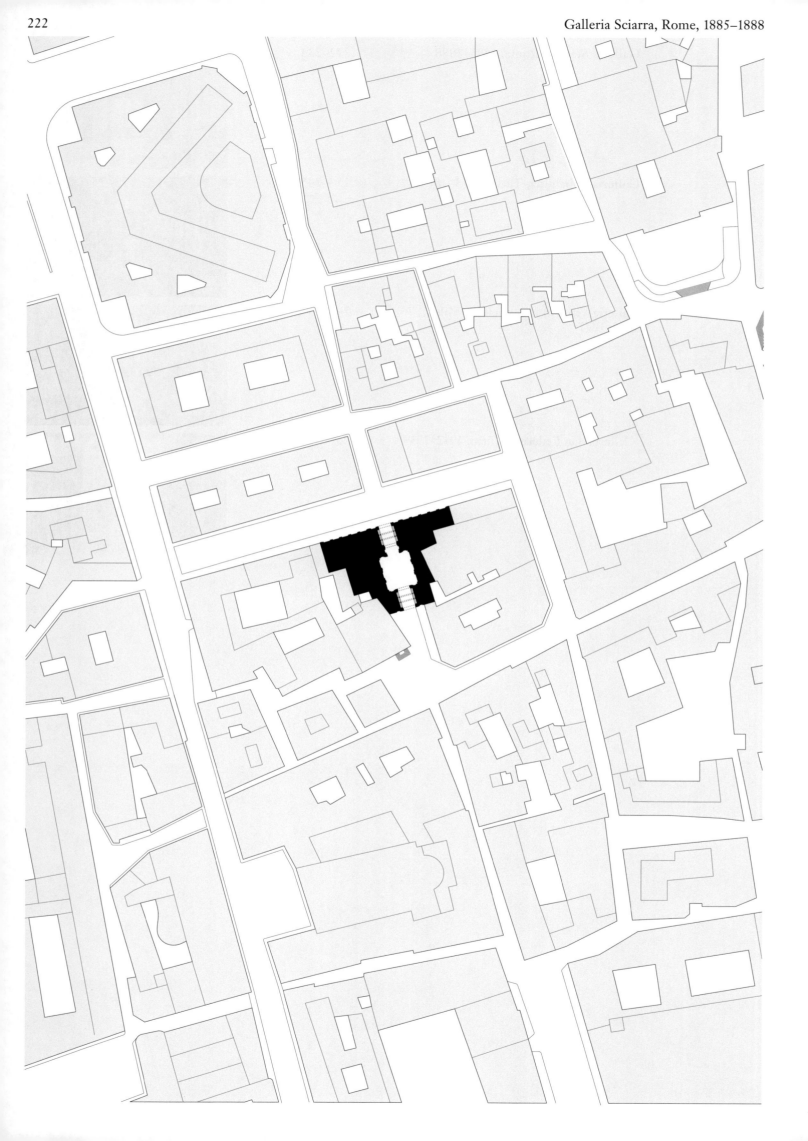

Galleria Sciarra, Rome, 1885–1888   222–233

Galleria Sciarra is a covered pedestrian passage that connects Palazzo Sciarra to Teatro Quirino. It was built by order of the Prince Maffeo Barberini-Colonna di Sciarra, with the aim of linking Palazzo Sciarra with various activities and properties of the family.

Though the language and materials utilized remind us of the passages of Paris, Galleria Sciarra differs from the French prototypes in terms of both shape and function. With respect to the passages, the Roman galleria has a prevalently vertical extension, therefore not configured as a covered street faced by cafés and shops, but as a vertical joint of access and circulation for the buildings it connects.

The project was carried out from 1885 to 1888 by the architect Giulio De Angelis—who had a particular focus on the use of cast iron in new constructions—while the decorations were created by Giuseppe Cellini.

The galleria, whose longitudinal span is equal to 35.5 meters, has a triple organization in its plan: at the ends there are two opposing atriums, each with a height of about 6 meters, featuring coffered ceilings and cast-iron columns; the central part, the vital fulcrum of the galleria, is forcefully vertical and is topped by a luminous pavilion vault in iron and glass. This space, measuring 13.1 × 11.3 meters, by a height of 28 meters, is vertically divided by three orders of composite Ionic-Corinthian pilaster strips, alternating with four orders of windows decorated with moldings, frames, and aediculae; on the short sides, besides the same windows, there are four orders of trifores in the center.

The internal space was completely decorated by Giuseppe Cellini, in the year of its construction, with terracotta and frescos created with the encaustic technique. The central theme of the decoration is the "Glorification of Women" and particularly of the mother of the prince, Carolina Colonna Sciarra, indicated by her seal in the wall paintings, with Greek, archaic, and Etruscan motifs mixed with Renaissance figures with oriental and Egyptian references.

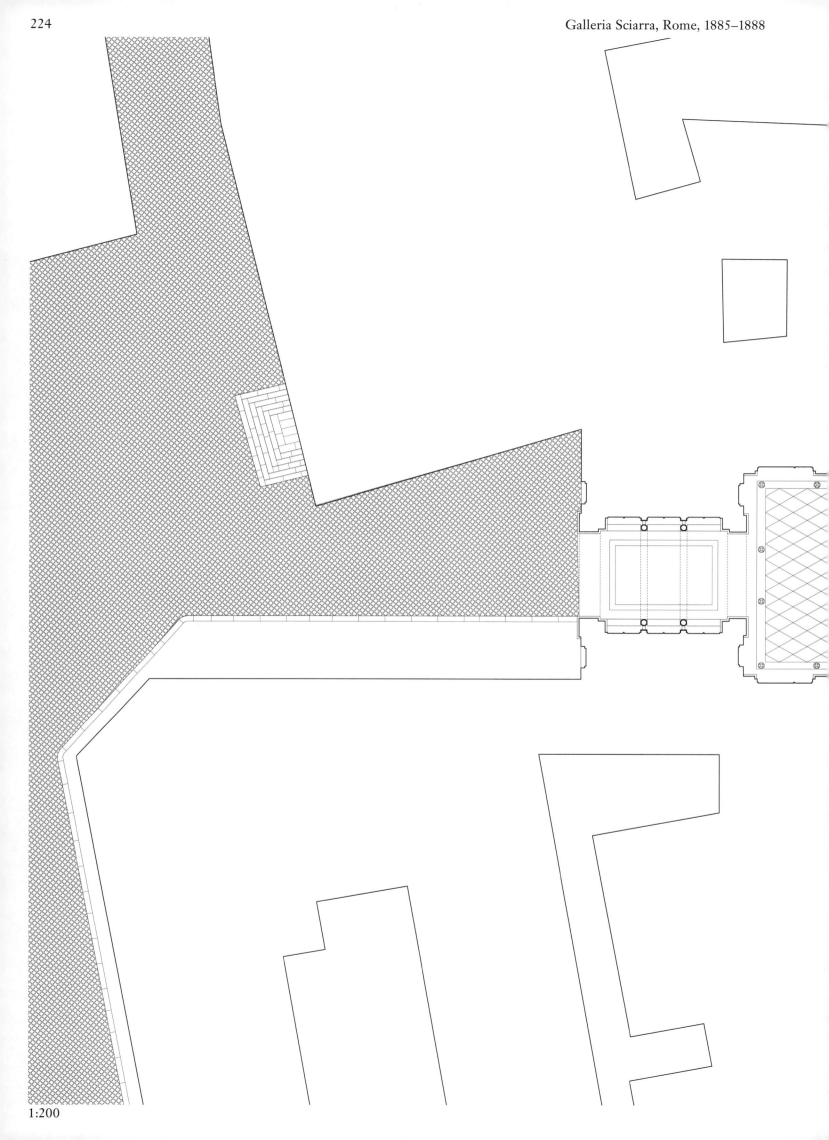

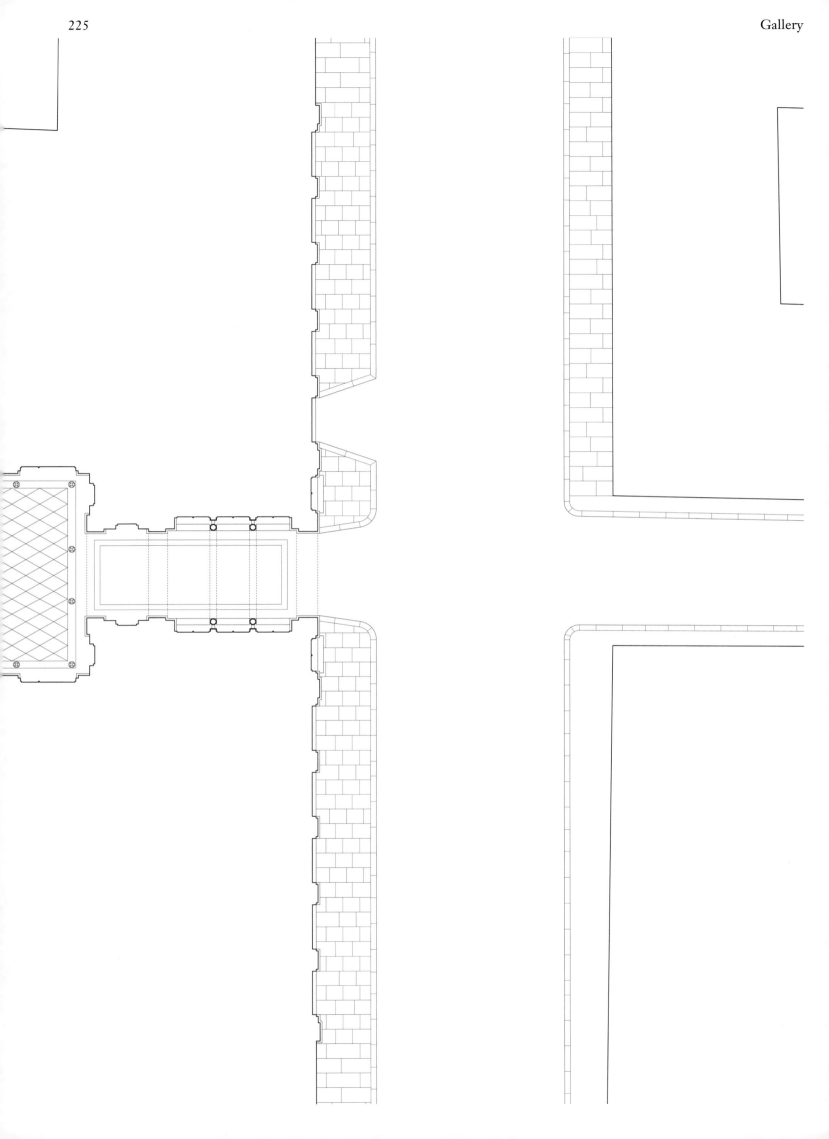

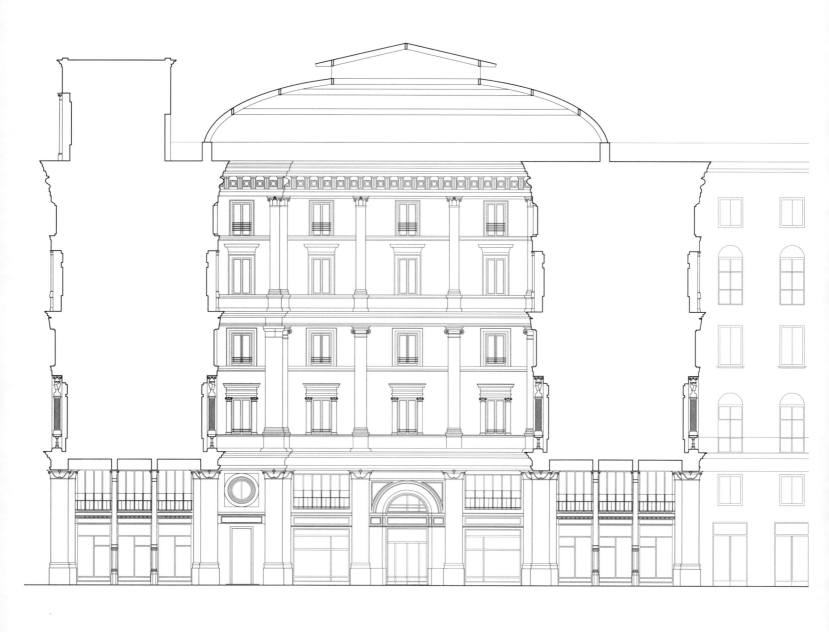

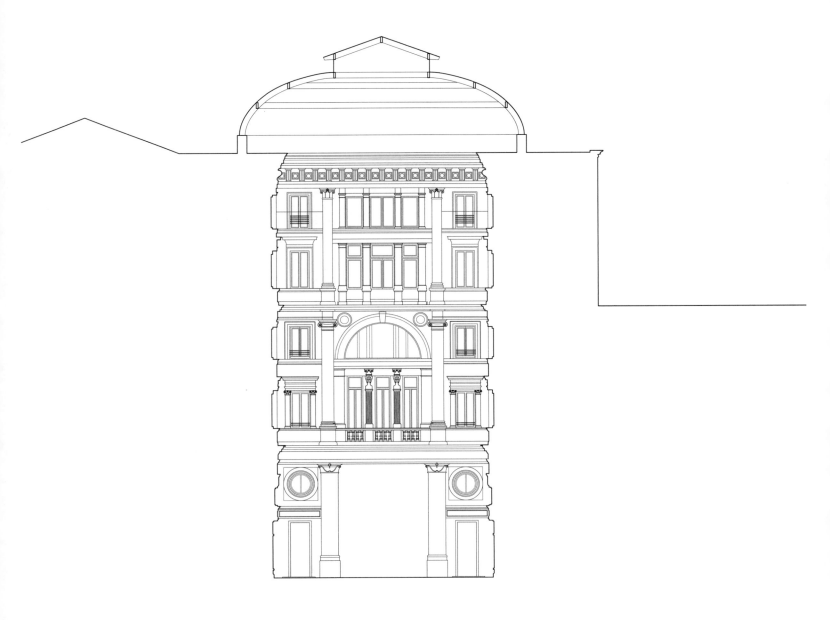

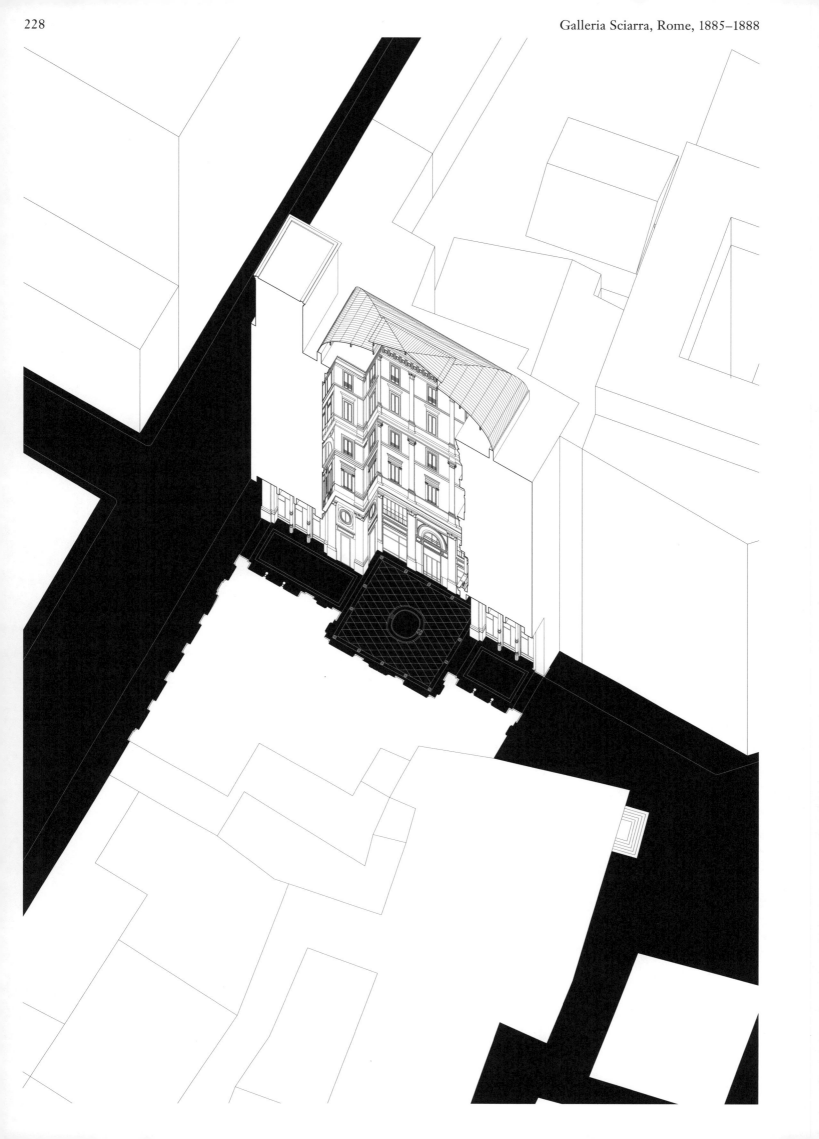

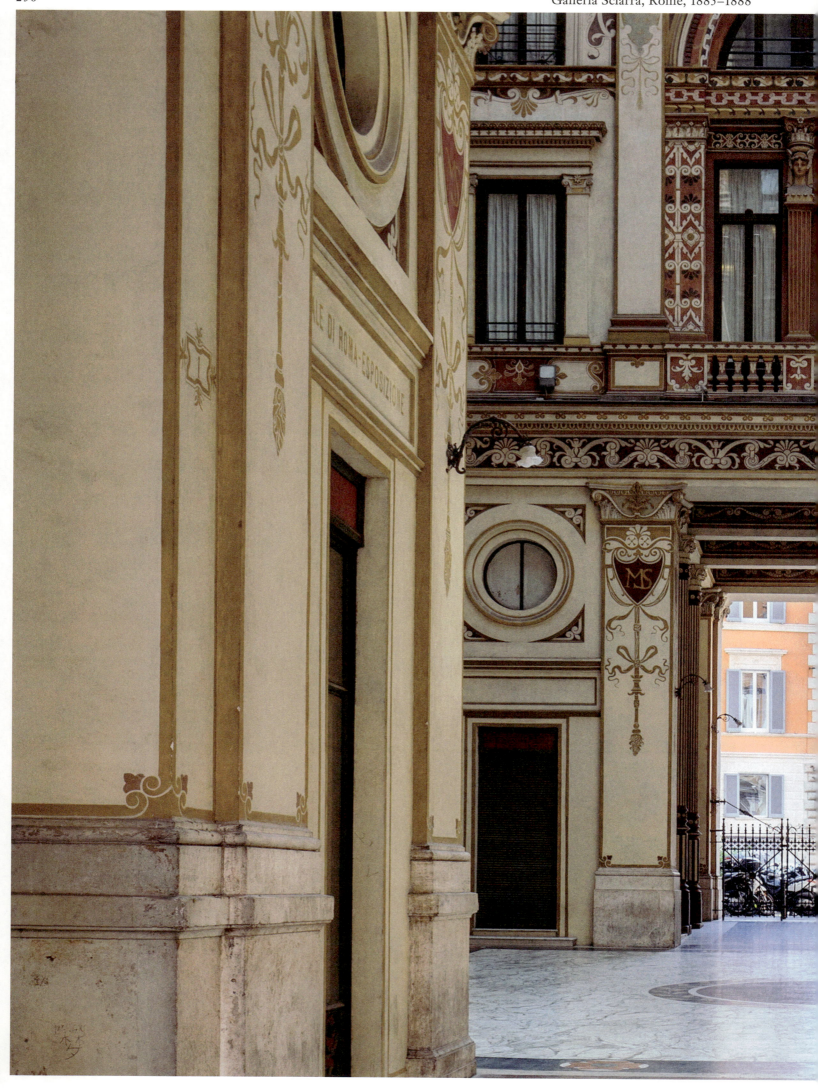

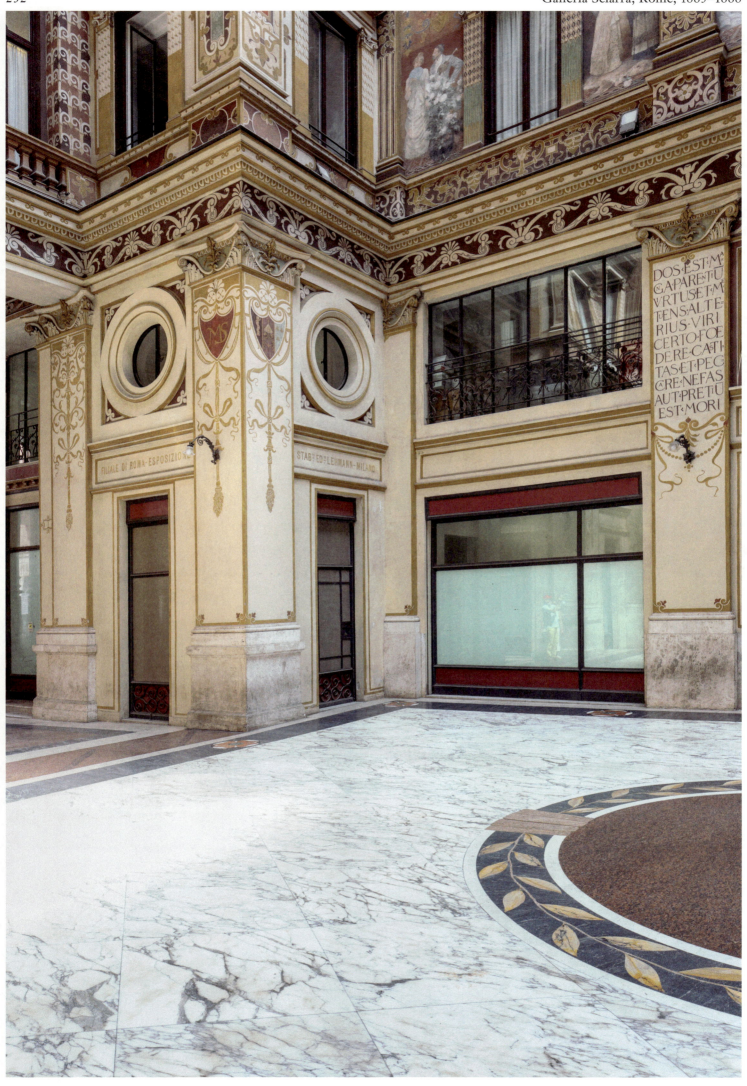

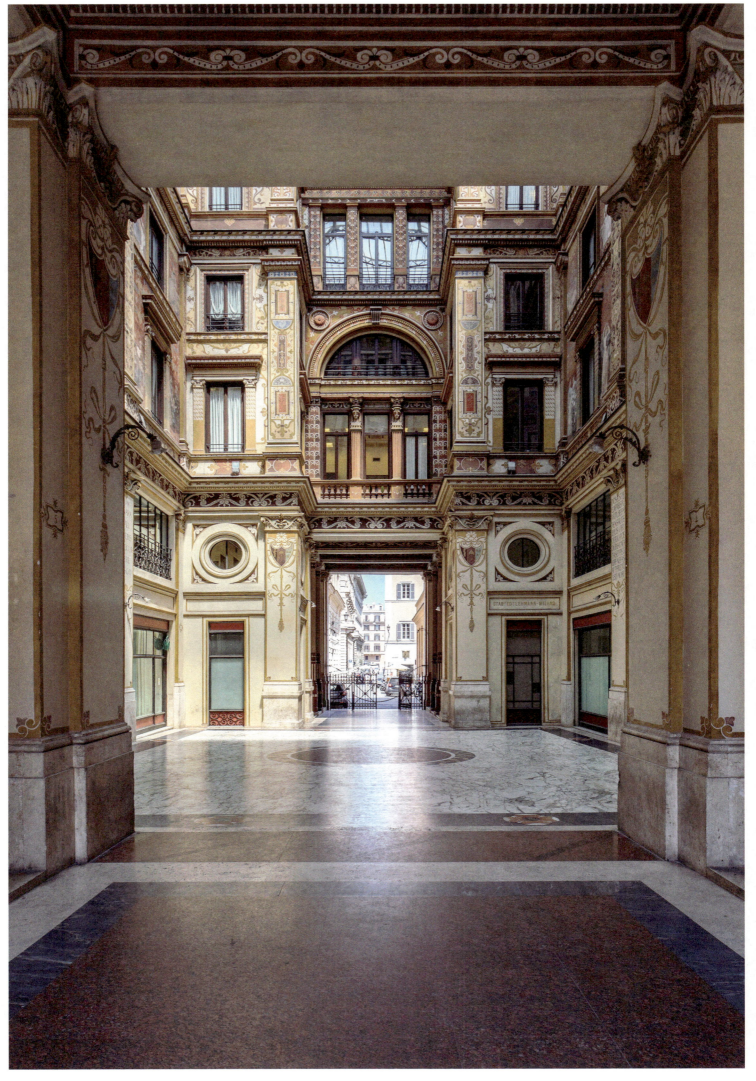

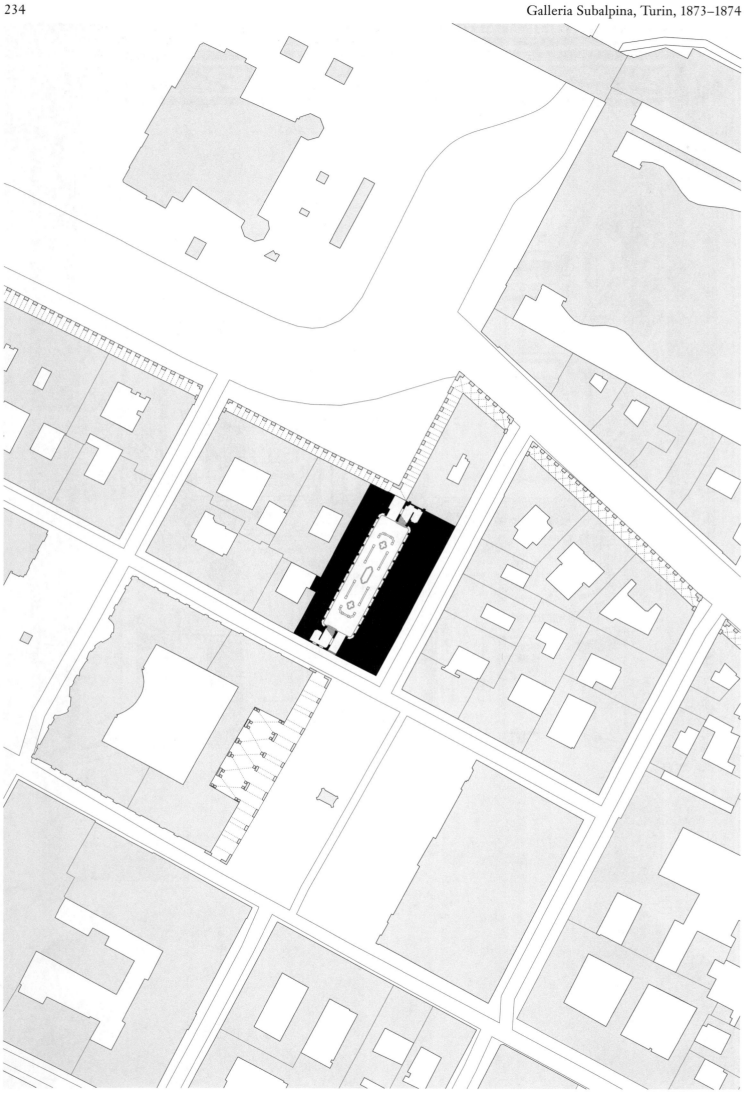

Galleria Subalpina, Turin, 1873–1874   234–245

Galleria Subalpina, one of the most important shopping passages built in Italy in the 19th century, takes its name from the Banca dell'Industria Subalpina, which entirely covered the costs of construction.

Clearly based on the Parisian passage type, Galleria Subalpina was created for the leisure time of the new bourgeois class, but it differs from the French model in terms of the breadth and proportions of the central space, conceived not just as a place of passage, but as a true covered square. At the same time, though it apparently blends into the urban setting, the galleria can be seen as a device of connection between two important public places in the city: Piazza Castello and Piazza Carlo Alberto, respectively the birthplaces of the first Subalpine Parliament and the first Senate of the Kingdom of Italy.

Designed by Pietro Carrera in 1873 and completed one year later, the galleria hosted several venues that took on historic importance, such as the Caffè Baratti & Milano, the Caffè Concerto Romano, which later became the Cinema Nuovo Romano, as well as restaurants, bookstores, and art galleries, which were an integral part of the project from the outset.

The internal space with a rectangular form measures 11 meters in width by 46 meters in length. The roof is composed of 11 longitudinal spans and 2 crosswise spans, joined by 4 corner bays at the extremities. On the vertical axis, the space is subdivided into two main levels, marked by the presence of a continuous balcony at a height of 7 meters. The glass roof with wrought-iron ribbing extends to a height of 20 meters and allows abundant natural light to enter, producing the impression of being in an outdoor space. The galleria is enhanced by eclectic decorations, blending Renaissance and Baroque features, created by the sculptor Pietro Rubino.

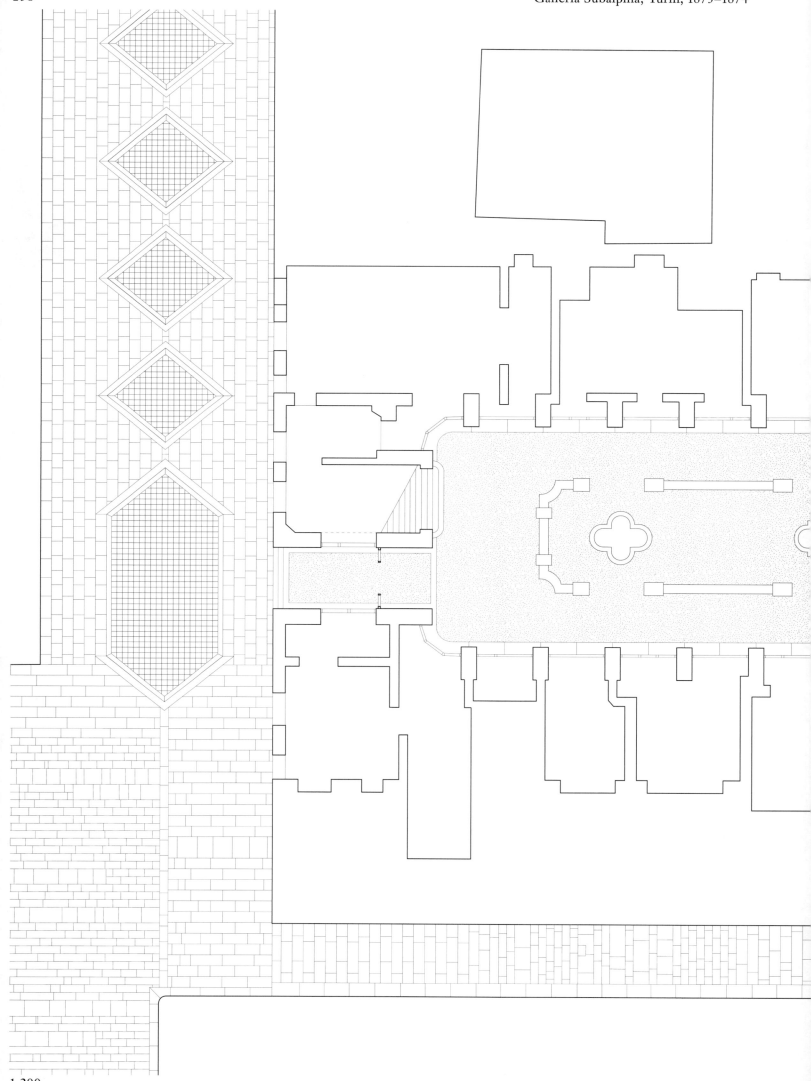

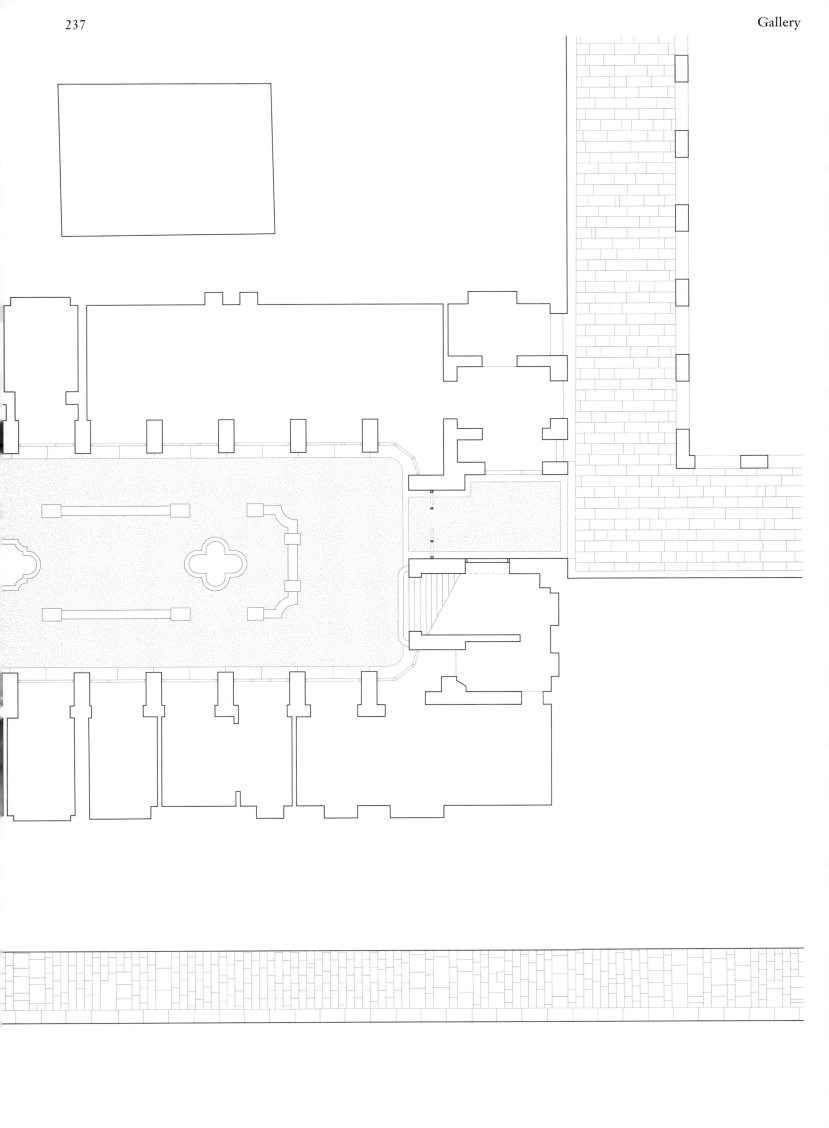

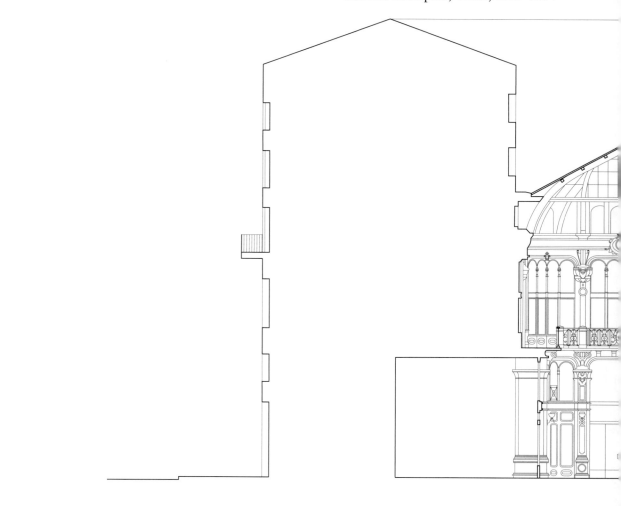

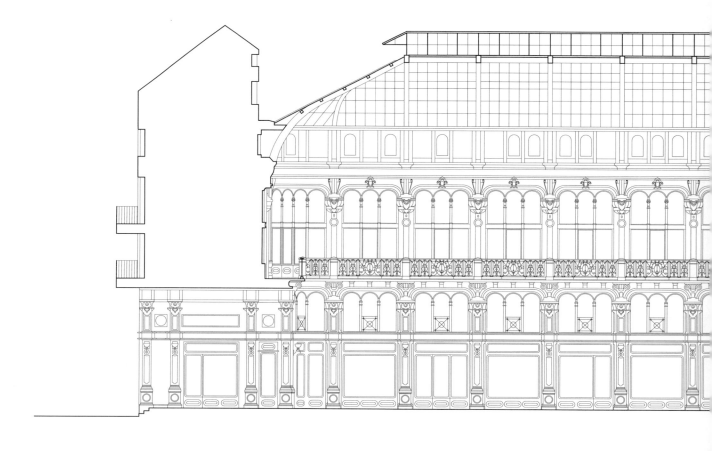

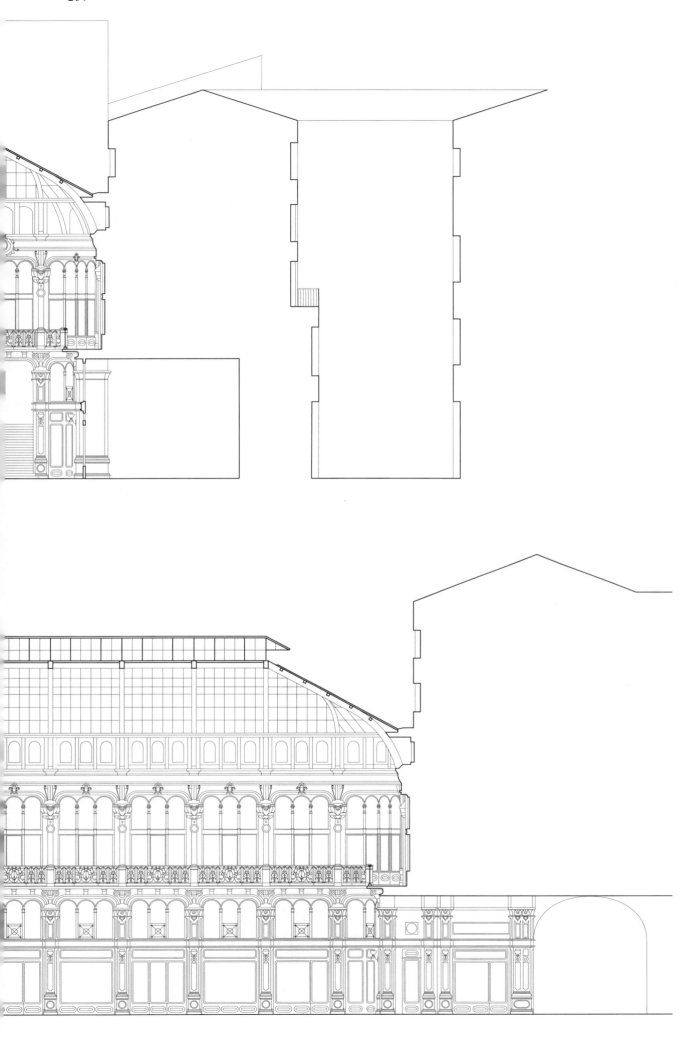

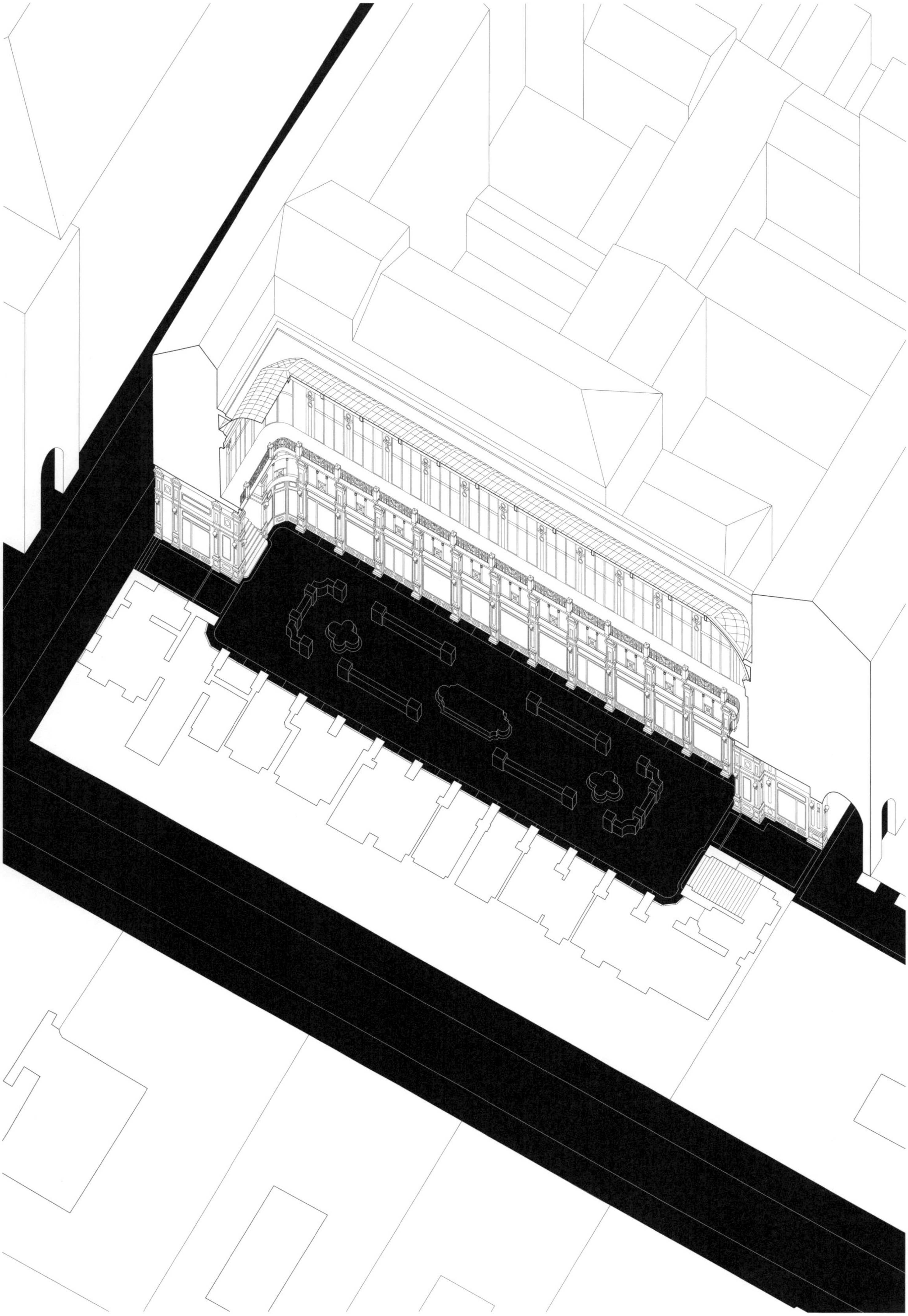

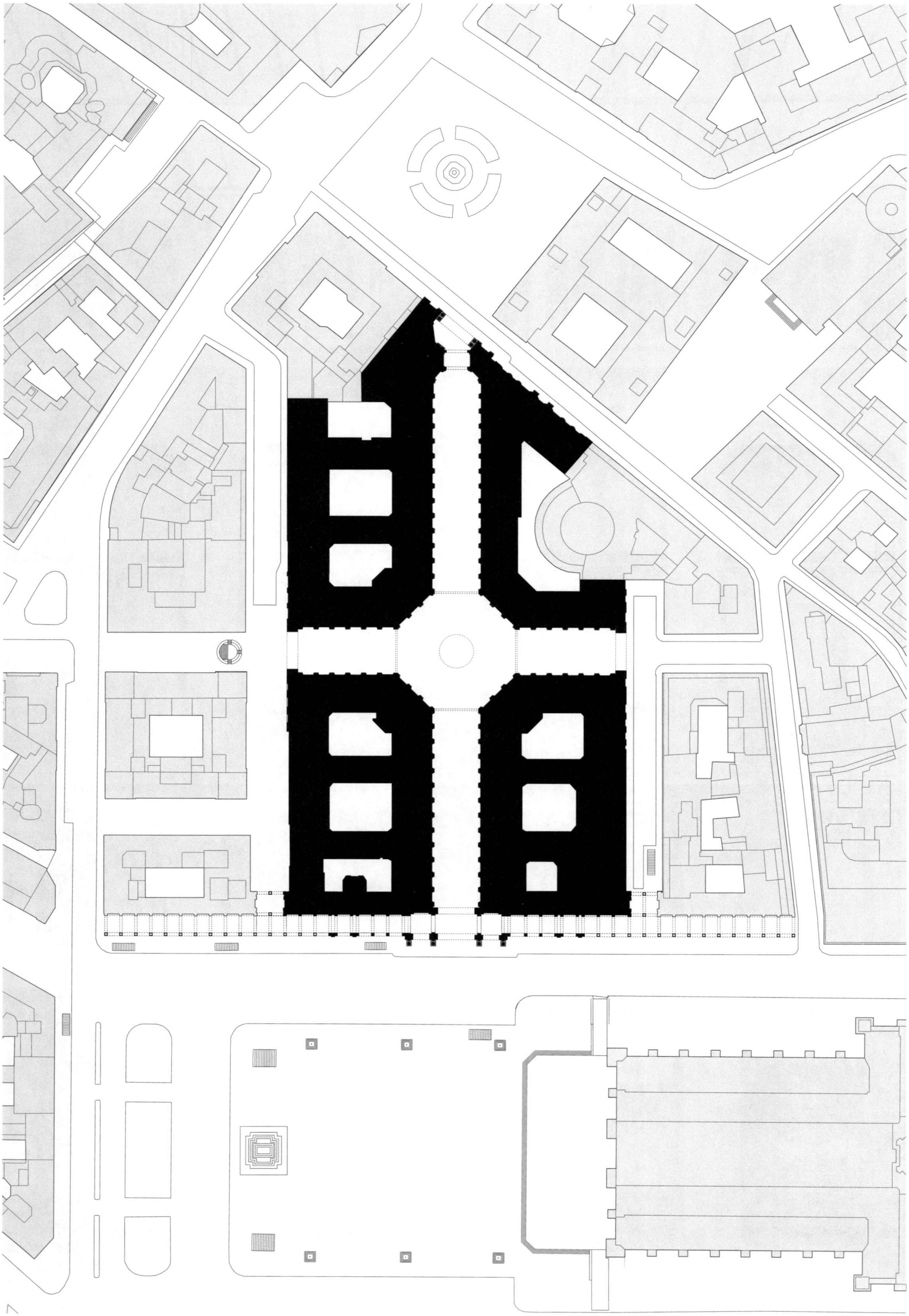

Galleria Vittorio Emanuele II, Milan,   246–257
1865–1877

Built from 1865 to 1877, Galleria Vittorio Emanuele II in Milan is one of the largest covered pedestrian streets in Europe; a walkway of almost 200 meters that connects two of the most important places in the city: the Duomo (cathedral) and Teatro alla Scala.

With respect to the archetype of the passages of London, Paris, and Brussels, Galleria Vittorio Emanuele stands out for its monumental size, making it a prototype of reference for the galleria typology all over Europe; a place set aside for shops, strolling and leisure, the rites of the new bourgeois class during its period of origin.

The idea of a route connecting Piazza Duomo and Piazza della Scala arose in the wake of one of the many debates taking place in Milan at the time, regarding the refurbishing of the piazza in front of the cathedral, which was smaller than it is today, irregular in form, and deemed by many to be unsuitable in its role as the square in front of the cathedral. After two competitions without winners, held in 1860 and 1861, the project was assigned to Giuseppe Mengoni, as the result of a third competition held in 1863; the definitive project was completed in 1864, and construction began in 1865. The work, excluding the building of the central entrance archway and the northern porticos of Piazza Duomo, lasted only three years, leading to an initial inauguration in 1867. Full completion of the project, however, came only in 1878.

The galleria is perfectly oriented on the cardinal axes and has a cruciform layout with four arms of different lengths: on the north-south axis it has a length of about 196 meters, while the east-west axis measures about 105. At the intersection there is a large internal piazza with an octagonal form. The planimetric structure is obtained by repetition—92 times—of the same modular span: 14.5 meters in width and 32 meters in height. The single module is composed in its elevation by three levels topped by a mezzanine, with a large round arch opening on ground level and three orders of windows on the levels above,

decorated in Lombard Neo-Renaissance style. The modules are separated by Ionic pilasters on high pedestals, with a second order of caryatids and telamons. The forceful vertical rhythm is softened by two protruding trabeations that form the balcony and the upper cornice that conceals the roof supports.

A barrel vault with a height of 29 meters, entirely in iron and glass, covers the arms of the galleria, while the crossing is protected by a glass dome reaching a level of 47 meters from the floor, with a diameter of 39 meters, inspired by the drawings of the Crystal Palace of New York. The ends of each arm are underscored by the presence of a monumental portal that creates a theatrical entrance and marks the presence of the gallery seen from the city.

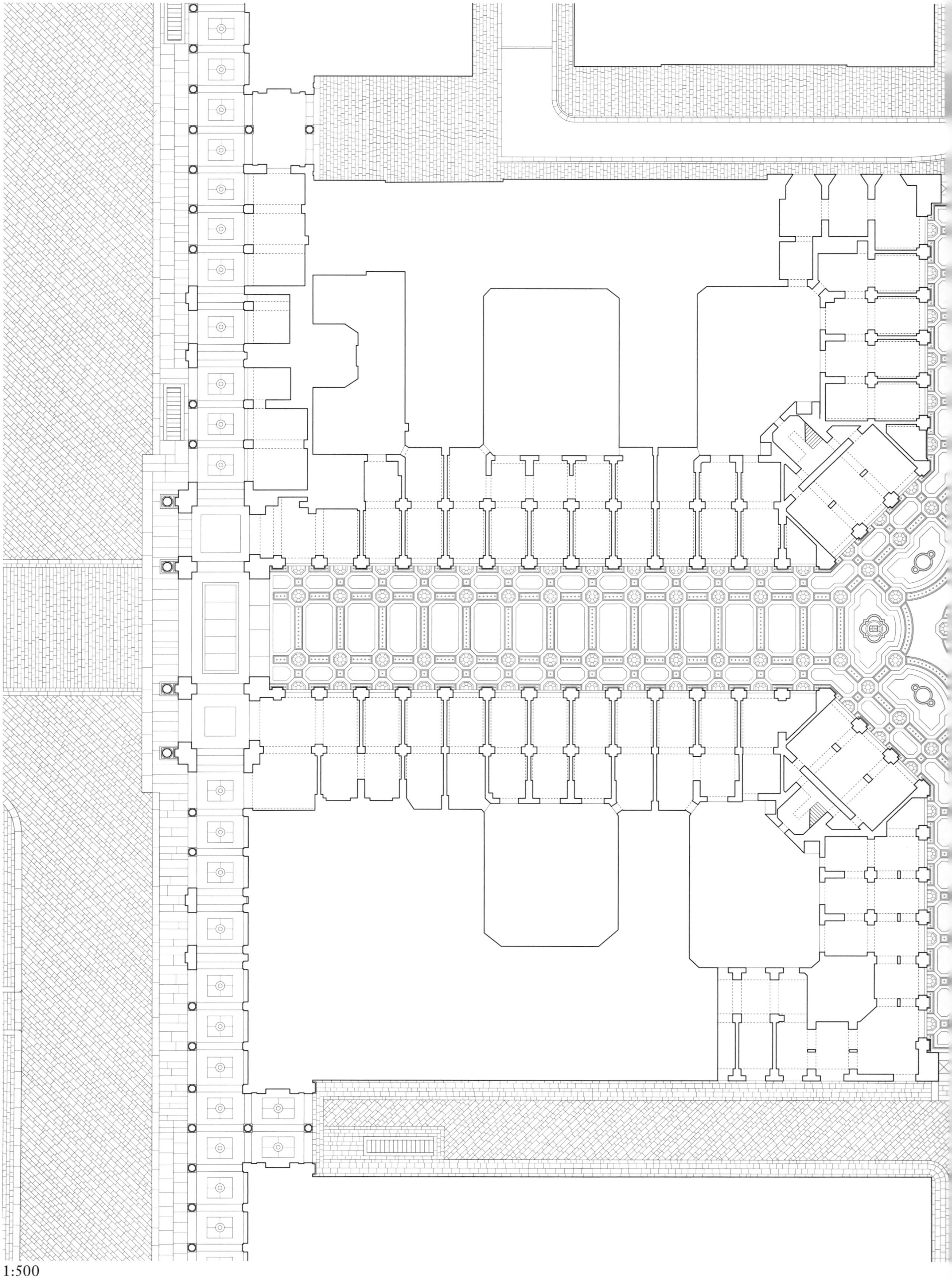

1:500

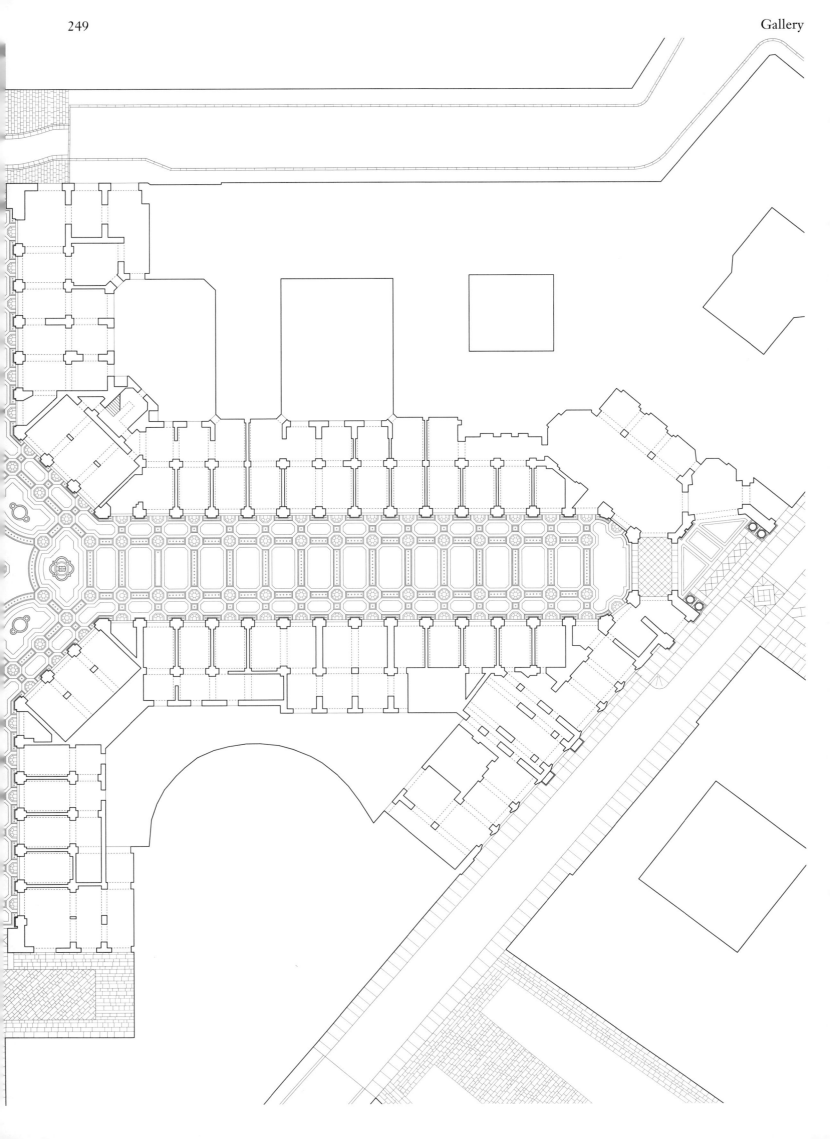

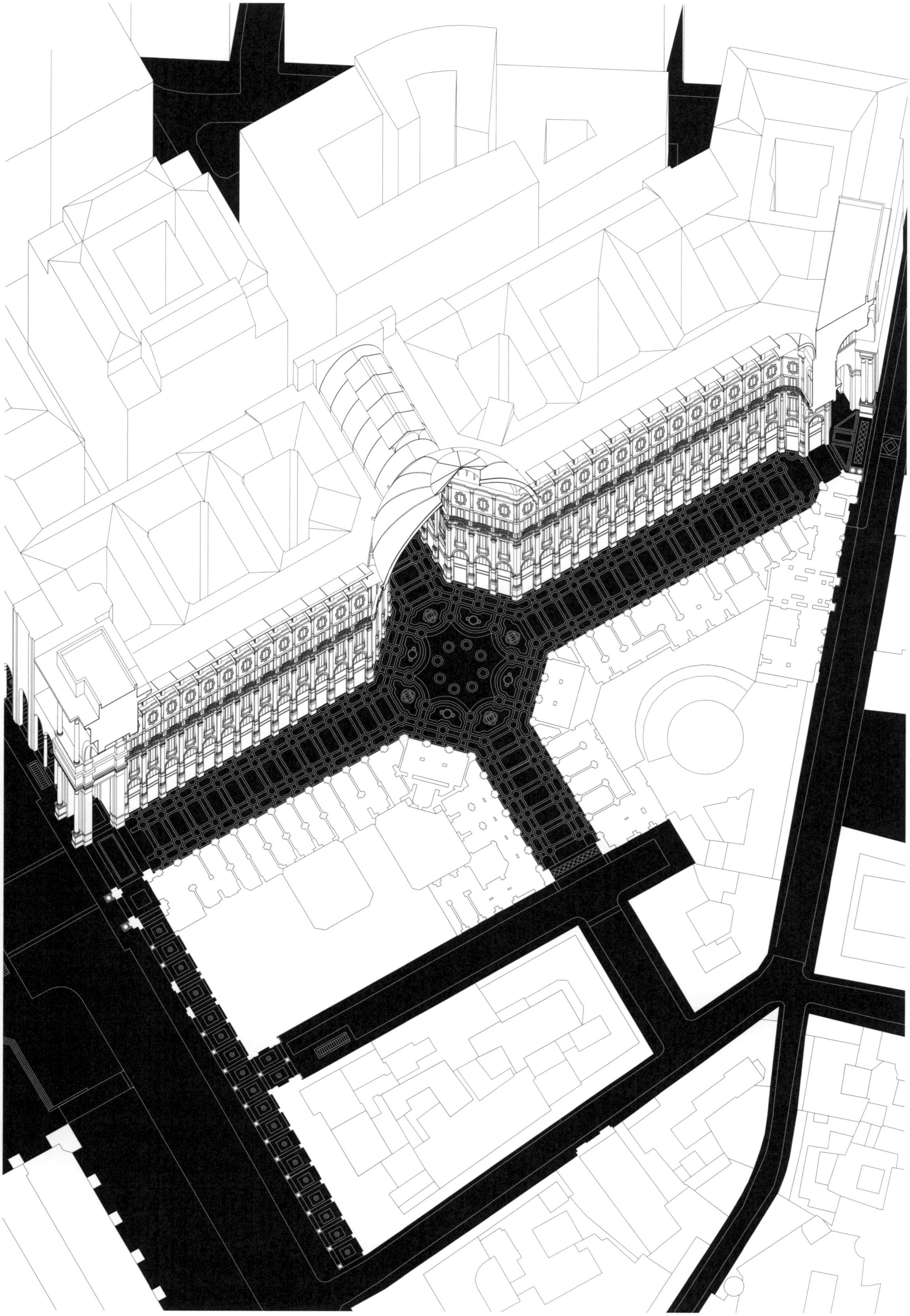

Galleria San Federico, Turin, 1932–1933   258–269

Galleria San Federico, designed in 1933 by the architect Federico Canova and the engineer Vittorio Bonadè Bottino, takes its name from the saint to which the entire block on which it stands was once dedicated.

 The typology of reference is the 19th-century galleria, based on the example of Galleria Vittorio Emanuele in Milan. Nevertheless, from the Parisian passages the galleria in Turin inherits the character of a place for leisure, strolling, and shops, in keeping with the new lifestyle that had been consolidated in the leading cities of central and northern Europe.

 In the context of the extensive refurbishing of Via Roma and the surrounding blocks carried out from 1931 to 1937, the mayor Paolo Thaon di Revel proposed the replacement of the existing Galleria Natta, which had been built in 1856 based on a design by Barnaba Panizza, with a new galleria that would establish a dialogue with the other projects being implemented at the time in the city center. Construction began in 1932 and was completed in 1933. The galleria issues onto Via Roma, the important artery that connects two of the most important places in the city: Piazza Castello and Piazza San Carlo.

 The galleria is organized with three arms of about 45 meters each, with a width of 12 meters, respectively connecting Via Roma, Via Antonio Bertola, and Via Santa Teresa. At the point of intersection, the central, symbolic space of the gallery, there is the entrance to the Cinema Rex (today's Cinema Lux), the historic movie theater of the city of Turin.

 The internal elevations of the galleria, rising for two levels, feature eclectic decorative motifs and facings in multicolored marble. The roof made with glass tiles, supported by reinforced concrete depressed barrel vault ribs, provides natural diffused lighting inside. At the position of the three entrances the vault is interrupted by the presence of octagonal domes set on a rectangular base; the vault corresponding to the central intersection is also octagonal, and set on a square base.

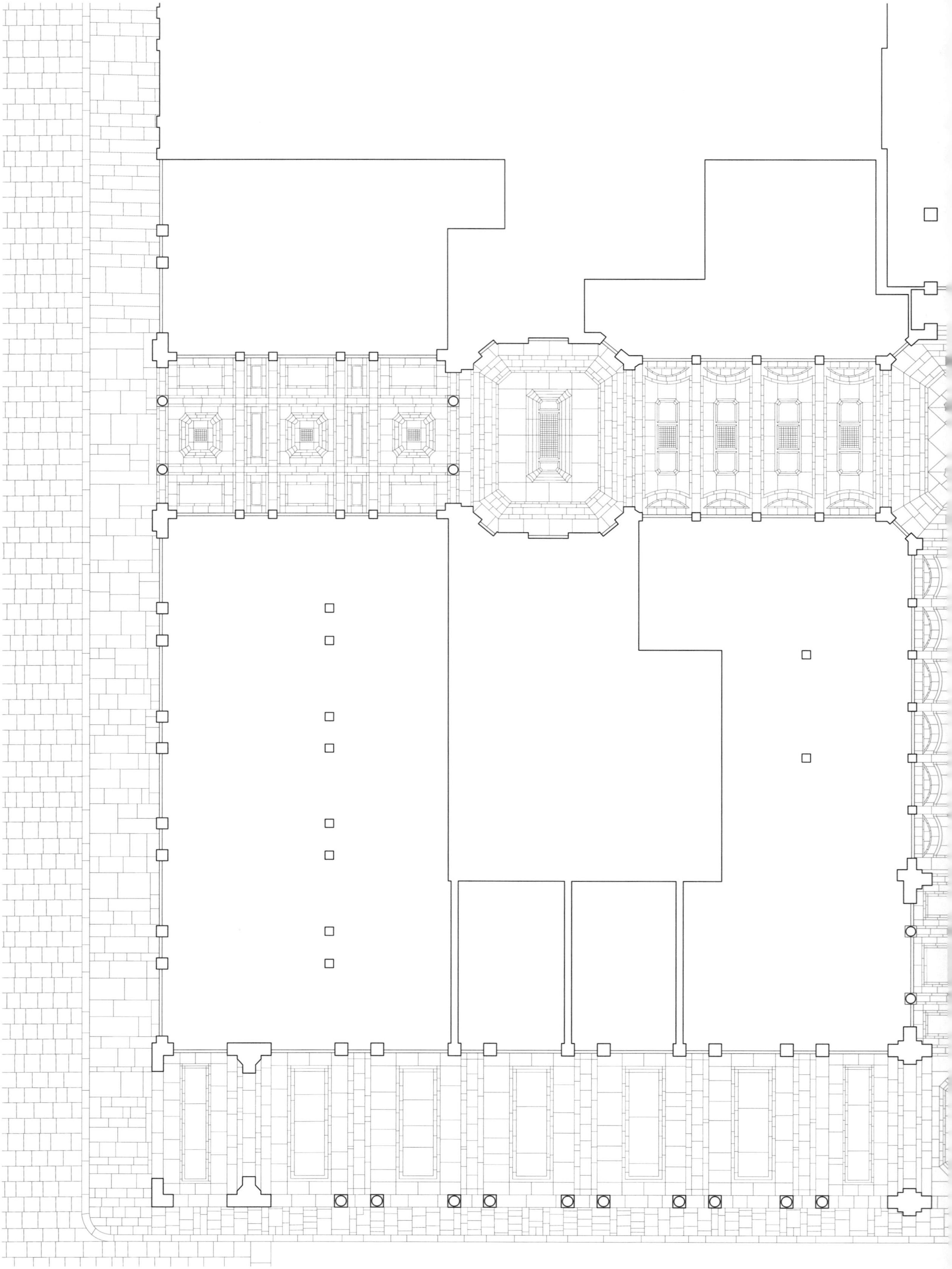

1:350

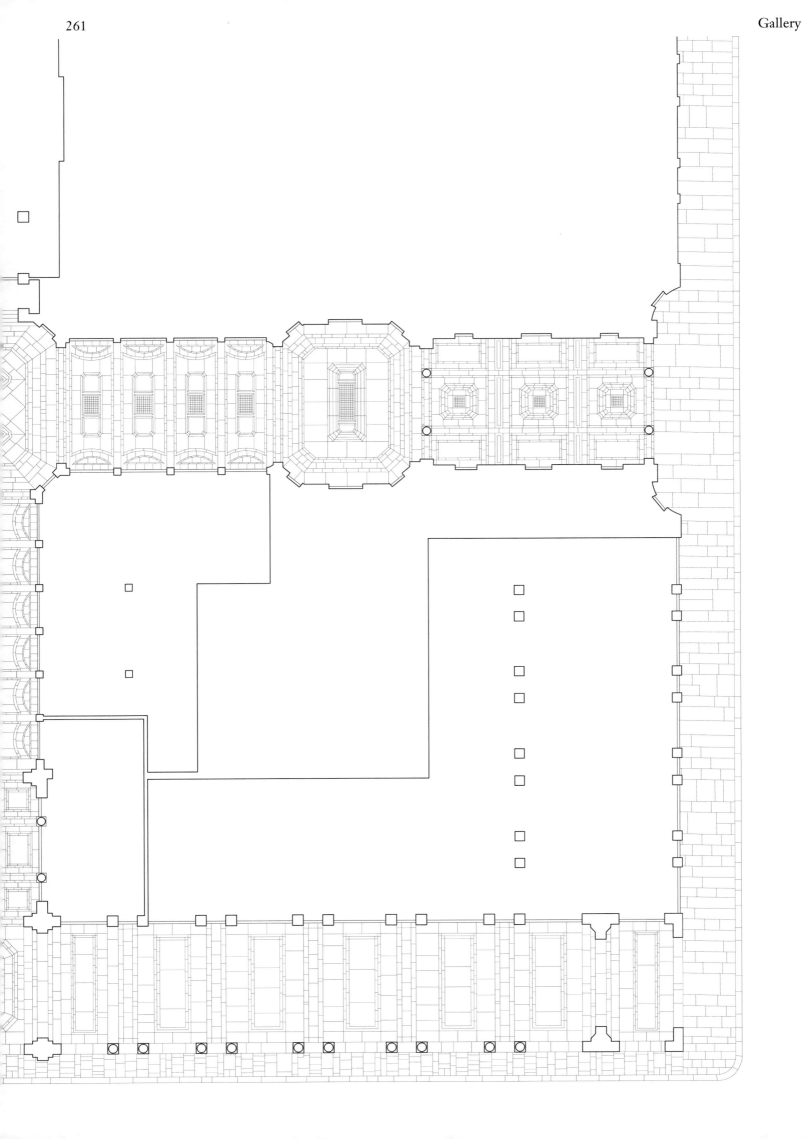

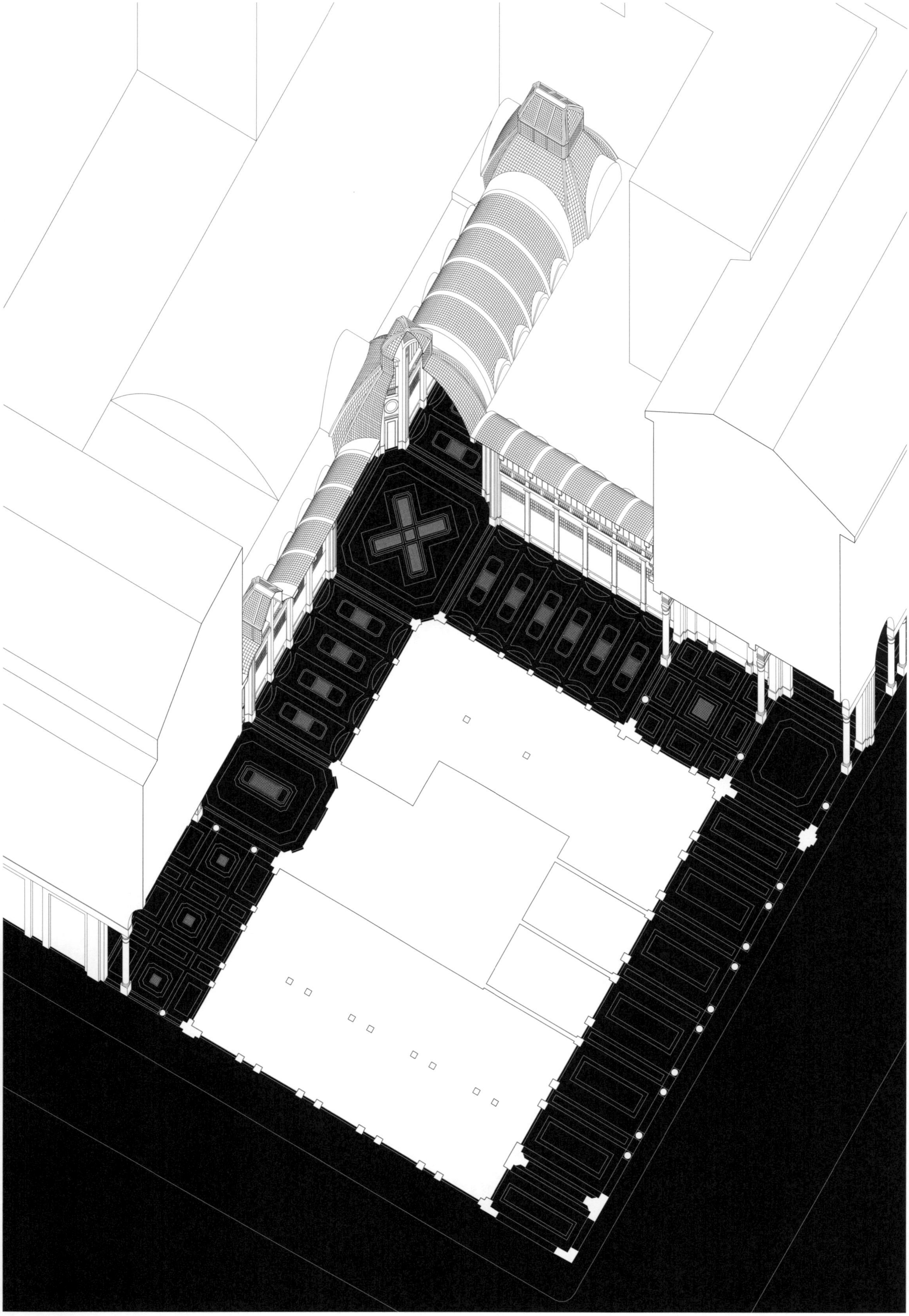

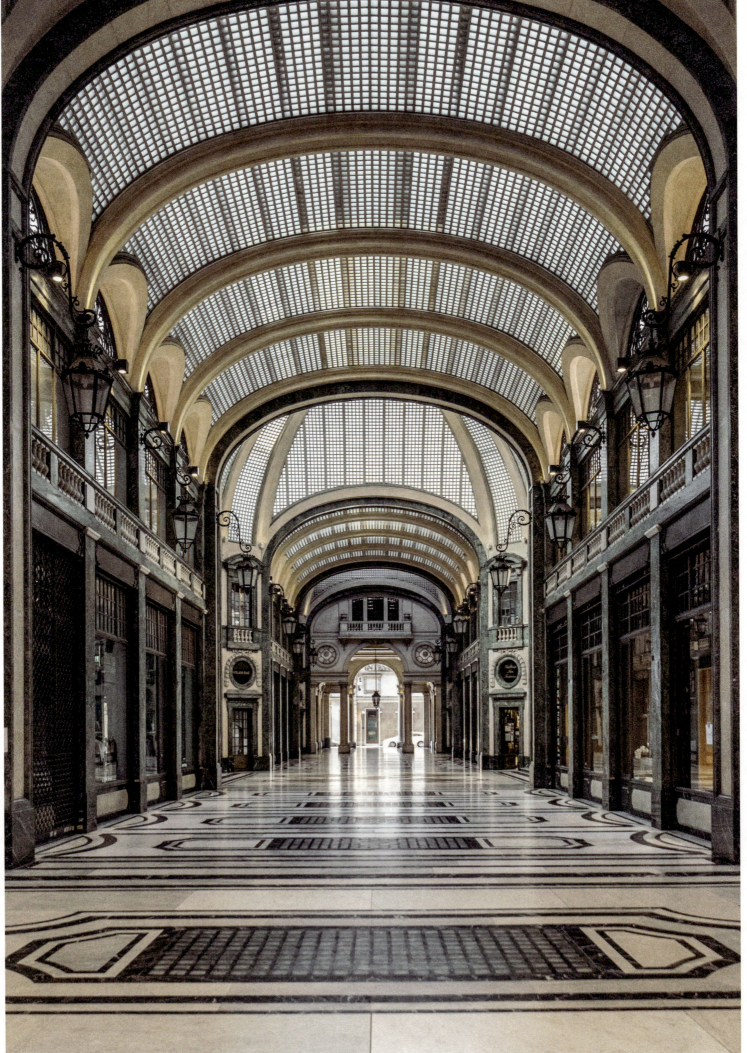

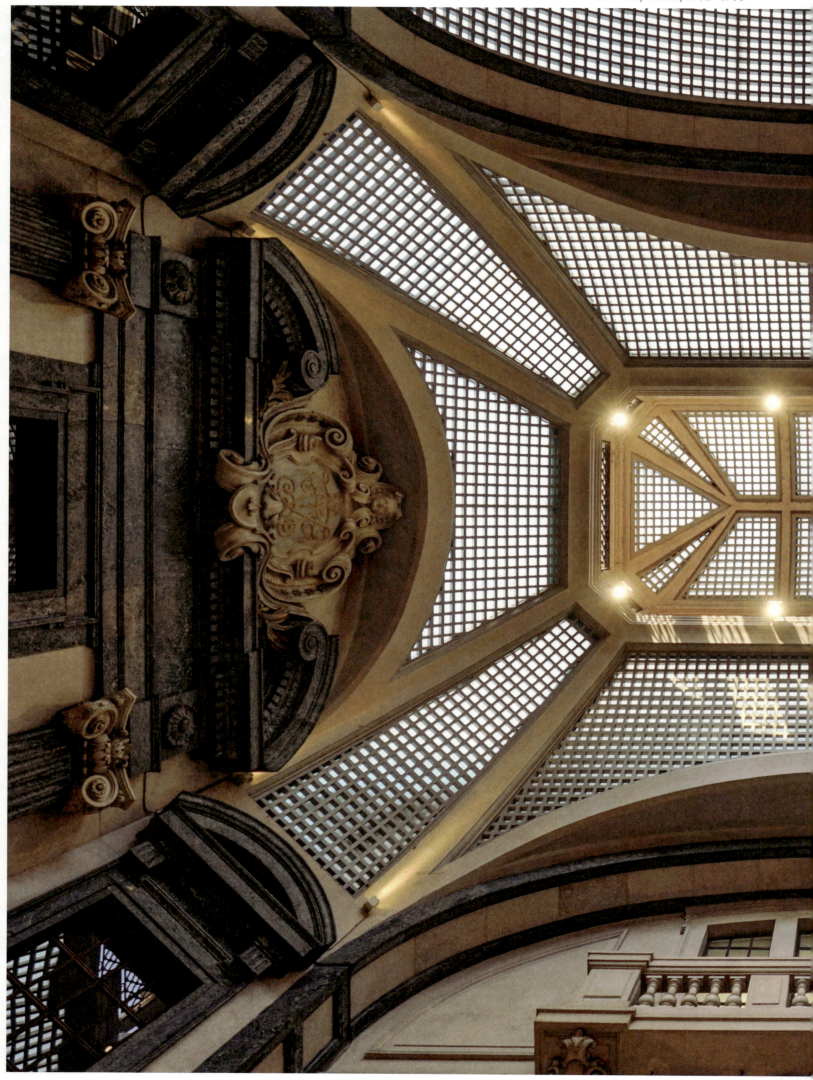

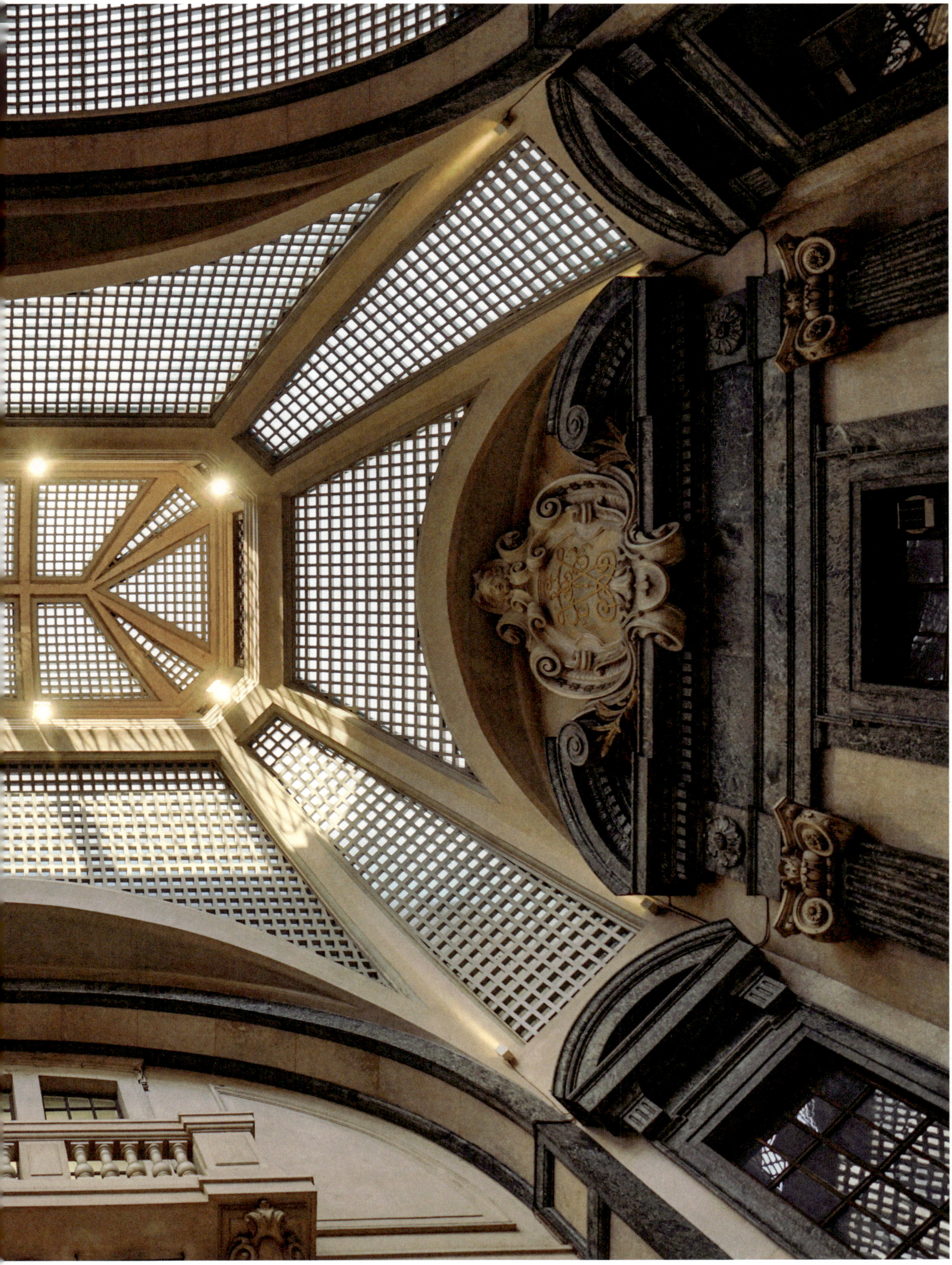

An architectural device placed in front of a building of primary importance in the city, necessary in order to compensate for a level shift through the alternation of horizontal planes, the treads, and vertical segments, the risers.

In other words, when the access stairs of a building become a device of topographical organization of public space.

Steps

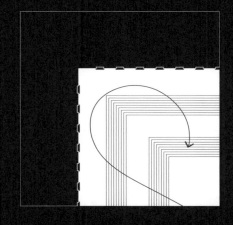

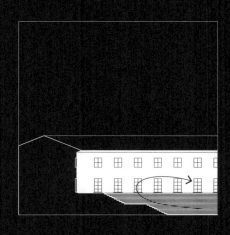

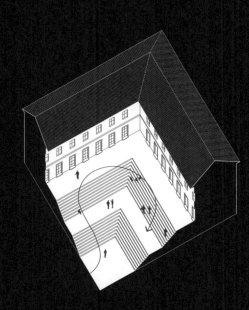

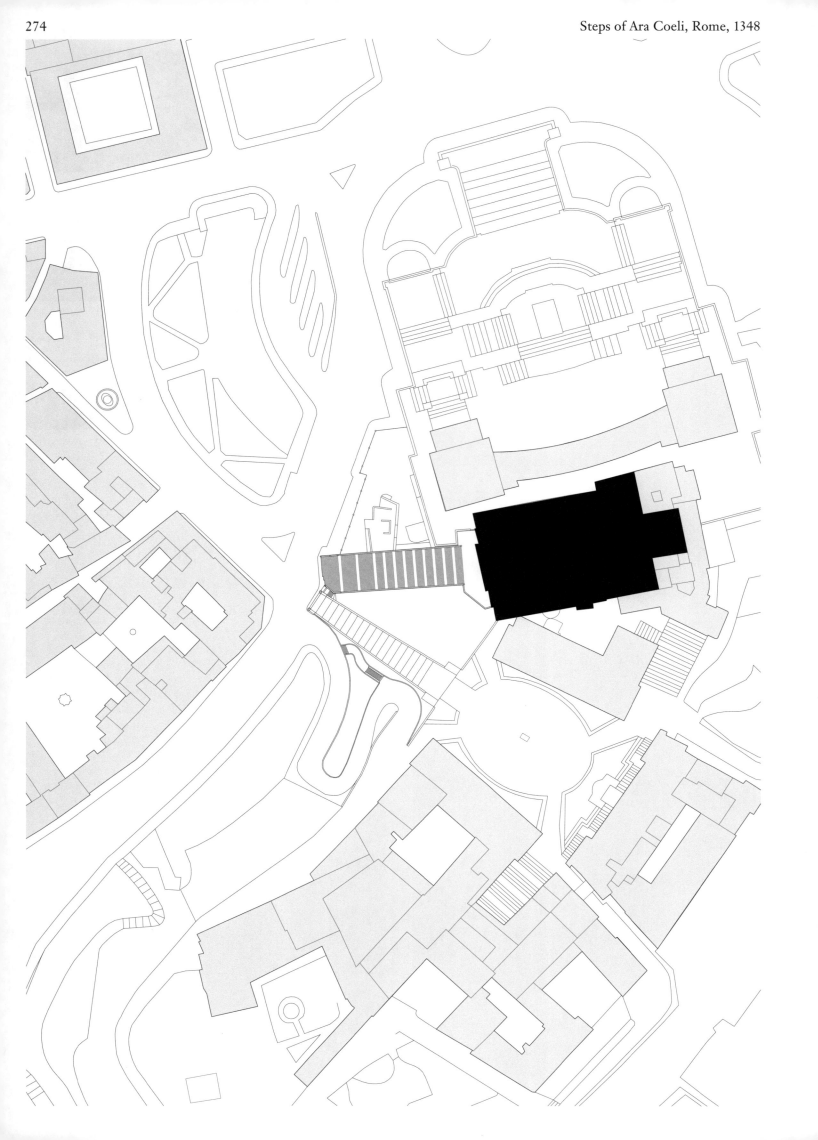

Steps of Ara Coeli, Rome, 1348 274–285

One of the most important urban projects of 14th century Rome, the Ara Coeli steps connect the slopes of the Campidoglio with the basilica of Santa Maria in Ara Coeli.

Given its size and monumental presence, the flight of Ara Coeli steps soon became a place of vivid symbolic value, a distinctive urban landmark capable of changing the physiognomy of the northern margin of the Capitoline Hill.

The flight of steps was built in a dark period in Roman history, as a votive offering to the Virgin to mark the end of the plague of 1348; the site was inaugurated that same year, according to legend, by the Tribune of Rome Cola di Rienzo. At the time of construction, the Franciscans, to whom Popo Innocent X had assigned ownership, altered the orientation of the church at the top, no longer facing towards the Forum but instead towards Christian Rome. They also completely changed its image through refurbishing in Roman-Gothic style. Built by Lorenzo di Simone Andreozzi, the steps were perceived at the time as a true *scala sancta*, ascended by the faithful on their knees in the hope of miraculous events. The name Ara Coeli—the "altar of heaven"—stems from the legend of the apparition to the emperor Augustus of a virgin on an altar, later interpreted as a pre-Christian sign of the birth of the church.

In 1546 the construction of the ramp of access to the summit of the Capitoline Hill, designed by Michelangelo, led to the cutting of the southwestern corner of the staircase.

The flight spans a level shift of 21 meters with 124 marble steps, salvaged from the remains of the Temple of Sarapis on the Quirinal Hill, grouped in 12 ramps with a variable number of steps: the first three ramps have 20, 15, and 14 steps, respectively, while the others have 7 steps each. The dimensions are impressive: 53 meters in length and 14 meters in width.

At the end of the steps one reaches a small terrace with an irregular polygonal form, offering access to the church and to the terrace of the Victor Emmanuel II Monument. This space, at the conclusion of the long staircase, also becomes a factor of geometric connection between the longitudinal axis of the Basilica and that of the steps, rotated by 7 degrees.

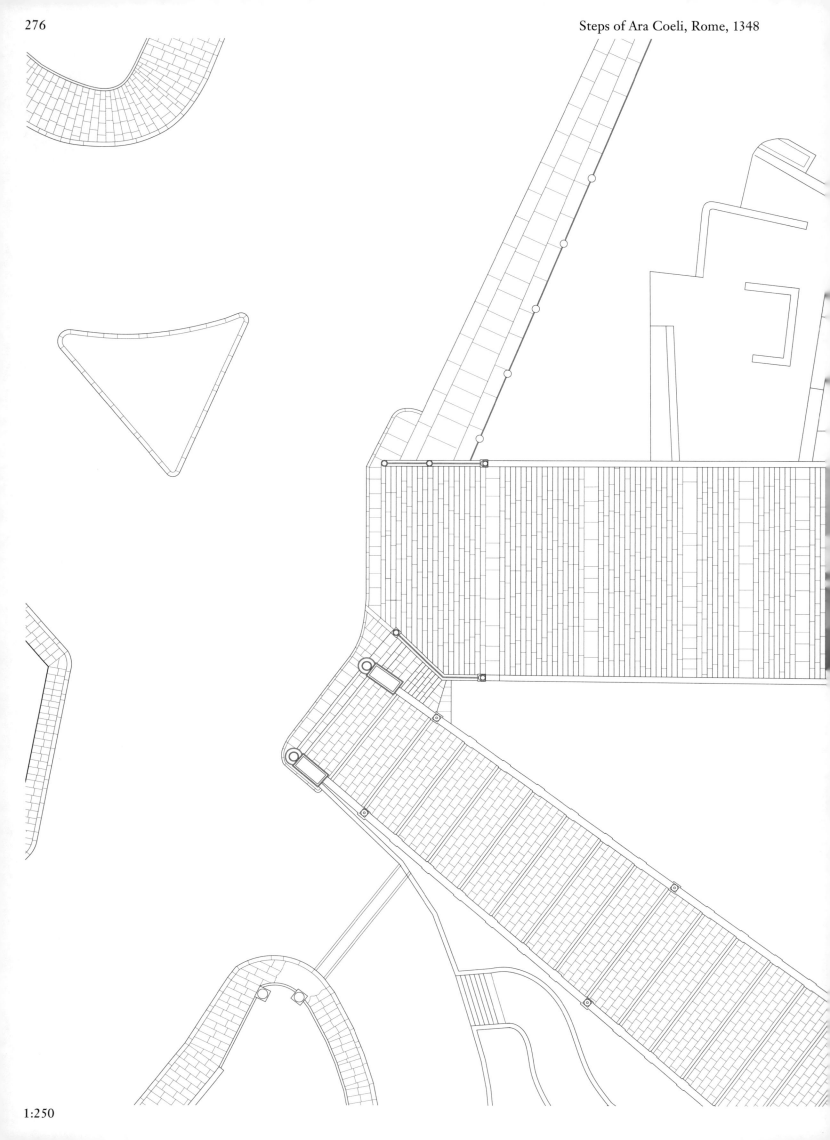

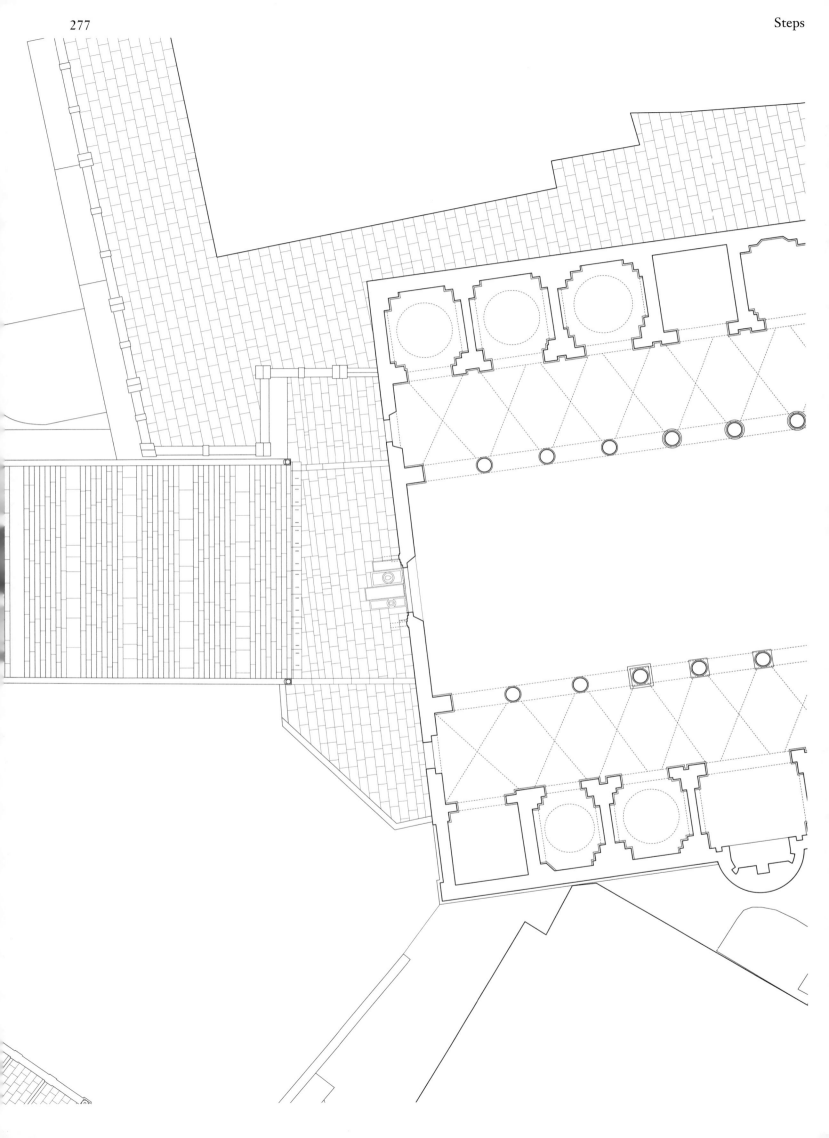

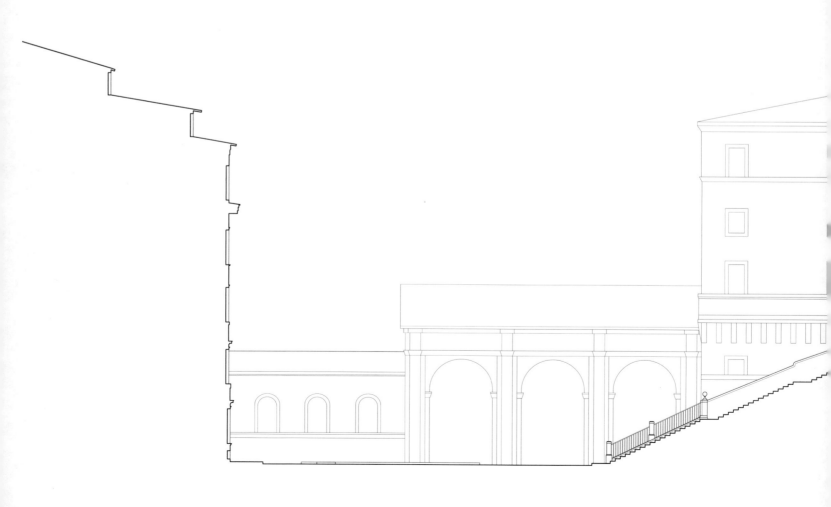

1:250

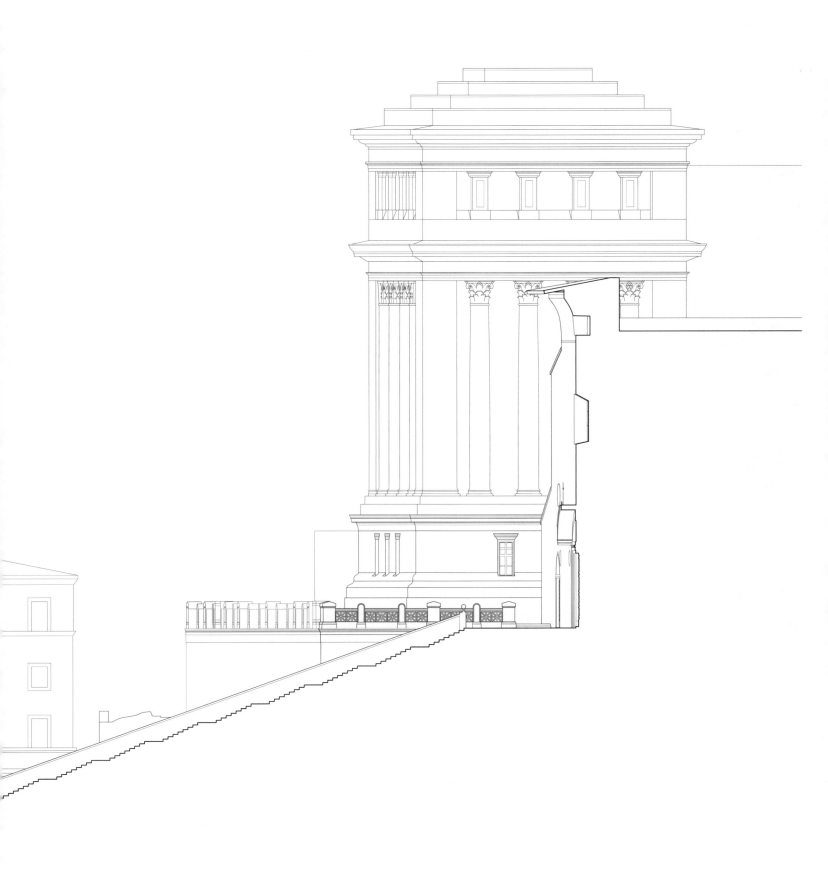

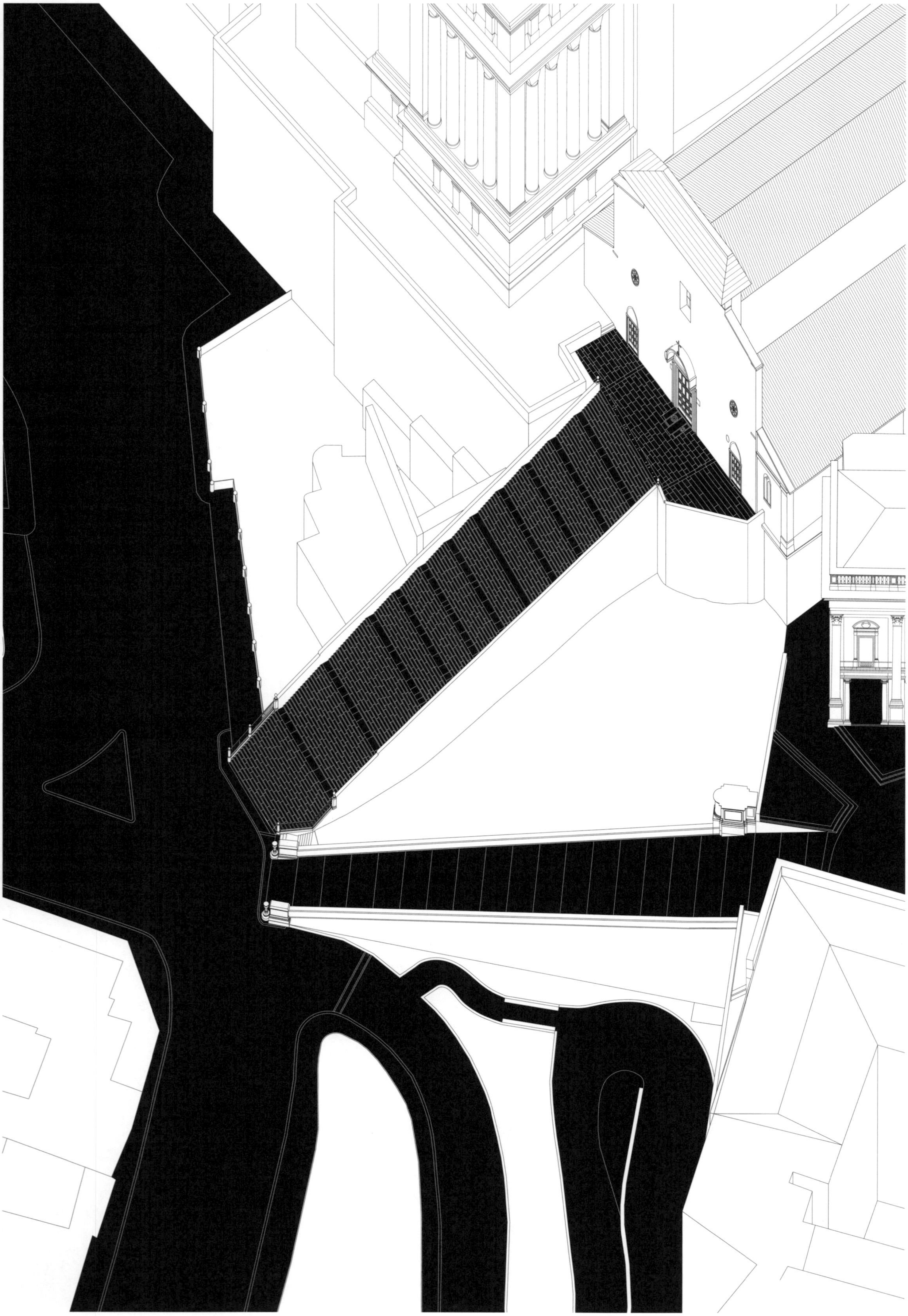

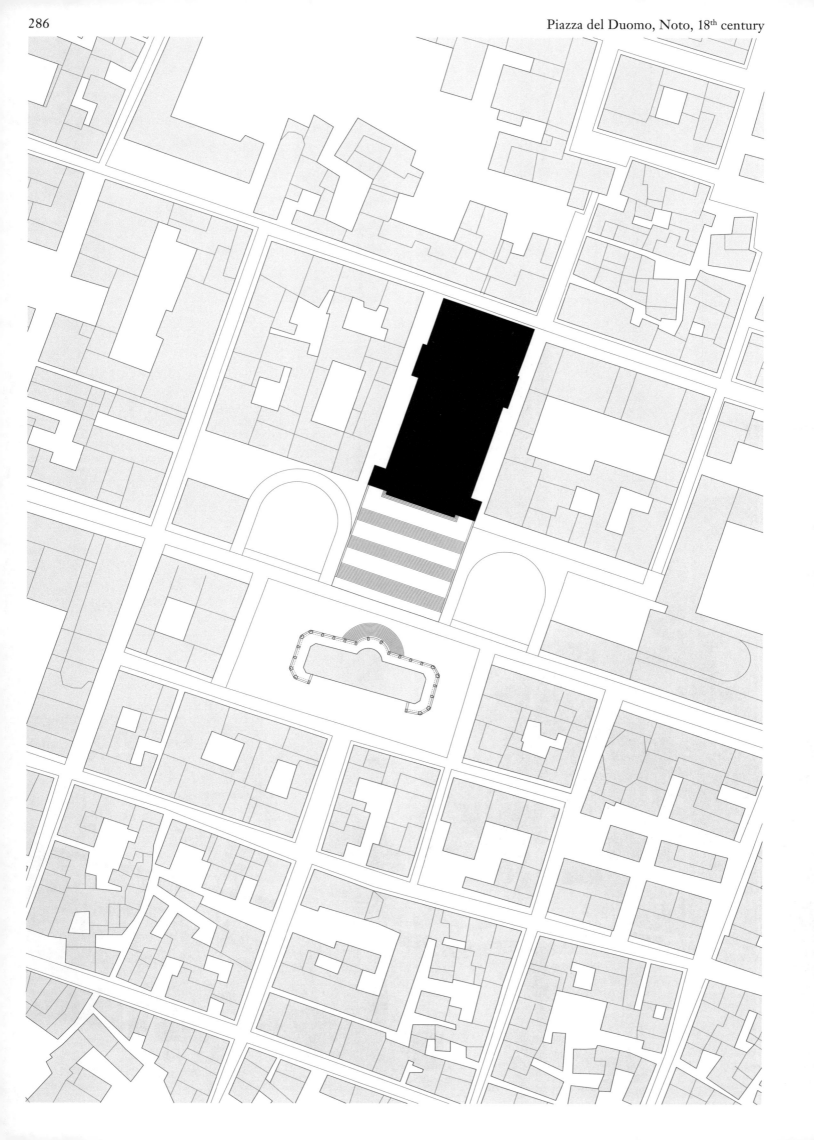

Piazza del Duomo, Noto, 18th century   286–297

Piazza del Duomo in Noto is a sloping square entirely occupied by a grand flight of steps that connects the cathedral of San Nicolò, to the north of the piazza, with the city hall to the south.

The impressive staircase, conceived in unison with the design of the cathedral, is an inseparable feature of the urban setting formed by the church of San Nicolò and the city hall. Due to its proportions—the overall level shift is small with respect to the widely spreading plan—the flight of steps of Piazza del Duomo can be considered a square with terraced steps; an urban device that goes beyond the mere functional necessity of spanning the level difference between the church and the city hall, and becomes a sort of large outdoor theater.

The background of the staircase is inevitably linked to the rather troubled history of the cathedral: built at the start of the 1700s, the church was inaugurated for the first time in 1703, but in the years to follow it was forcefully modified, reaching plausible completion only towards the end of the 18th century. In the 19th century, due to earthquakes, the dome collapsed and was then reconstructed in neoclassical style based on a project by the engineer Cassone. The cathedral was further damaged during the earthquake of 1990, and partially collapsed due to a structural defect in 1996. In 2000 reconstruction began, and after about six years of work the church was reopened for worship in 2007.

The façade can be traced back to a late Baroque language, made in soft limestone with neoclassical features. The scheme of the lateral towers, also found in certain French constructions of the 1700s, belongs in any case to the local architectural tradition, consolidated since the time of the Normans.

The flight of steps, dating back to the 1700s like the cathedral, was renovated and completed in the first half of the 19th century, with a project by the architect Bernardo Labisi.

The steps are organized in three ramps, respectively with 14, 12, and 11 risers, alternating with large flat portions. The plan is nearly square: with a length of 35 meters, it is 40 meters wide, exactly like the façade of the cathedral. Also in limestone to emphasize its unity with the cathedral, the staircase-piazza seems like the reflection of the church's façade on a horizontal plane. The design of the steps, beyond the relationship between riser and tread—a ratio of 1:2.75—emphasizes the horizontal extension of the project, accentuating the character of a sloping piazza.

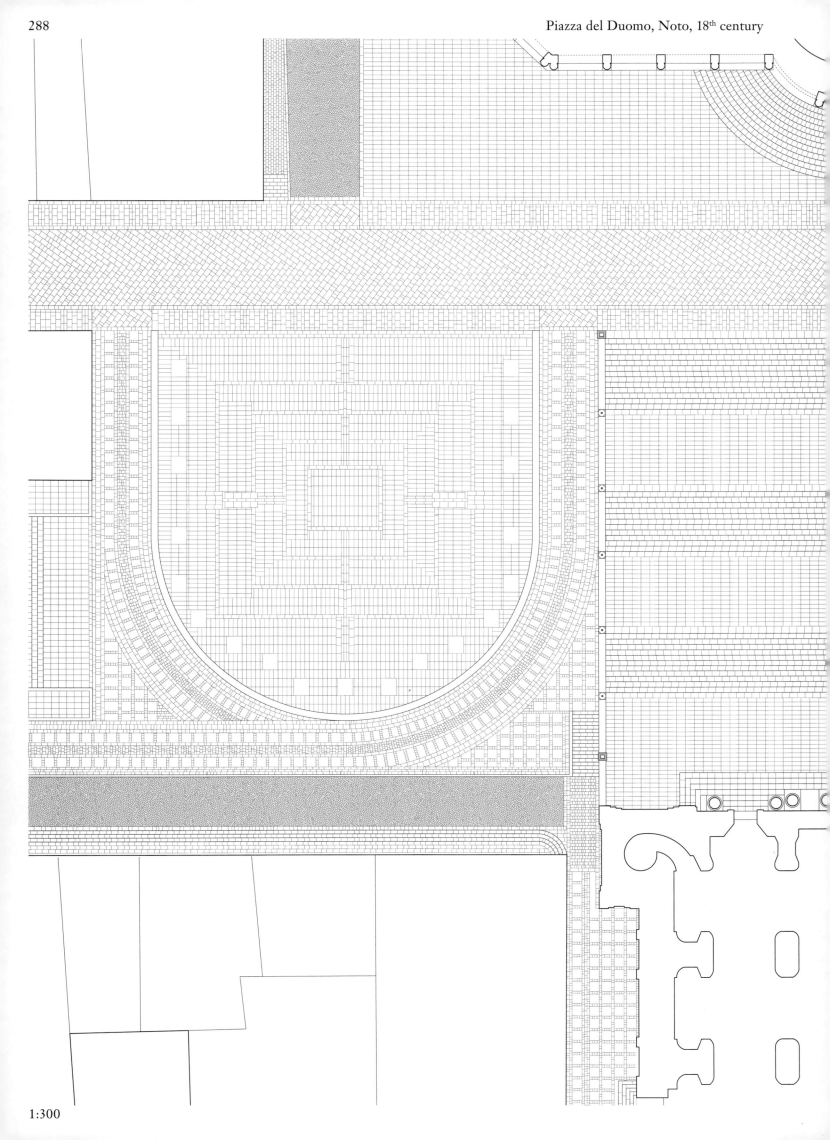

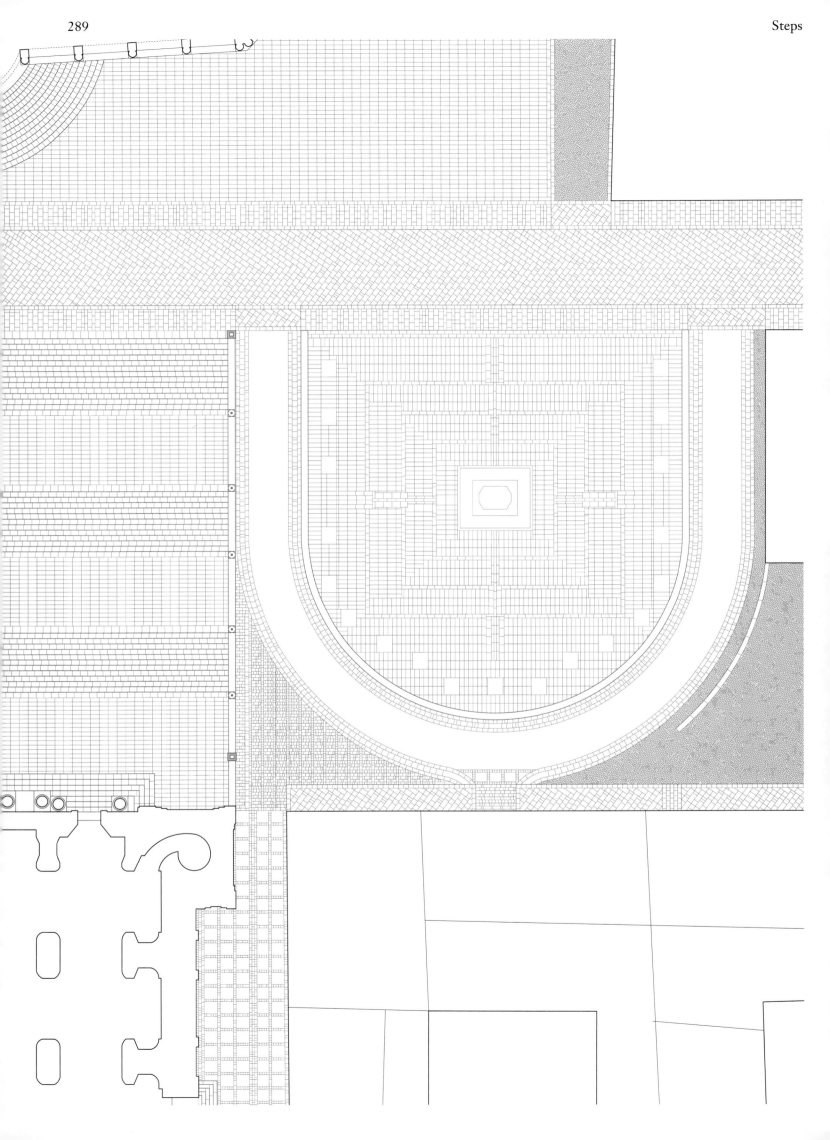

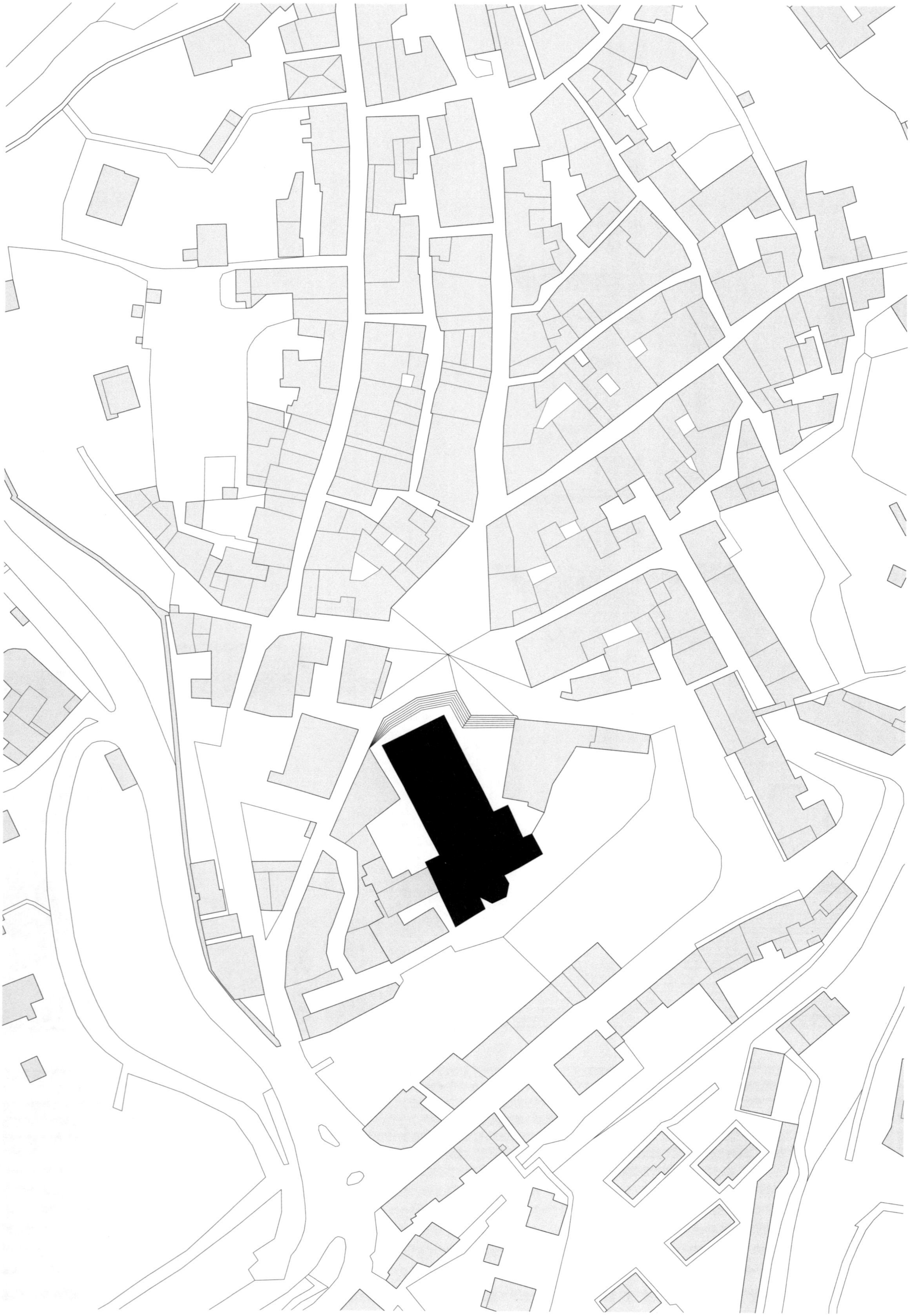

San Cerbone Cathedral, Massa Marittima,   298–309
1287–1304

The steps of the San Cerbone cathedral form
a detailed urban device that connects the various
architectural episodes facing Piazza Giuseppe
Garibaldi in terms of plan and elevation.
    The irregular shape in plan, the variation
of the number of risers, and the differing steepness
of the steps for each segment, make the staircase
a natural outdoor amphitheater harmoniously
inserted in the medieval settlement.
    The historical background of the staircase
is inseparably connected to that of the cathedral,
dedicated to Saint Cerbonius, bishop of Populonia
from 570 to 573, and the patron saint of the city.
Its construction dates back to the early years of
the 11th century, but over time it has undergone
a series of revisions and additions; its construction
continued, in fact, throughout the 12th and 13th
centuries. At the end of the 1200s, Giovanni Pisano
modified the third order of the façade and
extended the apse in its present form.
    The building is a remarkable example of
Romanesque-Gothic architecture; with their
works, great artists took part in its making: Giovanni
Pisano, Goro di Gregorio, Segna di Bonaventura,
Giroldo da Como, and Duccio da Boninsegna.
    The staircase-podium, following the
varying footprints of the buildings, becomes
an element of horizontal and vertical connection: in
a single base, it creates a relation between the
cathedral, the steeple, and the diocesan building,
connecting them with the irregular piazza.
    The staircase, whose linear length is equal
to 56 meters, has a variable number of risers: at
the position of the entrance to the piazza, arriving
from Via Ximenes, the steps of the base are
10 in number, after which they gradually increase
until there are 18, at the position of Via Butigni.
Adapting to the urban morphology, the steps are
also modified in the riser/tread relationship,
growing increasingly steep on the right side of the
cathedral, until they become a true vertical wall.

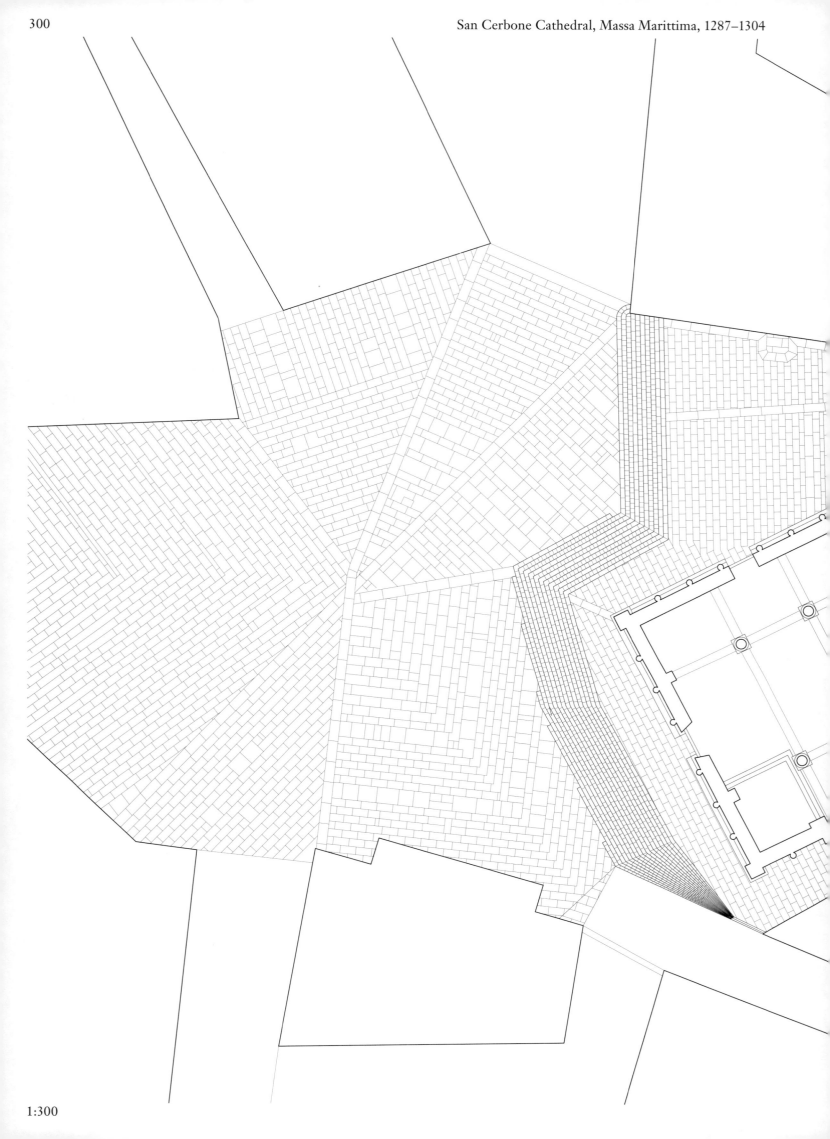

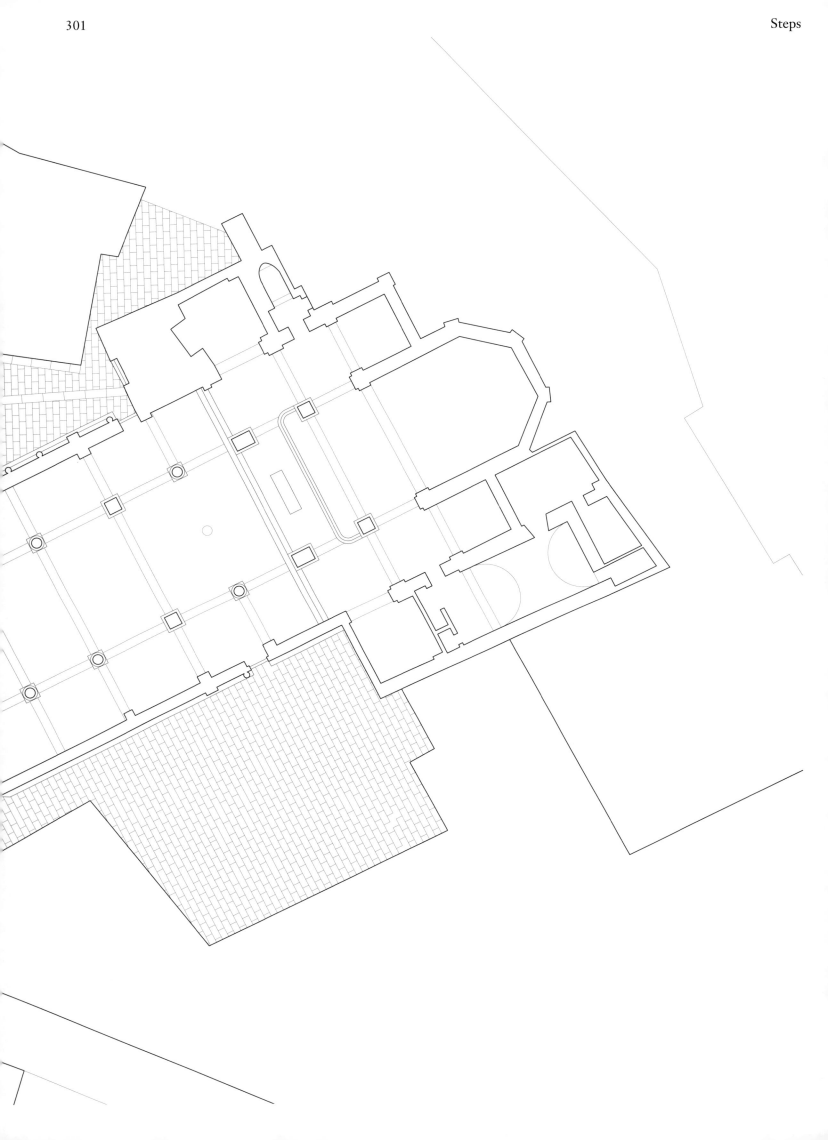

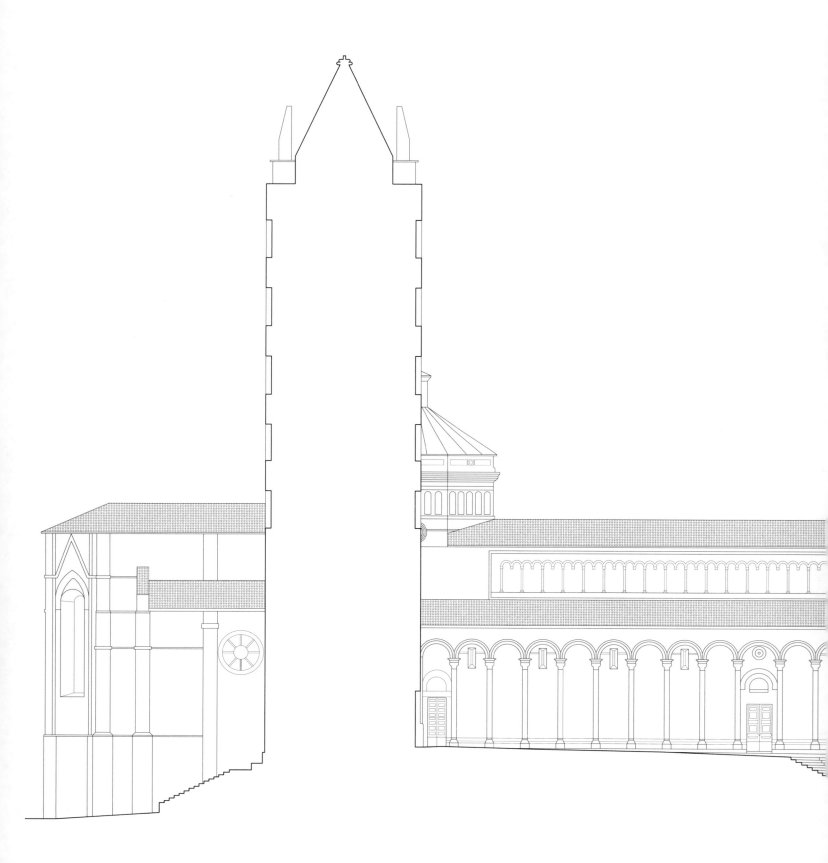

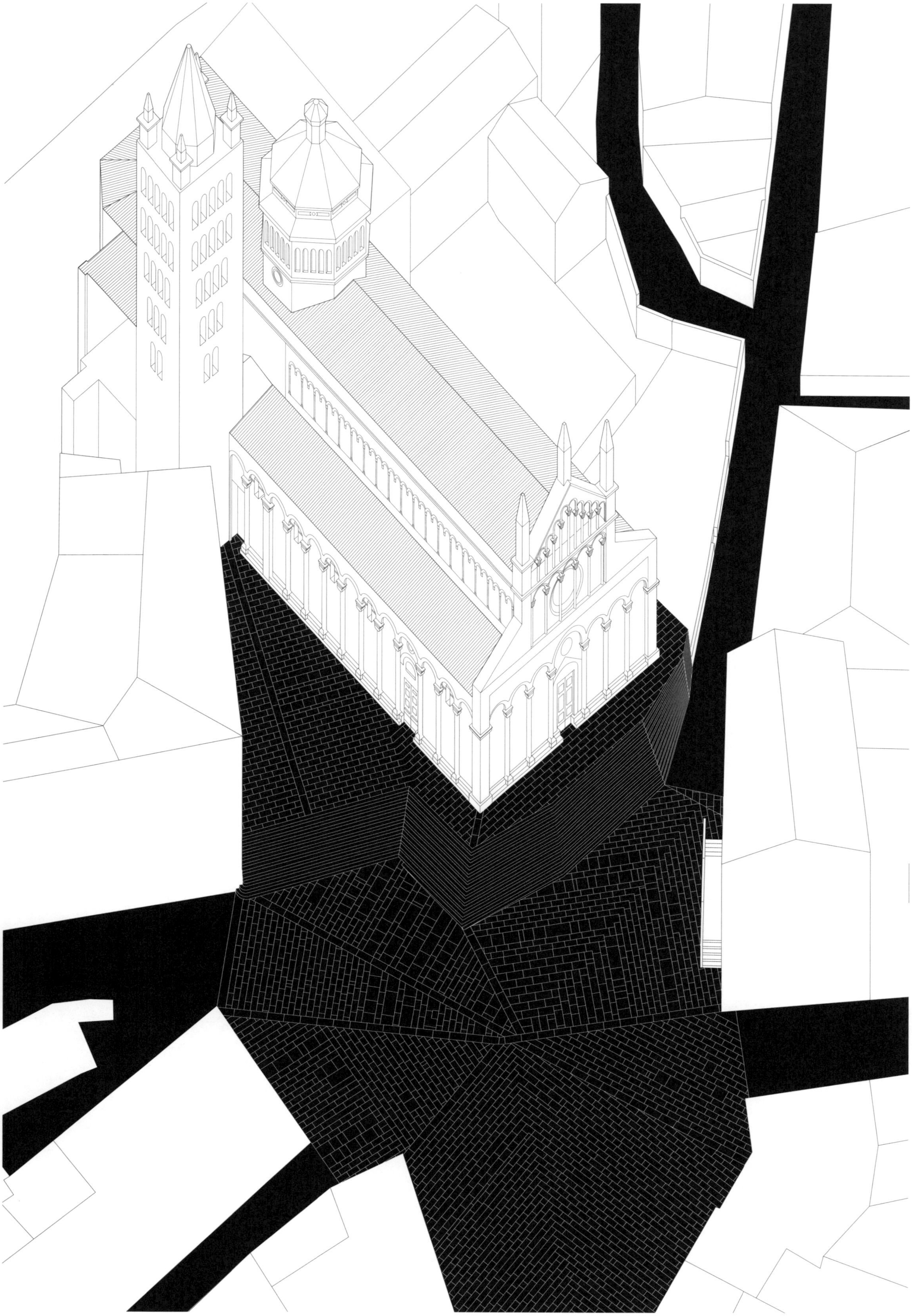

A horizontal roof of a building directly accessed from the public space of the city.
In other words, when the roof of a building can be utilized, and becomes part of the continuity of the surrounding urban spaces. This is the opposite of the Covered Square.

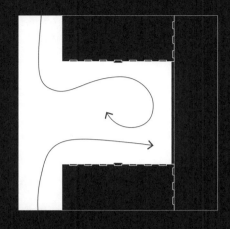

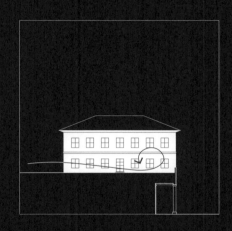

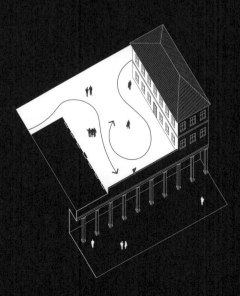

Urban Terrace

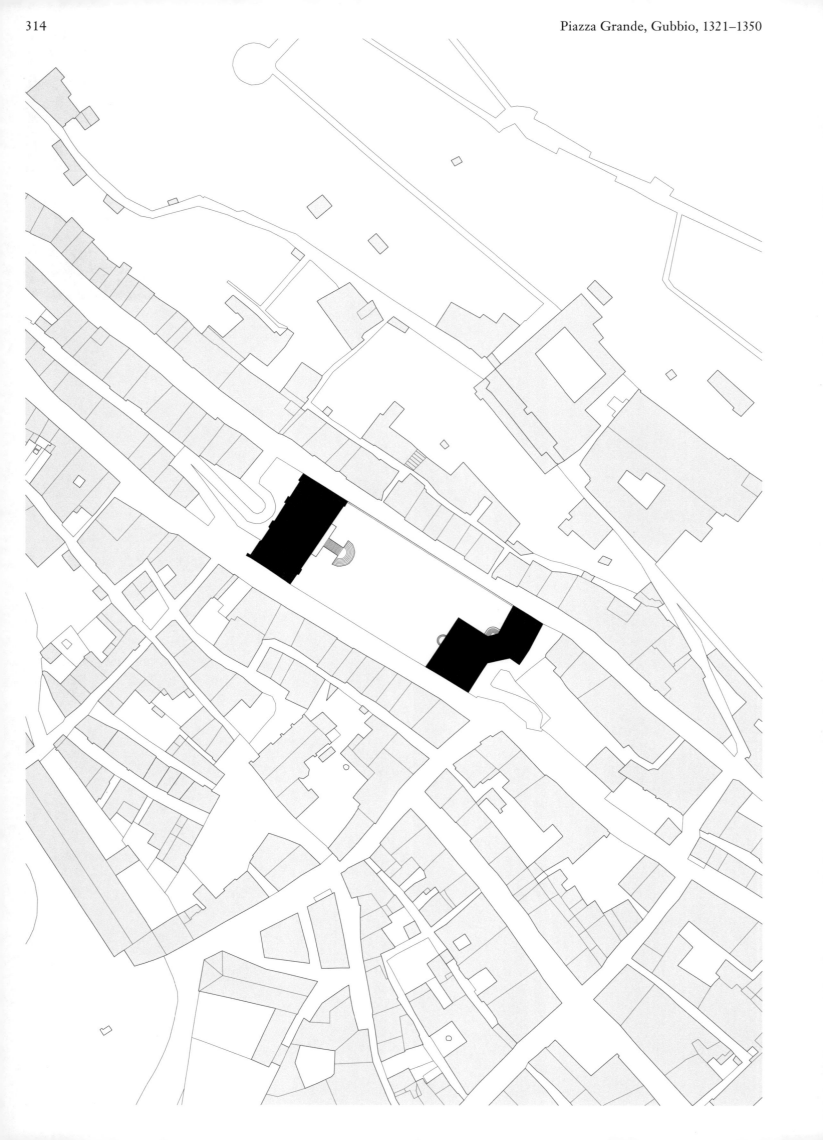

Piazza Grande, Gubbio, 1321–1350   314–325

Built starting in 1321 and completed in the mid-1300s, Piazza Grande in Gubbio is one of the largest elevated squares in Italy. Besides being one of the most modern and ambitious projects of urban transformation of the Middle Ages, it is also the result of exceptional engineering.

Piazza Grande is an urban device that is hard to classify: it is simultaneously a terrace from which to view the surrounding landscape, a square faced by the most important buildings in the city, and the roof of a system of spaces and substructures.

In the wake of the economic and administrative growth of Gubbio during the 13th century, the municipal government decided to create a new town center, in a position lower than the old settlement and closer to the increasingly lively and thriving productive community. It was decided to make the new center at the point of convergence of the city's four districts—Sant'Andrea, San Giuliano, San Martino, and San Pietro—to symbolically mark the point of union of the entire city.

The project was extremely ambitious for its time, calling from the outset for a large raised piazza around which to place the main buildings of the municipal administration: the Palazzo dei Consoli and the Palazzo del Podestà. The construction began under the supervision of the architect Angelo da Orvieto in 1332, and continued until the mid-1300s.

The end of communal independence, with the advent of the lordship of the Gabrielli (1350), also marked the interruption of the work: the Palazzo Pretorio (Podestà) remained unfinished, while the four great arches acting as the substructures of the piazza were not completed until 1482.

In the 16th century a loggia was built on the southwestern side of the square, a feature demolished in 1839, while on the opposite side the neoclassical Palazzo Ranghiasci was built.

The piazza has a rectangular form measuring 65 meters on the long side towards the landscape, and 42 meters on the short side.

To construct the project it was necessary to alter the natural state of the land in the higher zone, starting with the formation of an embankment, while towards the valley the raised square is supported by a system of buttresses, with 12 lower and 12 upper compartments. The wall towards the valley that supports the piazza is about 17 meters in height from the street below, and contains four large barrel-vaulted spaces with a structural role.

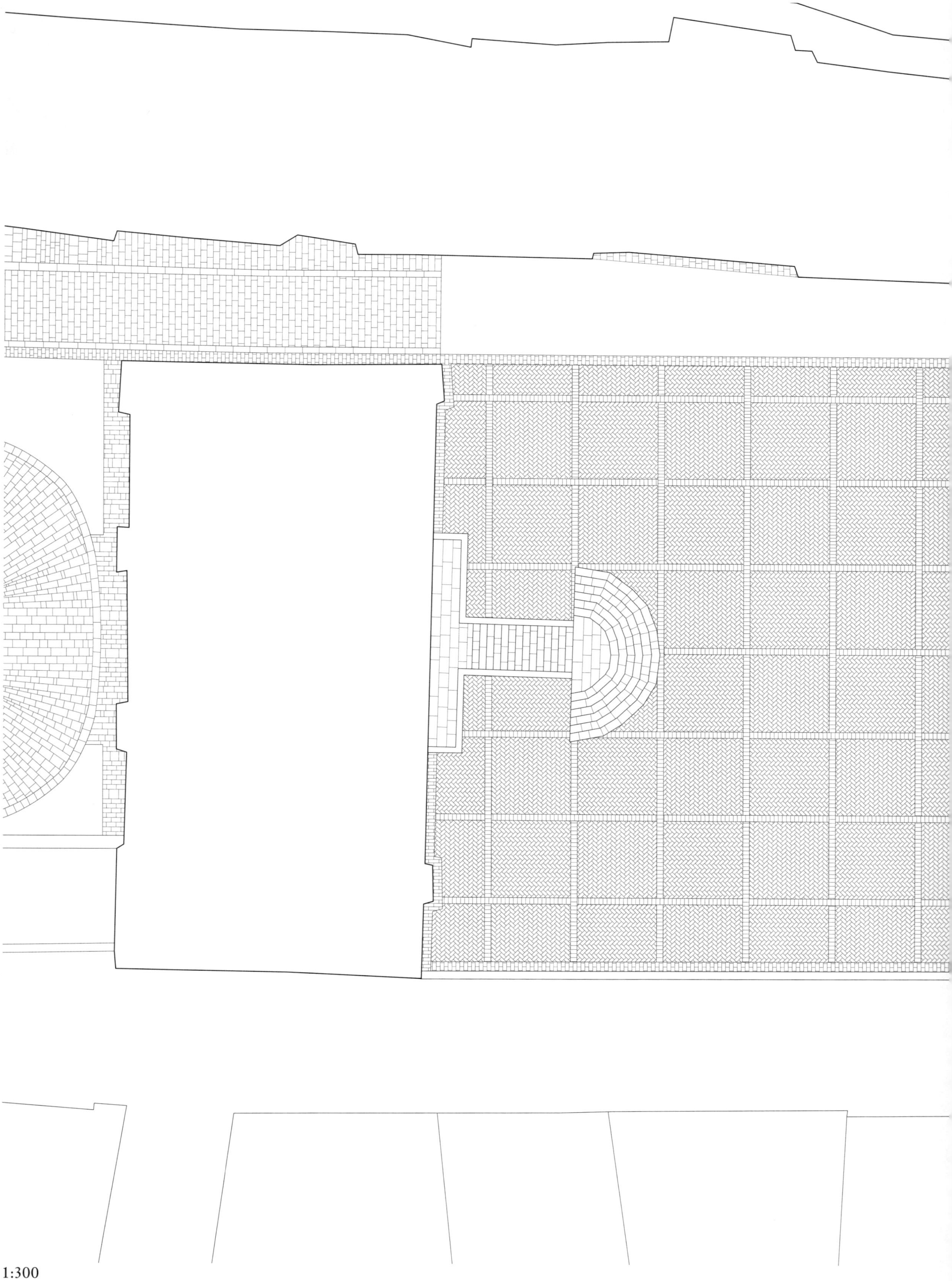

1:300

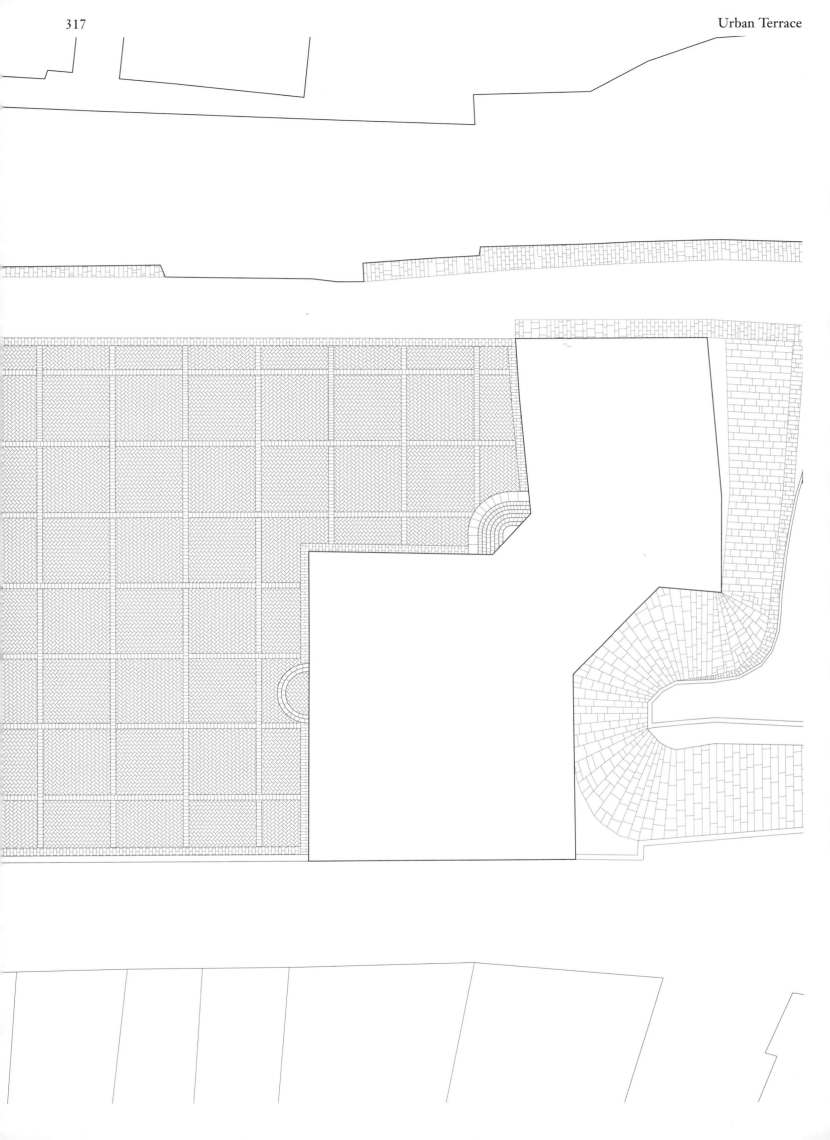

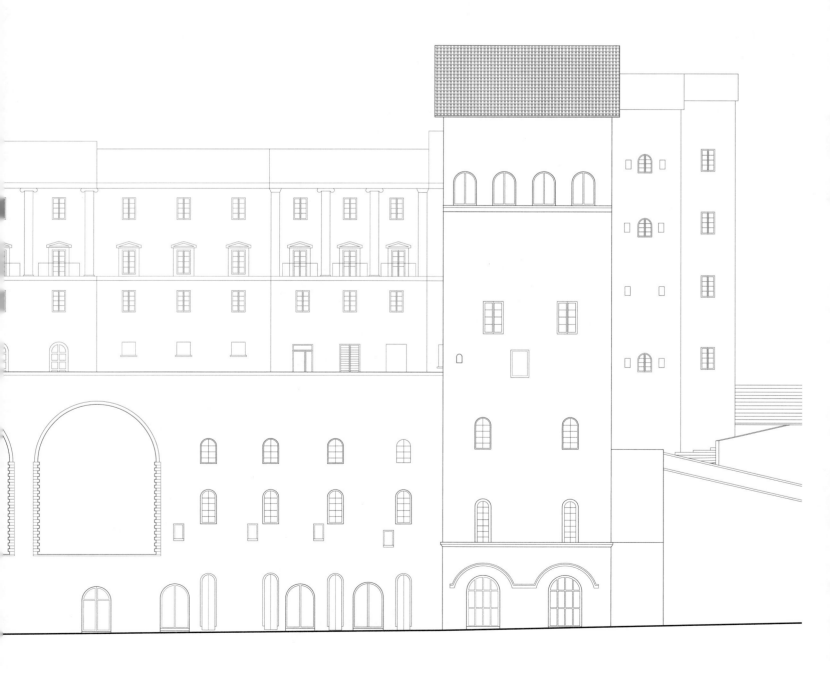

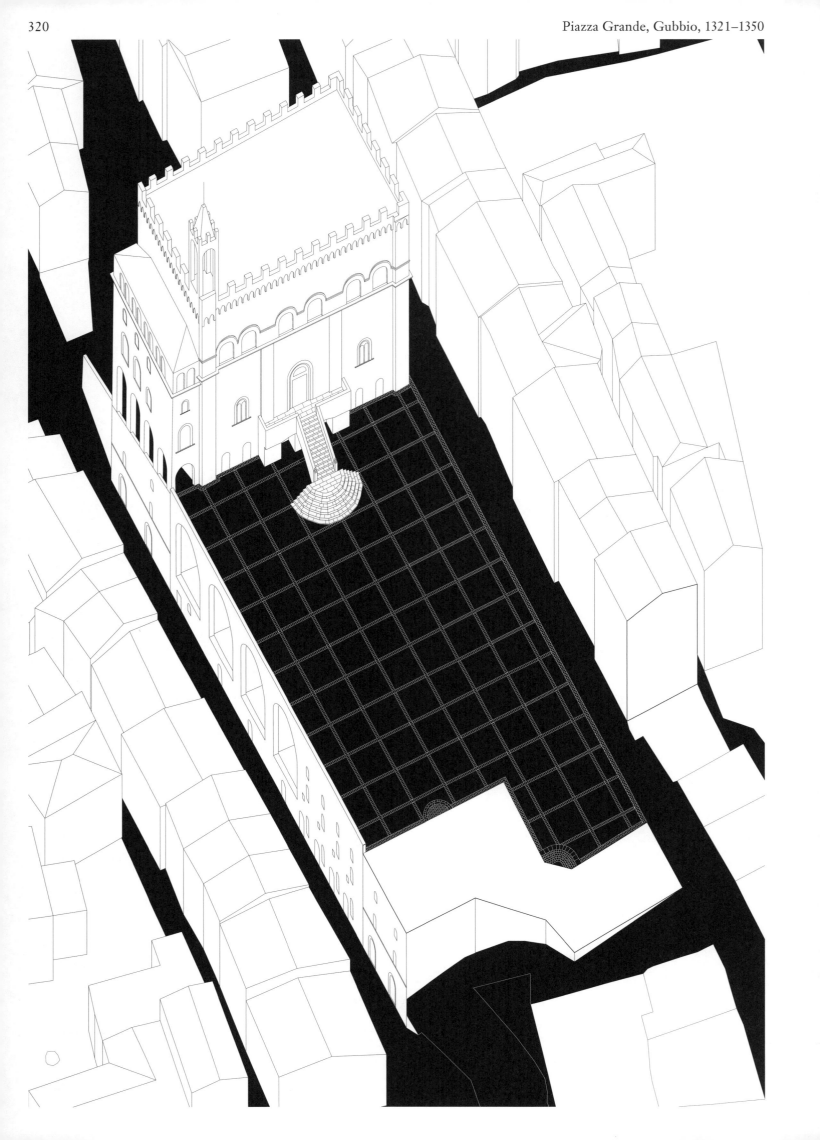

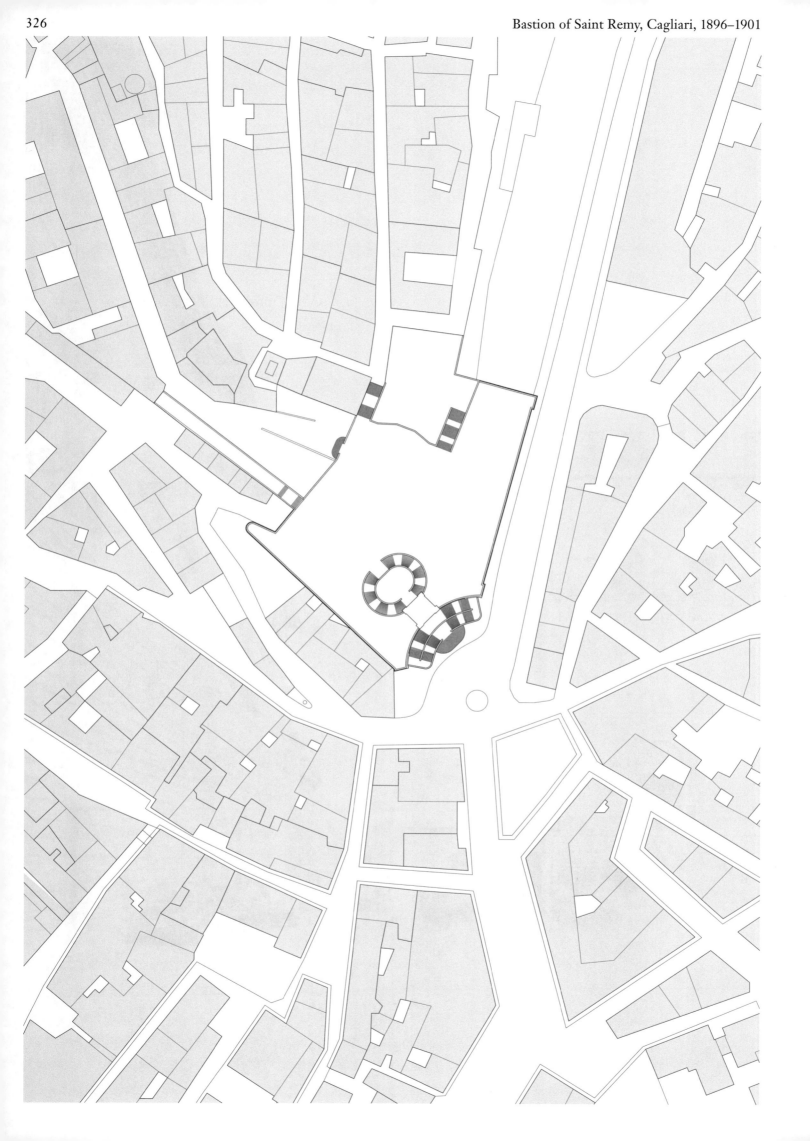

Bastion of Saint Remy, Cagliari, 1896–1901   326–337

Standing on the footprint of the detailed system of fortifications of the city dating back to the early 14th century, the Bastion of Saint Remy takes its name from the first viceroy of Piedmont, Filippo-Guglielmo Pallavicini, Baron of Saint Remy.

The Bastion of Saint Remy is a complex urban system composed of public spaces on multiple levels: a monumental staircase, a wide covered space, and large panoramic terrace.

Built at the end of the 19th century, the new bastion joins the three southern bastions dating back to Spanish rule—Zecca, Santa Caterina, and Sperone—in a single system. The monumental complex, built from 1896 to 1901 based on a project by Giuseppe Costa and Fulgenzio Setti, is an urban device that performs various functions: by means of a large flight of steps, it connects the Castello district with the lower Villanova and Marina zones, while at the same time creating a new system of outdoor and indoor public spaces.

The vertical connection is entrusted to a composite system of staircases rising to a height of over 20 meters, offering access to various levels of the city. The first staircase portion is a double ramp that connects Piazza Costituzione to a sheltered promenade placed on the eastern front of the bastion at a height of about 13 meters above the piazza below. The covered walkway is organized in three aisles formed by two rows of 16 round arches. The second portion of steps is composed of two ramps in a pincer formation leading to Terrazza Umberto I. At a still higher level stands the smaller bastion of Santa Caterina, existing prior to the neoclassical project but incorporated in it to become part of the same urban system.

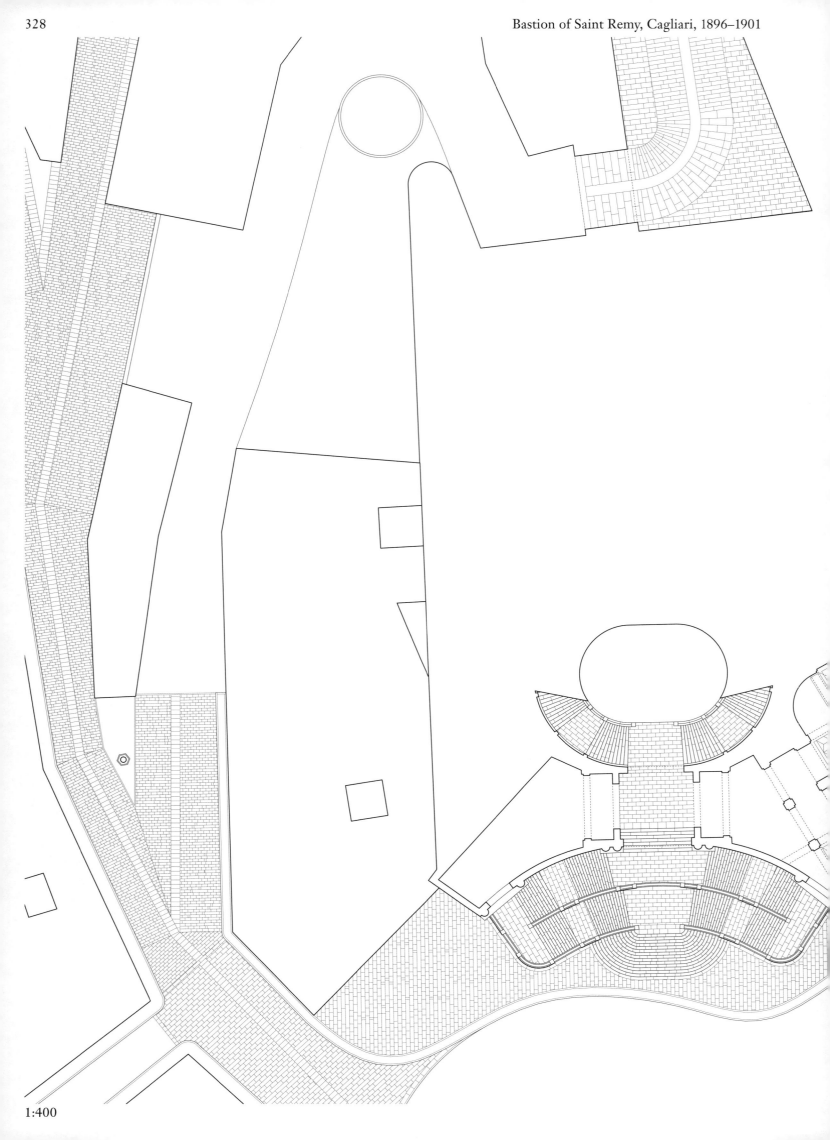

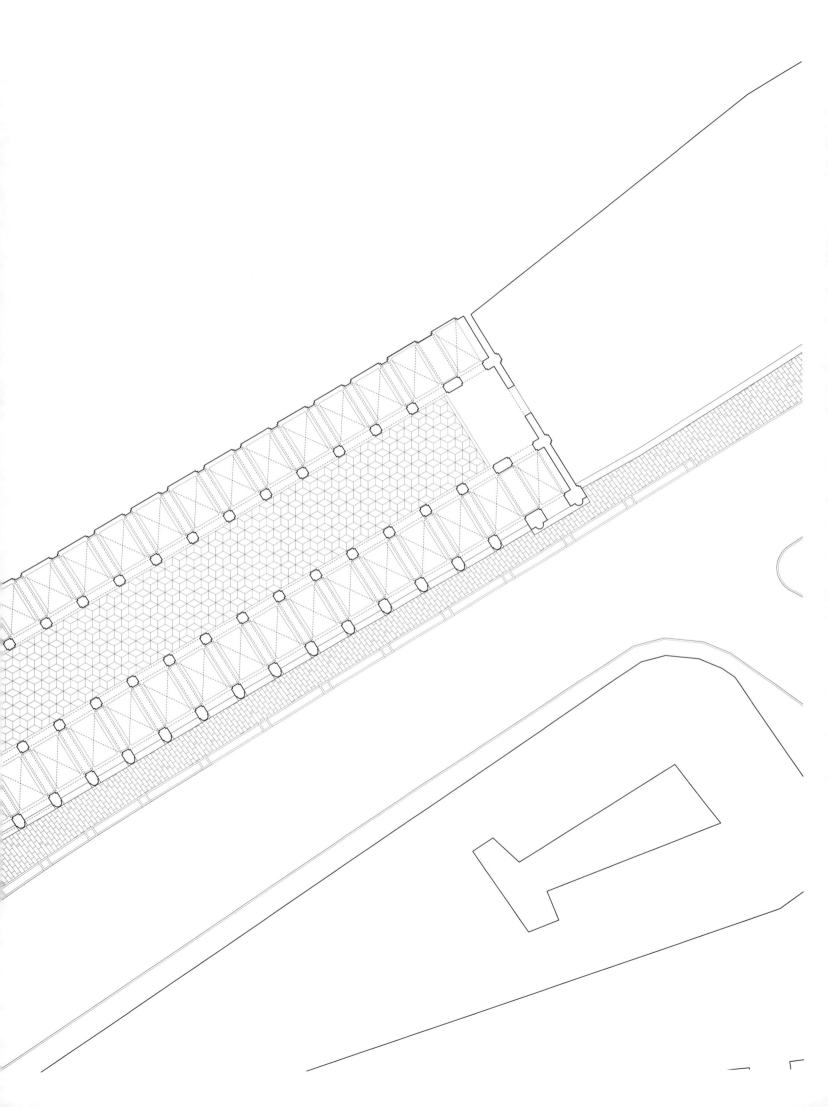

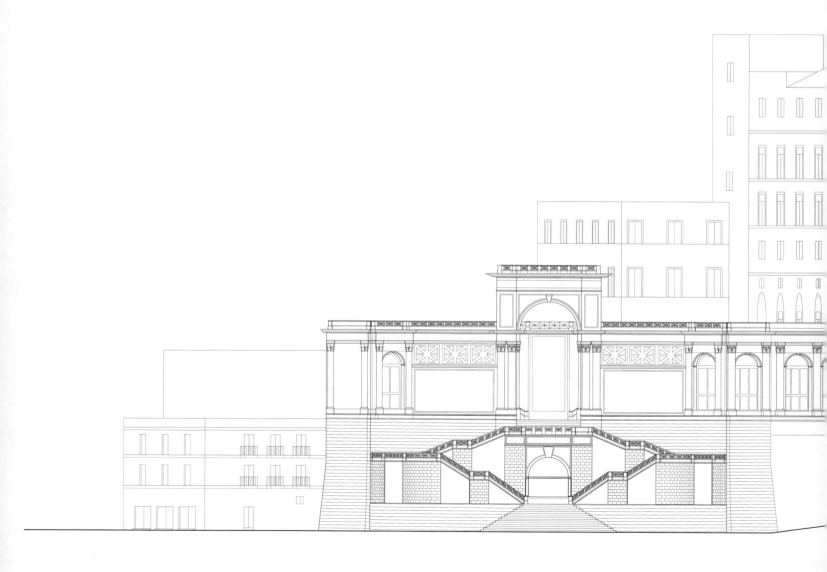

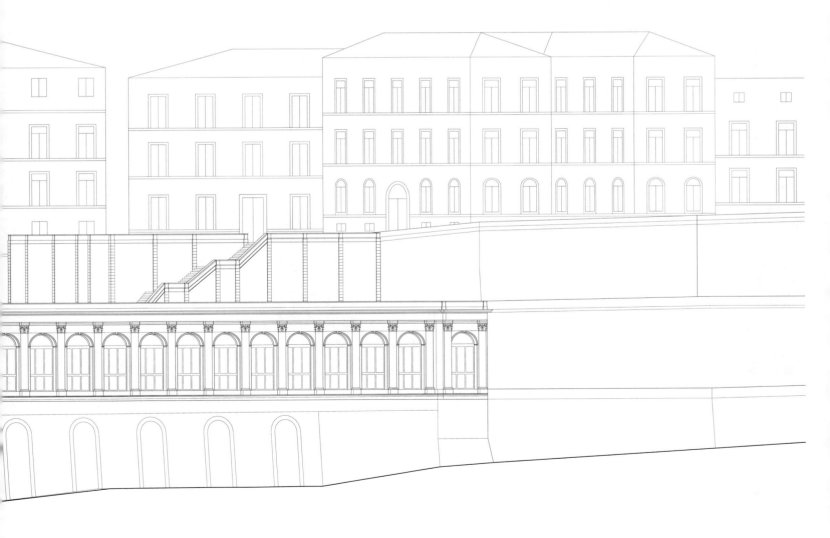

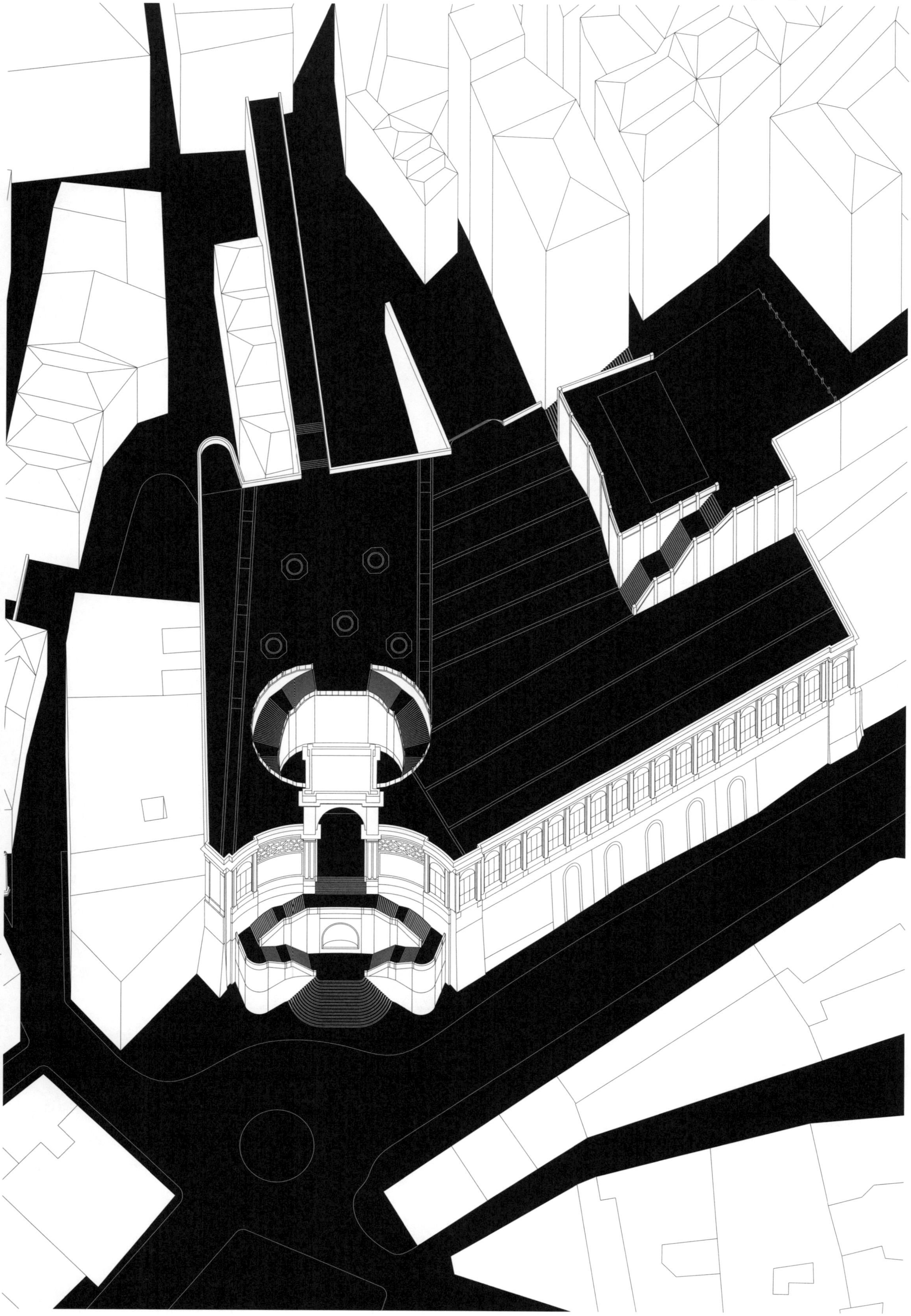

A structure in wood, iron, masonry, or reinforced concrete, equipped with one or more covered portions, serving to ensure continuity of the street when crossing a waterway or a lower portion of the terrain.
In other words, when a bridge goes beyond its purely functional nature to become an inhabited public space.

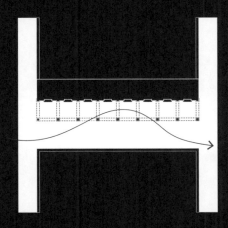

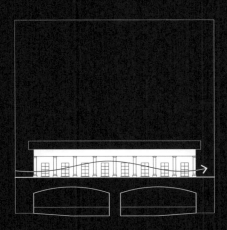

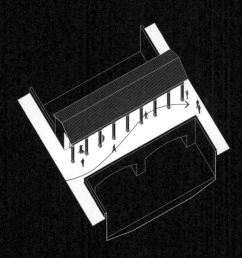

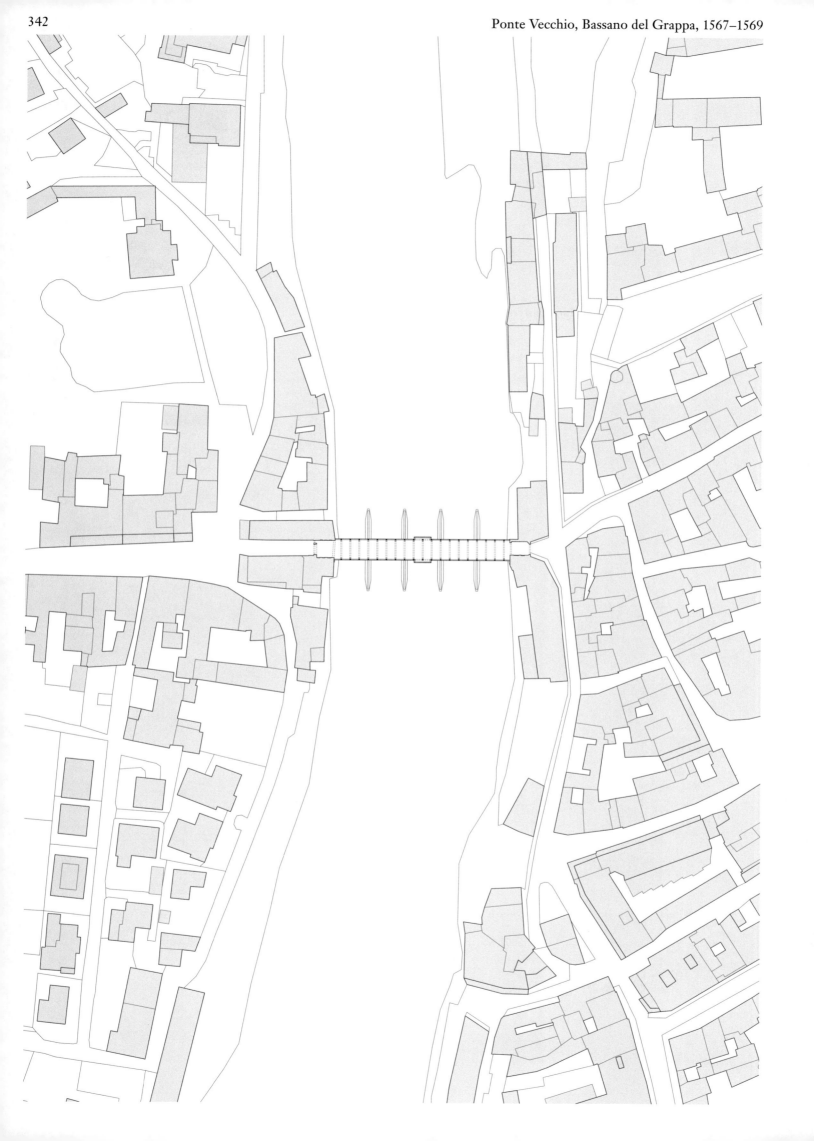

Ponte Vecchio, Bassano del Grappa, 1567–1569   342–353

The bridge on the Brenta River, known as Ponte Vecchio or Ponte degli Alpini, is a wooden covered bridge with five spans, whose original design dates back to Andrea Palladio.

The proportions of the structure and the trussed roof supported by slender pillars make this bridge an urban device that goes beyond its merely functional nature: it can be interpreted as a linear square, a terrace on the river or a covered passageway.

The first wooden bridge of Bassano dated back to 1209; various documents bear witness to its history of repairs or reconstruction of the original structure over the centuries, due to the intrinsic fragility of the material and the powerful force of the river. Extraordinary flooding of the Brenta in 1567 caused yet another collapse, leading to the commission assigned to Andrea Palladio for the design of a new structure. The first proposal was that of a stone bridge with three arches, based on a Roman model, but it was rejected by the city council, which asked the architect to create a bridge that would not differ too much from the original structure.

The wooden construction designed by Palladio lasted almost 200 years, undergoing its first collapse in 1748; after reconstruction based on the original project by Bartolomeo Ferracina, it collapsed a second time—again due to flooding—in 1813. The present structure, resulting from a third reconstruction after destruction in 1945 caused by an explosion, still complies with the original design.

The bridge, with a length of 64 meters and 8 meters in width, has five spans of about 13 meters, formed by large wooden beams with oblique crosspieces resting on four intermediate pylons and two lateral abutments. The four wooden pylons, designed to adapt to the river's current, are formed by eight piles with a diameter of about half a meter driven into the riverbed, and by a series of piles of decreasing height that generate the characteristic oblique profile. The roof, with a truss structure with a height of 4.5 meters, is supported by two rows of 19 Tuscan pilasters.

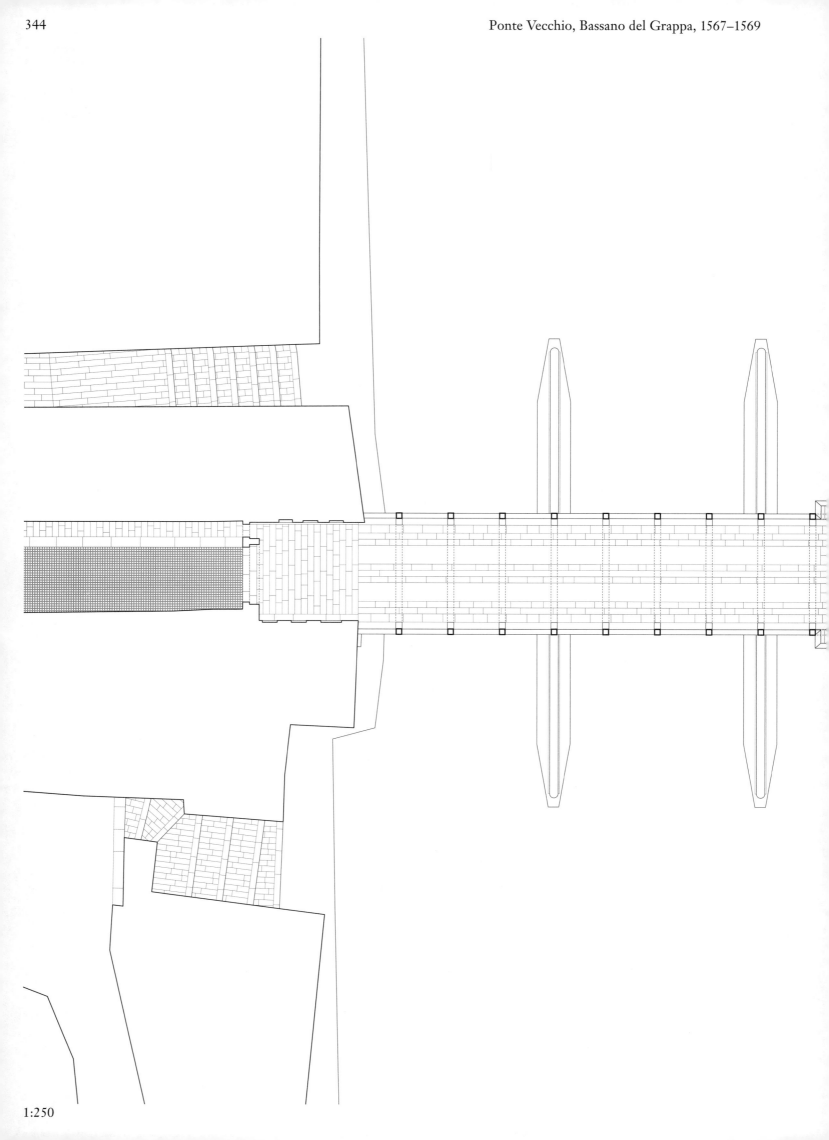

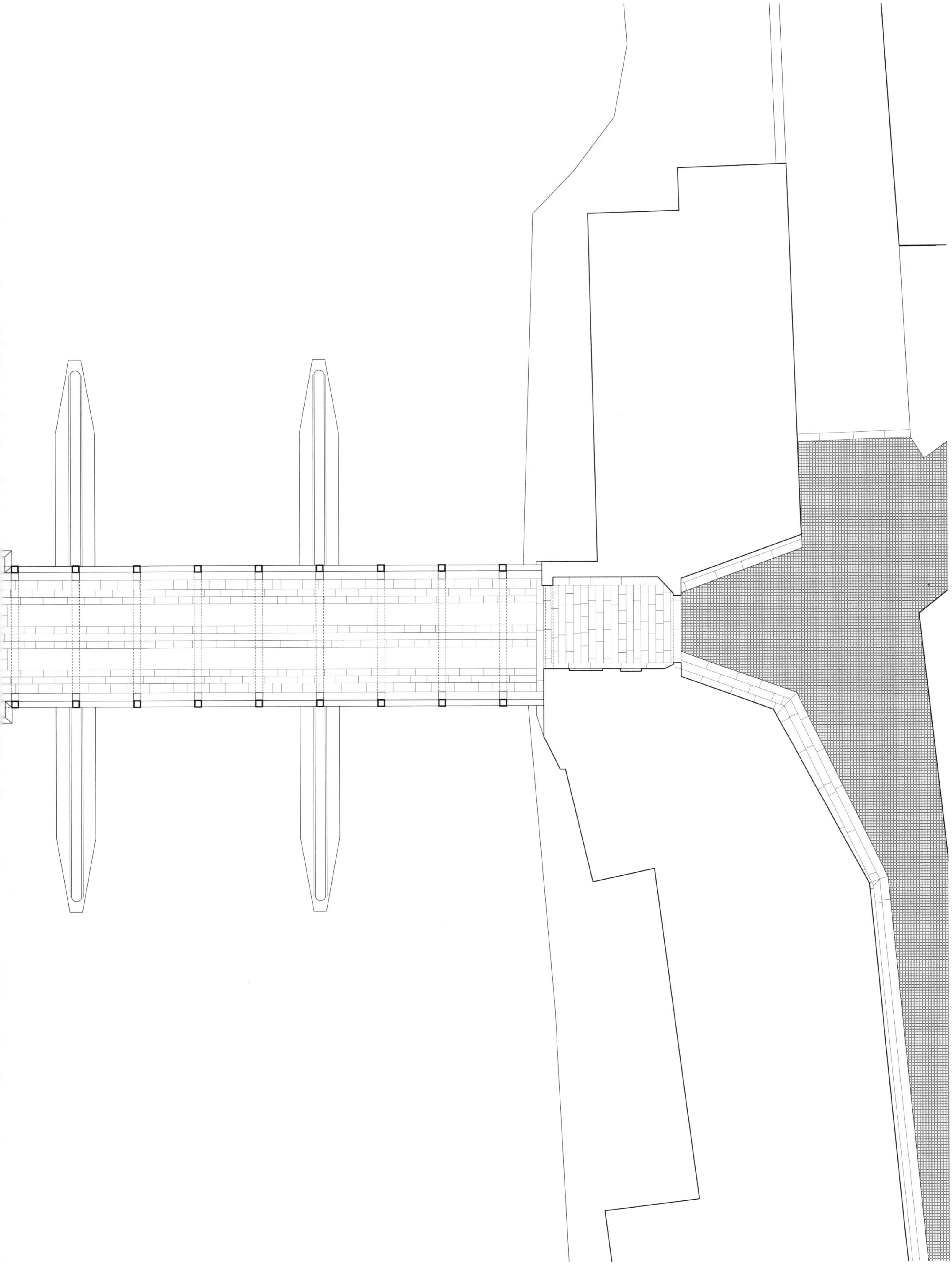

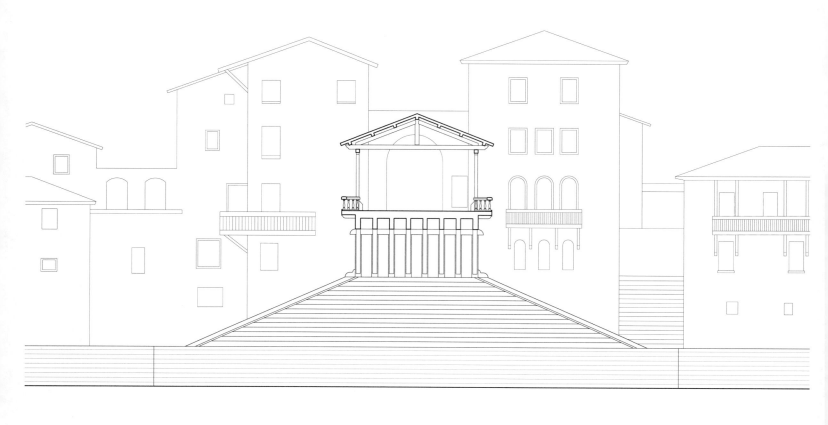

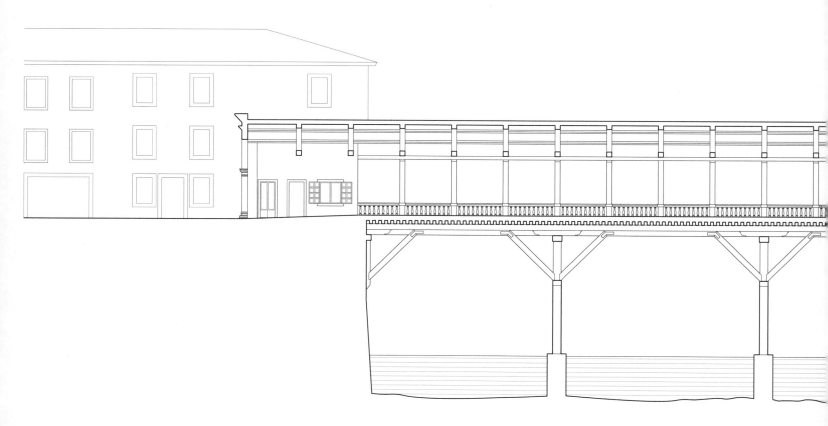

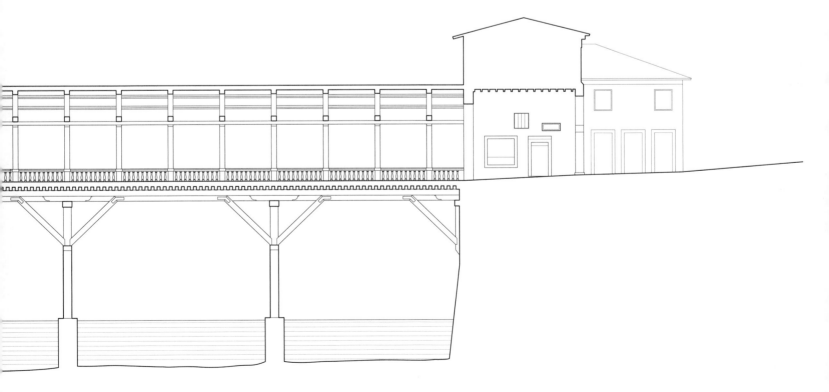

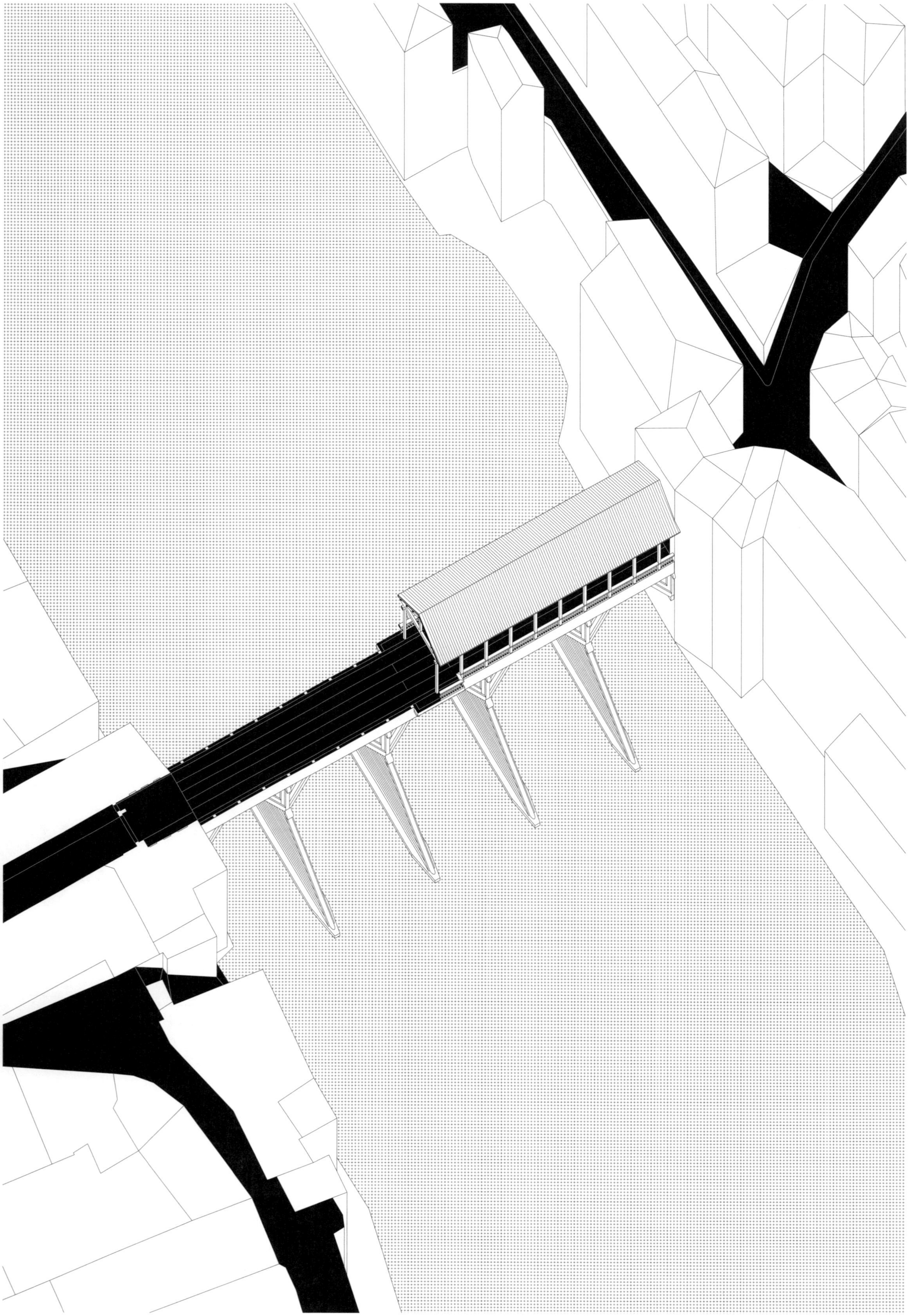

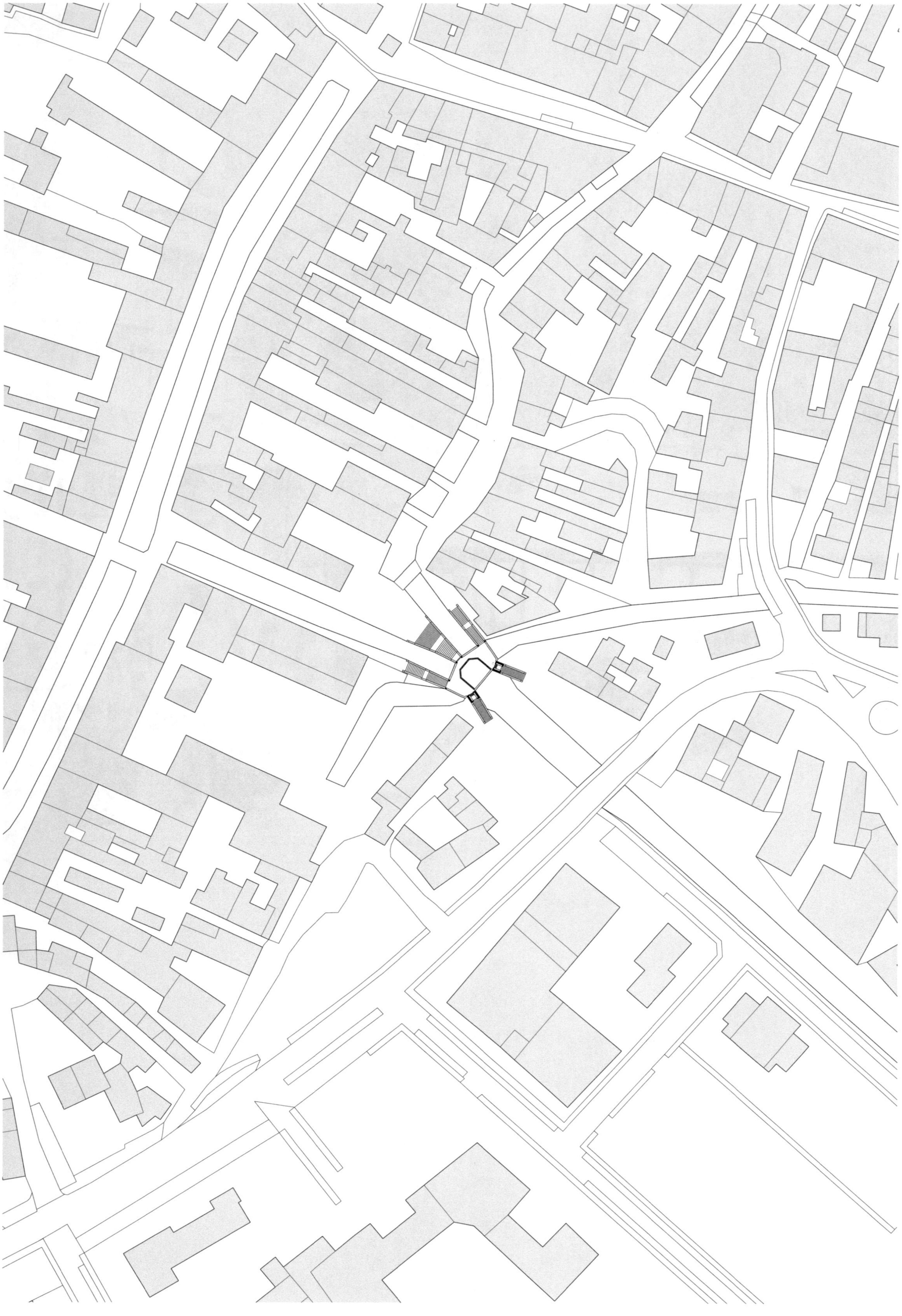

Trepponti Bridge, Comacchio, 1634   354–365

The Trepponti bridge, also known as Ponte del Teatro, is a work of engineering along the old navigable Pallotta Canal that led to the Adriatic Sea. The bridge constituted the fortified gate of the city.

The structure which connects the two banks of the canal through a detailed system of routes is an original urban device that can be interpreted as a simple bridge, but also an access gate, an outdoor theater, or a raised square.

The complex was built in 1638 by order of the Cardinal Giovanni Battista Maria Pallotta, based on a design by an architect from Ravenna, Luca Danese. Due to the direct involvement of Pope Urban VIII, Luca Danese worked at length on the renewal of the lagoon-front town of Comacchio, considered to be of strategic importance in the context of the improvement of Adriatic port facilities. Based on an orderly plan of public works of his own preparation, the architect designed the new waterway—canale Pilotta—connecting the city to the seas, and many projects created to regenerate local civil and economic vitality. These included the many canals and bridges, including the "pentarch" bridge, namely the Ponte dei Trepponti.

The bridge is composed of five ample brick staircases—three on one side and two on the other—that converge on a terrace over the water in Istrian stone. The largest staircase with a trapezoidal plan has 28 steps divided into two ramps, and reaches the level shared by the other ramps of 5.5 meters. The two staircases at the sides of the Pallotta Canal are specular, composed of 24 consecutive steps and 4 steps placed inside the turrets.

The raised part in Istrian stone has three steps that reach a level of 6 meters. Below the single vault, which reaches a height of 5 meters and is composed of five arches, the navigable Pallotta Canal comes to an end, spreading into the historical center to form four different canals known as Salara, Sant'Agostino, Borgo, and San Pietro. Across the centuries the bridge has been altered in various ways, above all for aesthetic reasons, as in the addition of the two guard turrets at the top of the two rear staircases, and of six small pillars placed at the top of the three frontal staircases. Both fortified towers bear plaques that display two significant quotations for the city of Comacchio.

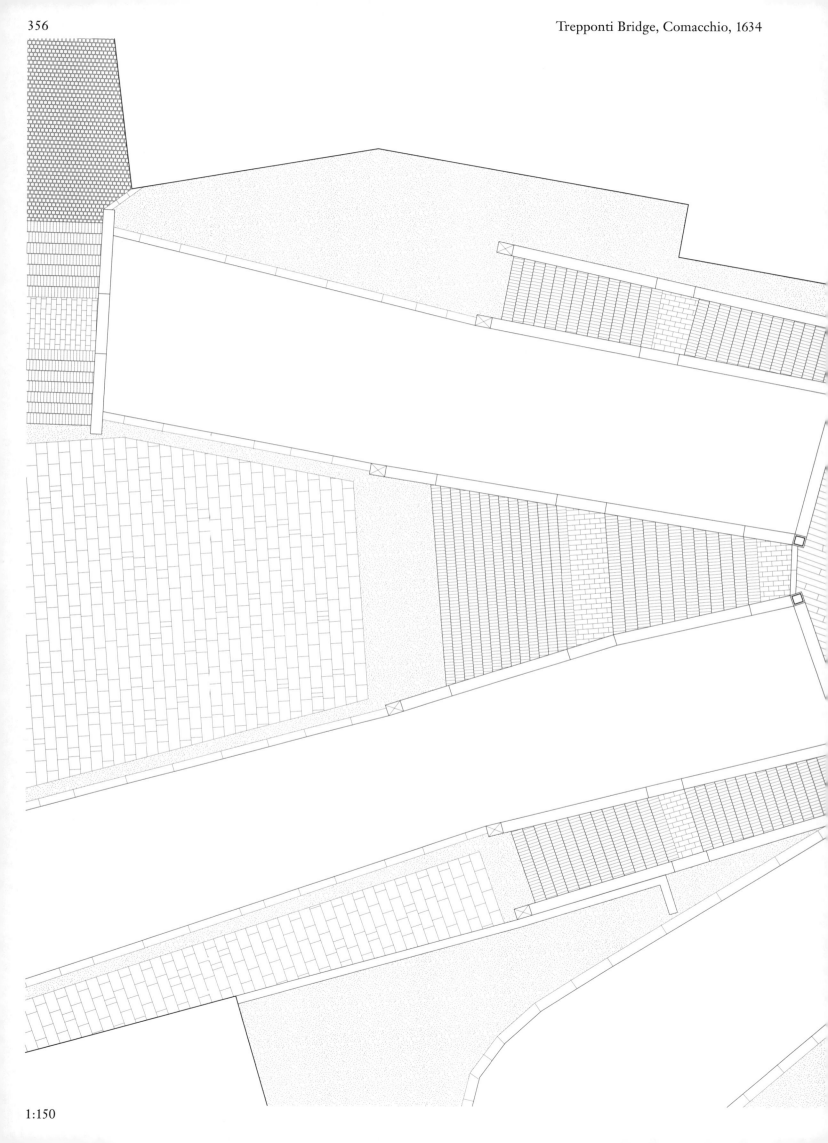

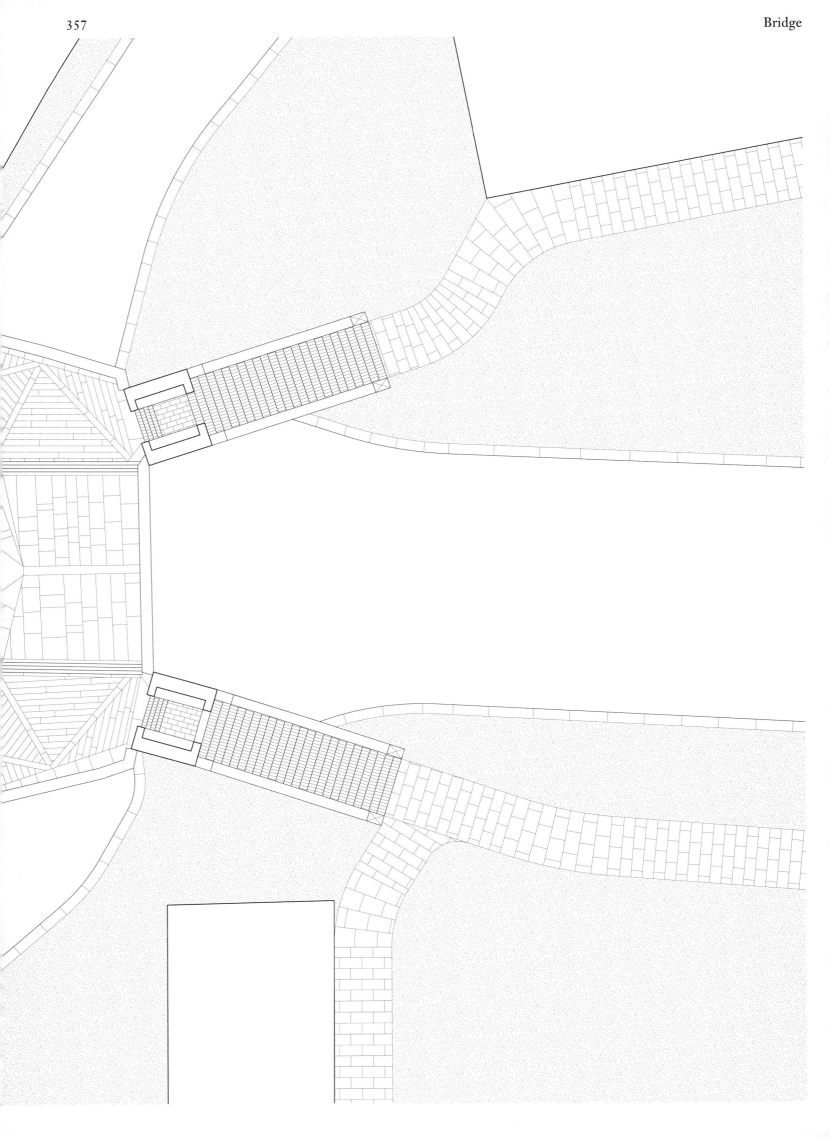

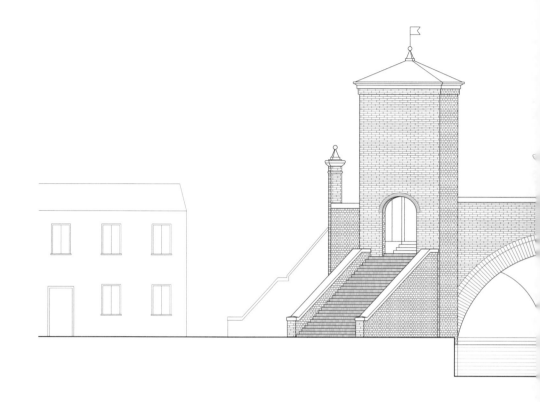

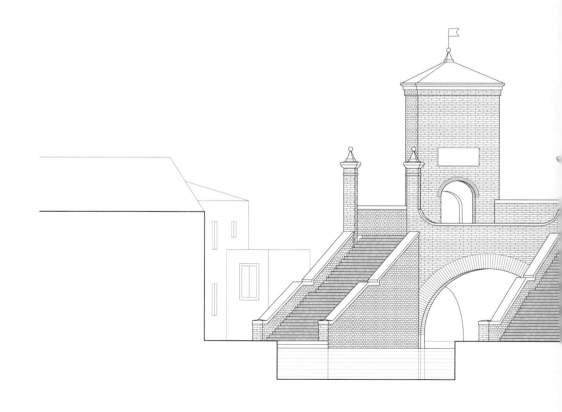

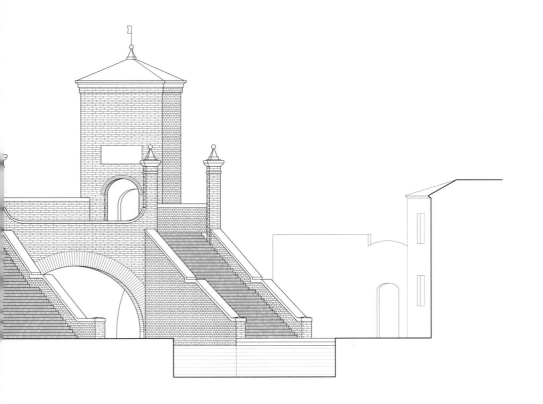

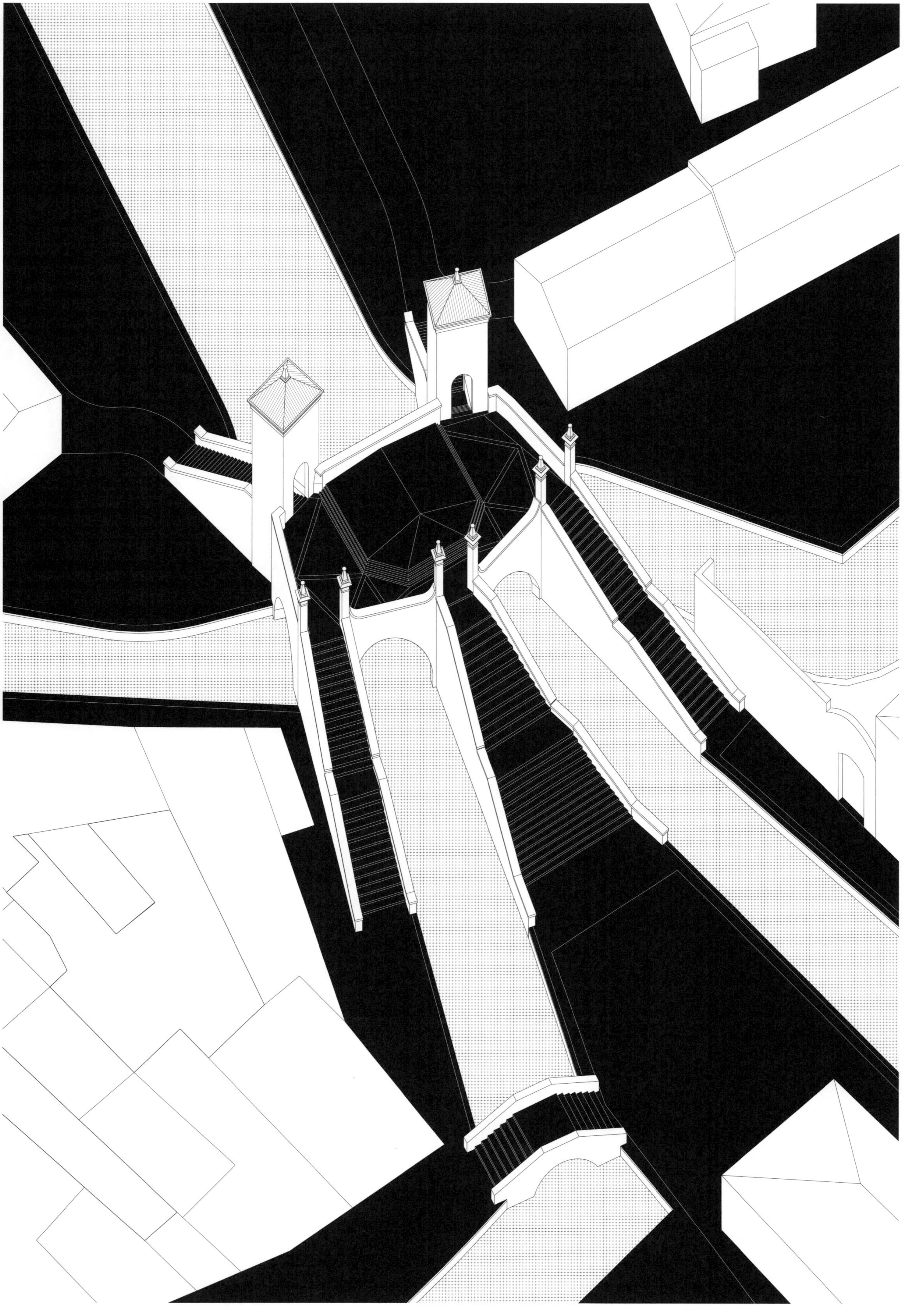

Ponte Vecchio, Florence, 1339–1345   366–377

Ponte Vecchio, the oldest bridge in the city, was built from 1339 to 1345 in the point where the banks of the Arno River are closest to each other, which was originally the location of a ford.

The presence of craftsmen's shops on both sides of a central piazza facing the river make Ponte Vecchio an architectural structure that can be interpreted as a fragment of the surrounding urban fabric, raised over the Arno.

The first crossing of the Arno, in a position not so different from today's, dated back to the Roman era. The bridge in its current configuration, built from 1339 to 1345, is attributed to one of two different figures: Taddeo Gaddi (as reported by Giorgio Vasari) or Neri di Fioravante (due to the fact that in those years he held the position of the city's master builder).

Unlike the bridges created until that time, which were based on Roman models with round arches and short spans, Ponte Vecchio was built with segmental arches that permitted a reduction of the number of piers in the riverbed, extending the size of the spans. This new solution—the first of its kind for a bridge in Europe—left more space for the river to flow, thus limiting its resistance to the current.

The original bridge featured four linear buildings placed at the four corners, with a small central plaza; over the roof of the buildings there was an upper walkway accessed through four doors placed in the central part and at the ends. The arcades of the lower level gradually filled up with small buildings on both sides. These constructions, already existing in a different form in the 1300s, were set aside in 1442 by the municipal administration as shops for greengrocers and butchers, where the latter could discard scraps from meat cutting into the river. Over time the shops expanded with overhangs above the river, forcefully altering the original image.

The last important alteration of the bridge was done by Vasari, who in 1565 designed the "corridor" for Cosimo I, bearing the latter's name, with the aim of connecting the political and administrative center of Palazzo Vecchio with the private residence of the Medici at Palazzo Pitti. The elevated corridor, about 760 meters long and built in just five months, extends on the eastern side of the bridge above the shops and along the Lungarno degli Archibusieri in a sequence of 14 arches with a height of 8.5 meters.

About 96 meters long, with an average width of 24 meters, of which only 8.7 form the width of the pedestrian walkway, the bridge is divided into four blocks of shops topped by small apartments. The portions of the bridge with buildings are interrupted at the center, where the space widens on both sides to form a piazza overlooking the river; the southern side of the piazza is bordered by a loggia with three round arches that supports Vasari's corridor.

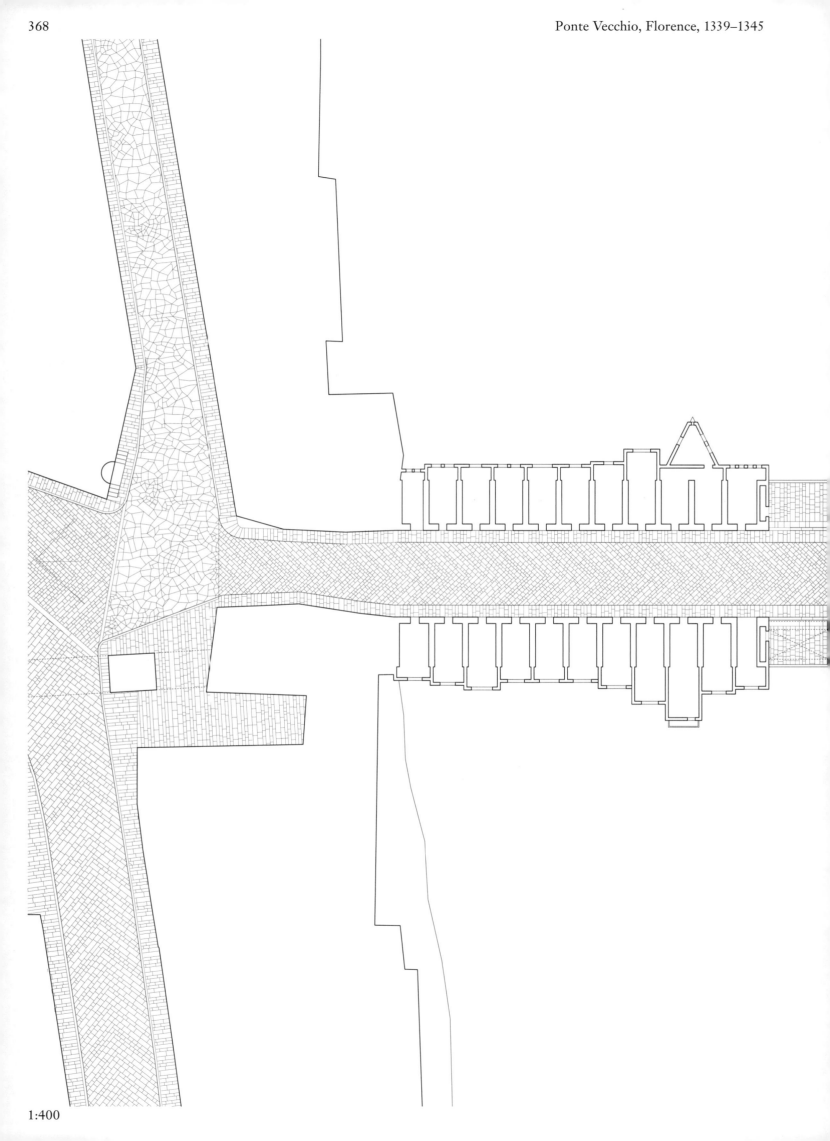

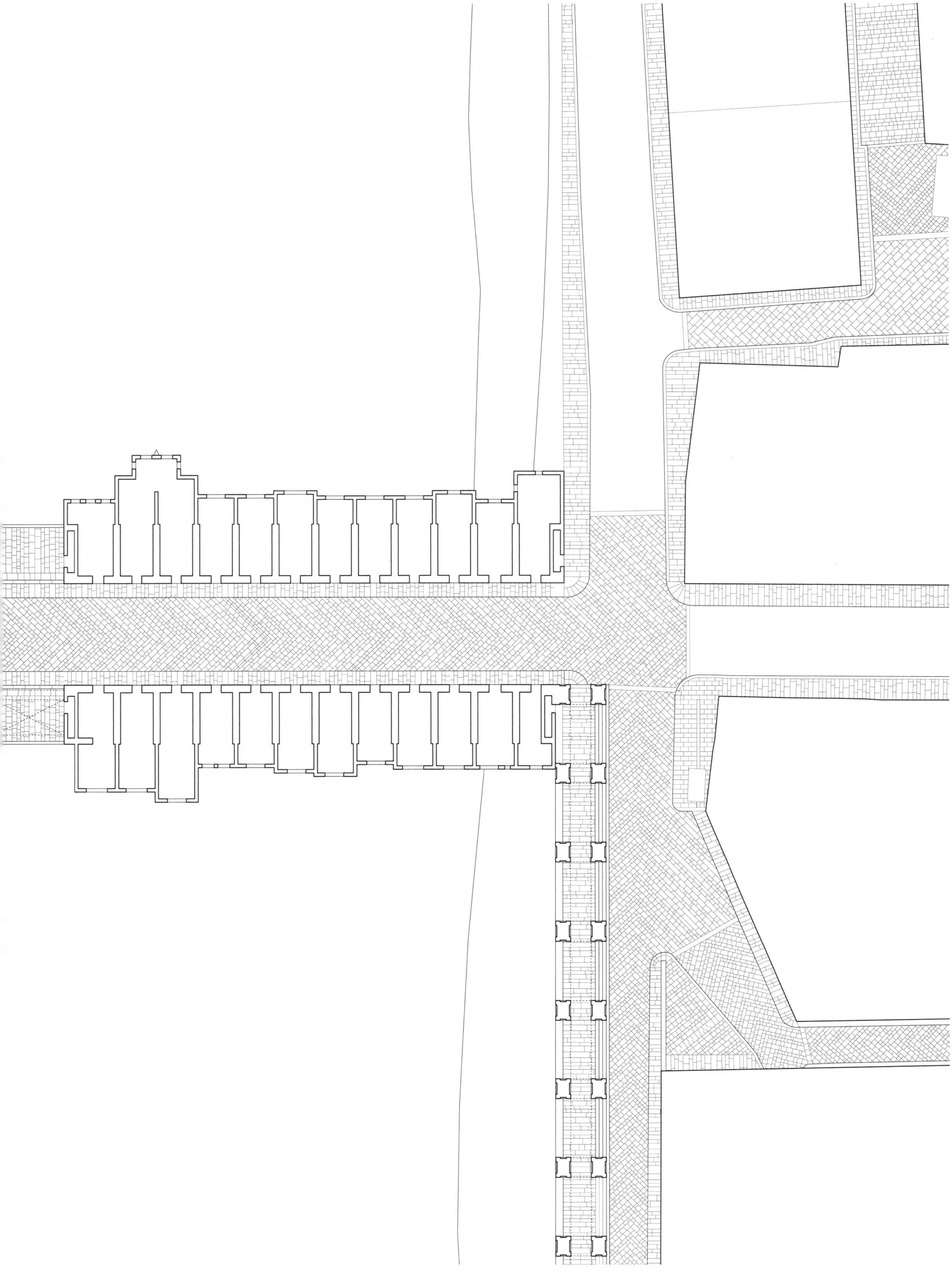

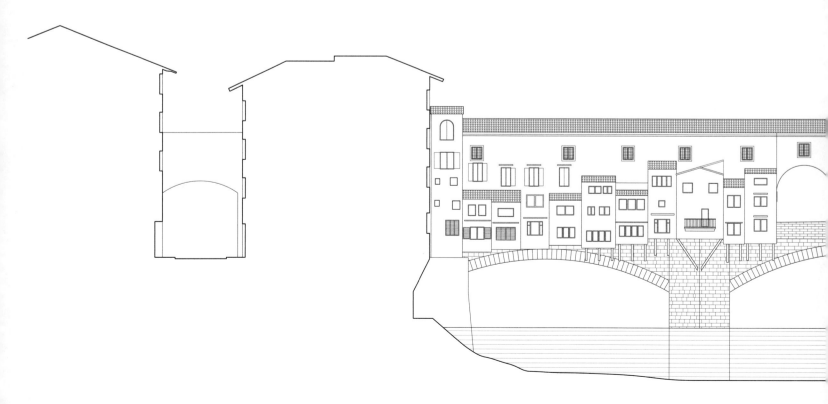

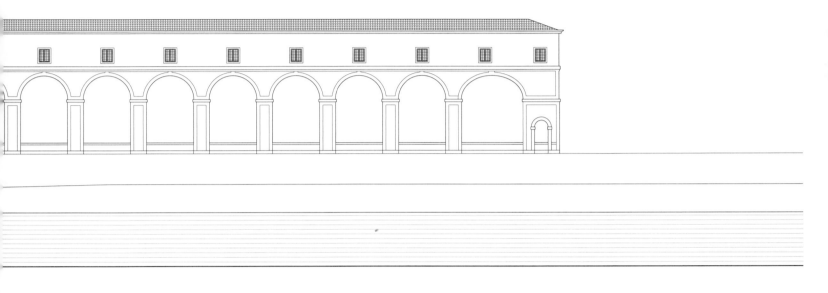

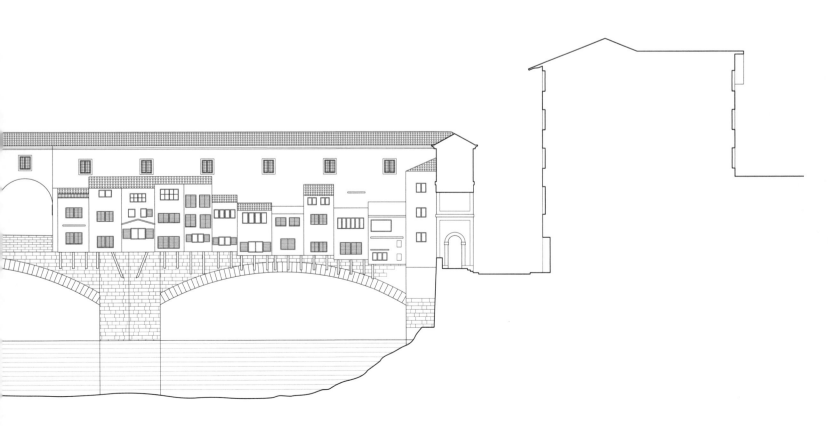

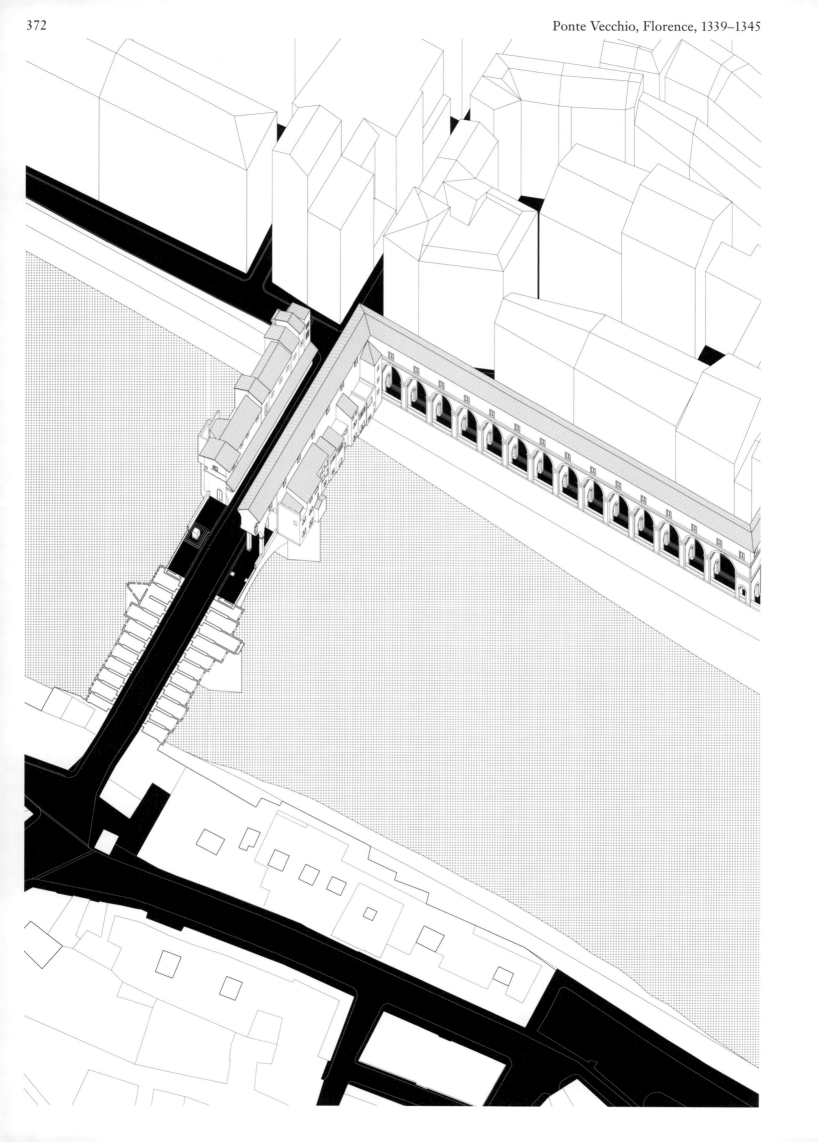

An open space bordered by artifacts whose coherent, unified design is capable of giving rise to a third, autonomous spatial entity.

In other words, when the design of the buildings facing a public space is able to generate an enclosure that has the characteristics of an interior, although it is an outdoor zone.

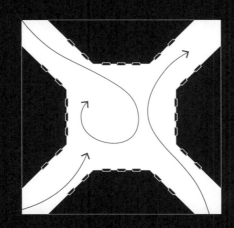

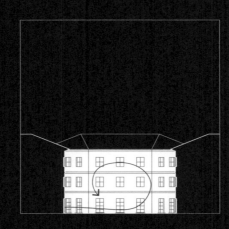

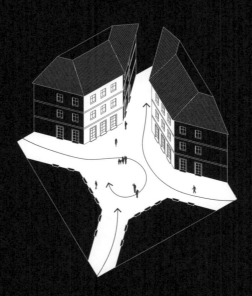

City Room

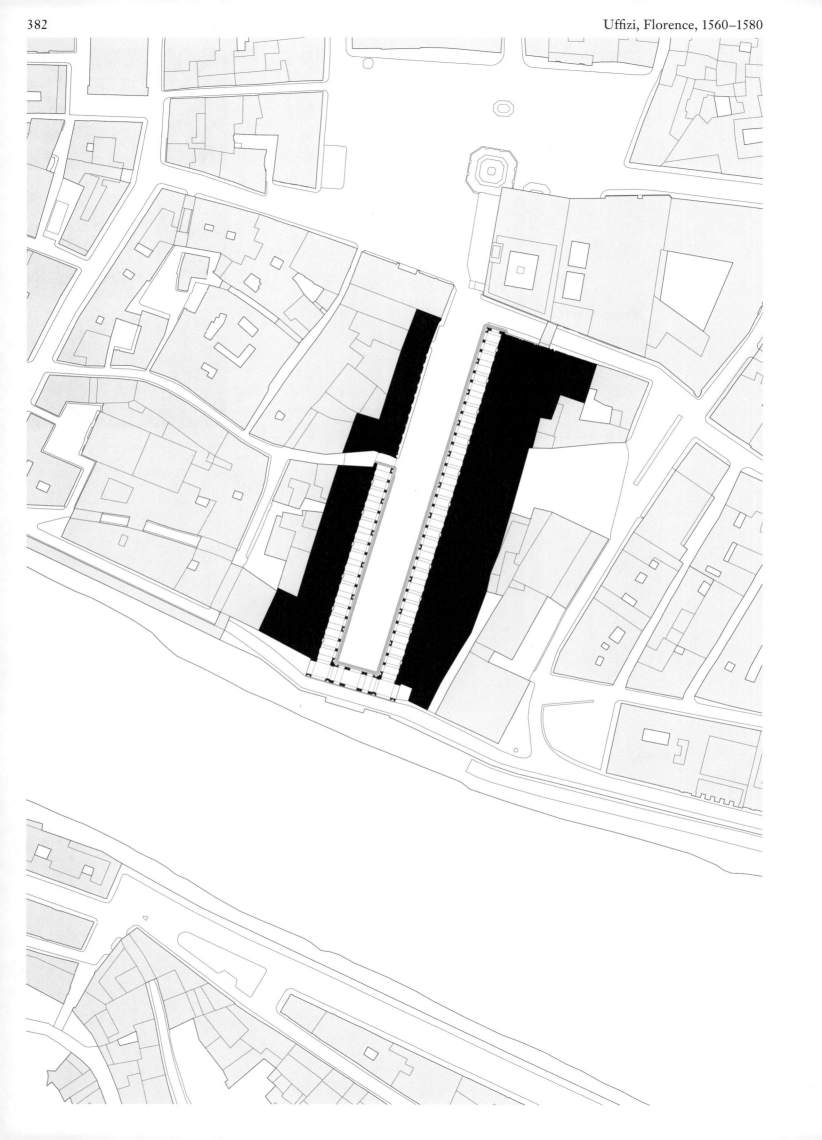

Uffizi, Florence, 1560–1580   394–405

The large Uffizi building is one of the most outstanding works of architecture of the Italian Renaissance, now containing an important museum complex.

With a radical gesture accentuated by the intense rhythm of the architectural parts and a layout of oblong proportions, Giorgio Vasari redesigned a portion of the city between Piazza della Signoria and the Arno River, creating a large open-air room.

Following the establishment of Duke Cosimo I de' Medici in the old city hall of Palazzo Vecchio, a policy of transformation of the city of Florence began, with the aim of granting visibility and prominence to the new government. Shortly after the midpoint of the century, Cosimo I commissioned Vasari to construct a complex that would bring together the 13 most important governmental offices of the city in a single head-quarters. The location chosen for the new construction was a parcel of land between the southern side of Piazza della Signoria and the Lungarno, in a strategic point of connection between the piazza of the seat of municipal govern-ment and the river port. When Cosimo I and Vasari died in 1574, the worksite was already close to completion, and the work was concluded shortly thereafter by Francesco I, son of Cosimo I, under the supervision of the architect Bernardo Buontalenti. The latter was responsible for the infill of the loggia running along the entire upper level, which became a personal gallery for the collection of 15th-century paintings of Francesco I.

The Uffizi has a linear form organized in two wings of different length: to the east, the *Uffizi lunghi*, and to the west the *Uffizi corti*, respectively measuring 150 and 90 meters. The two volumes are connected to the riverfront by a theatrical end composed of a double order of Serlian windows offering views of the river. The complex, with its oblong U-shaped plan, frames Palazzo Vecchio and its tower in a perspective view.

The volumes are externally attached to existing buildings, while the façade is limited to the internal front of the building, forming the perimeter of the courtyard-piazza of the Uffizi.

The 240 meters of internal façade stand out for a two-tone effective typical of Brunelleschi, a contrast between pale stucco and the gray hue of *pietra serena*. The three volumes are based on the same module, measuring 12 meters at the base and rising for a height of 24 meters; at ground level, a loggia with architraves covered by a barrel vault, whose key is at 11 meters, is formed by spans bordered by pilasters with niches, and subdivided into three intercolumniations with Doric columns placed at intervals of 3.5 meters from each other. Three openings in the false mezzanine above correspond to this module, serving to bring light to the portico. Three windows on the first floor present the alternation of a triangular and curved tympana, including the pilaster strips. Finally, at the upper level, a loggia replicates the tripartite module, as the location of the original "galleria" of the Uffizi.

The trabeated portico on the ground level, the pronounced overhang of the stringcourse cornices, and the corbels of the false attic clearly reveal the influence of Michelangelo. The internal floor of the loggia is raised with respect to the piazza thanks to four steps that define the inner perimeter.

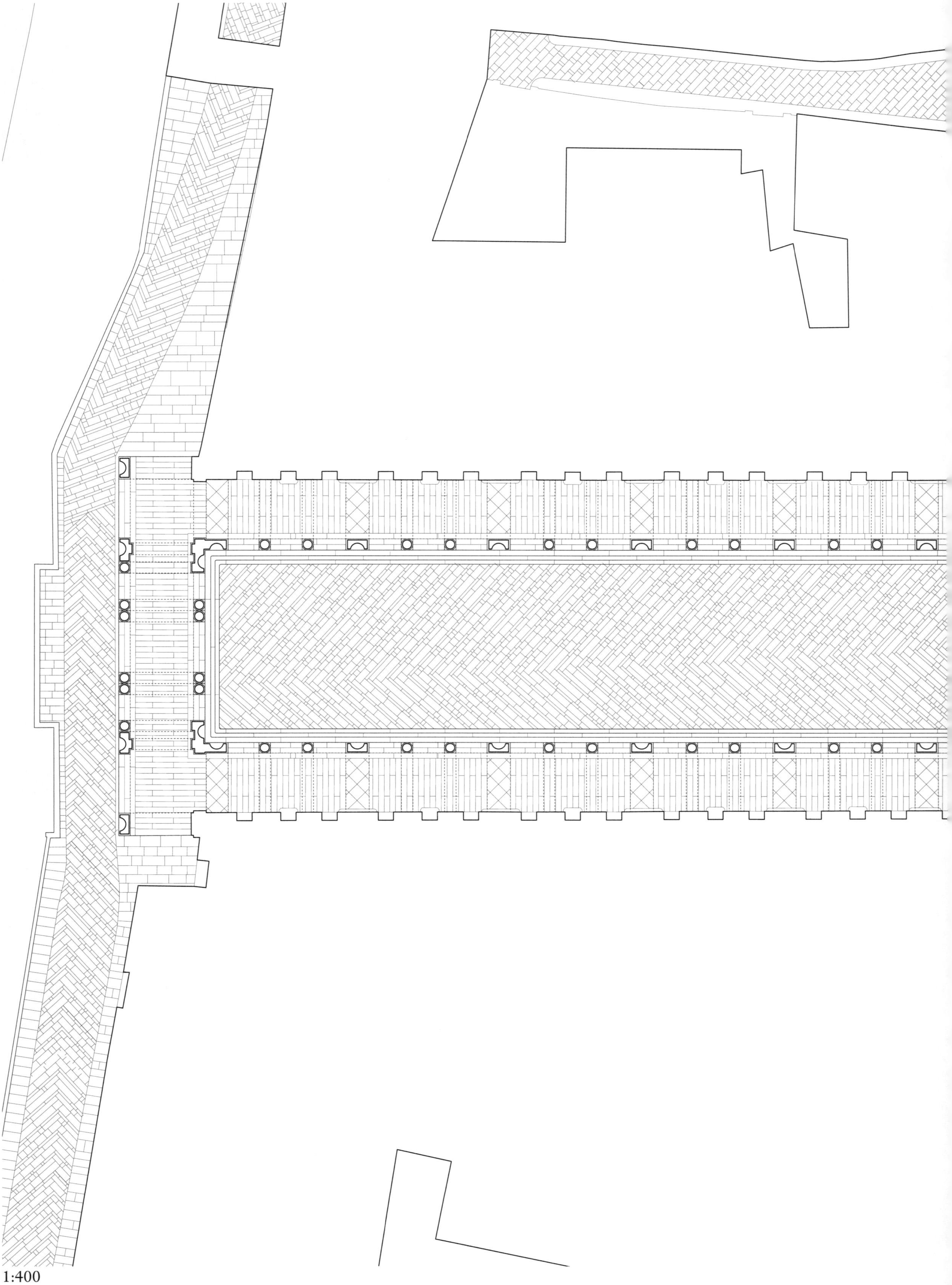

1:400

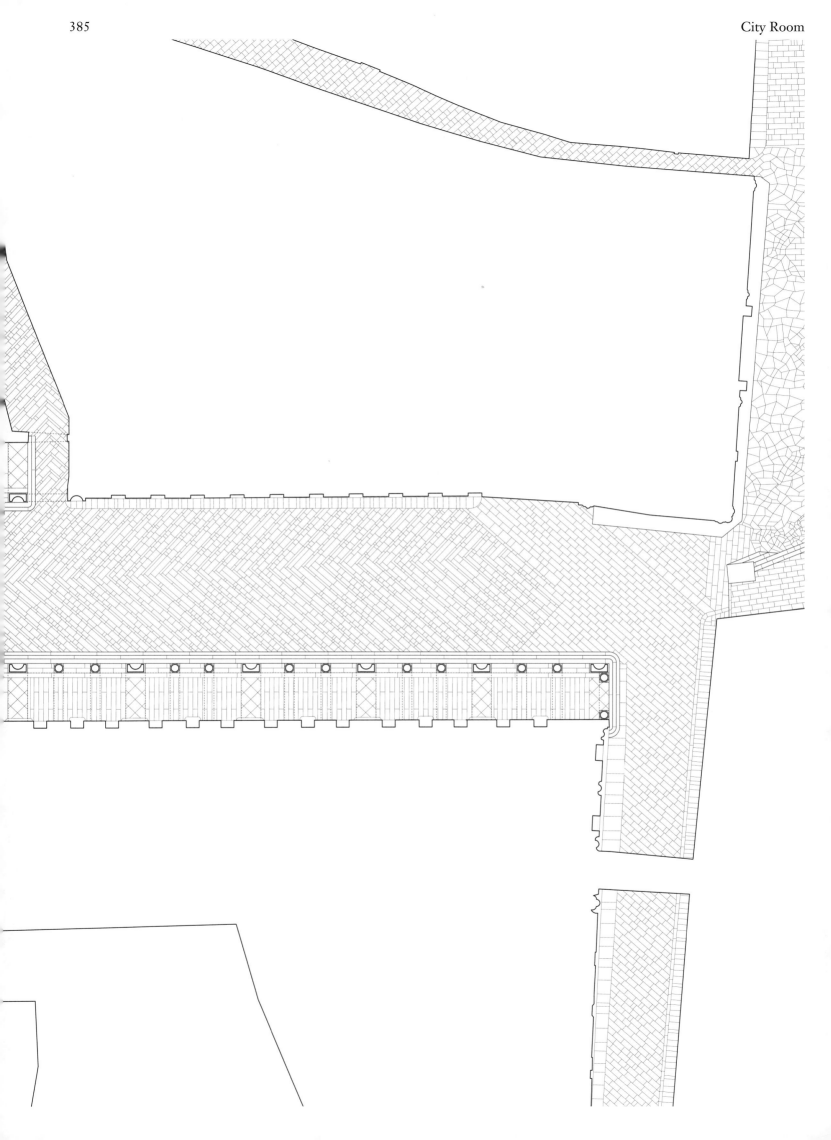

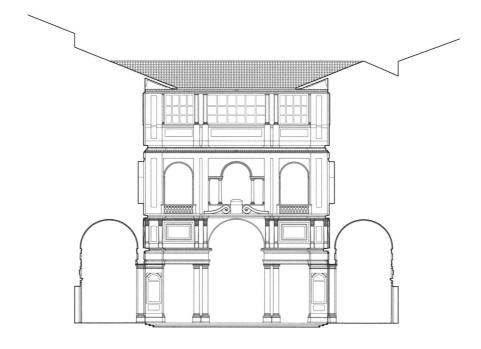

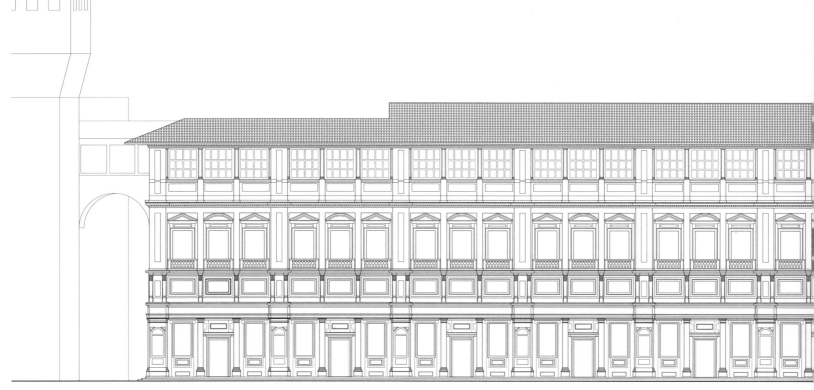

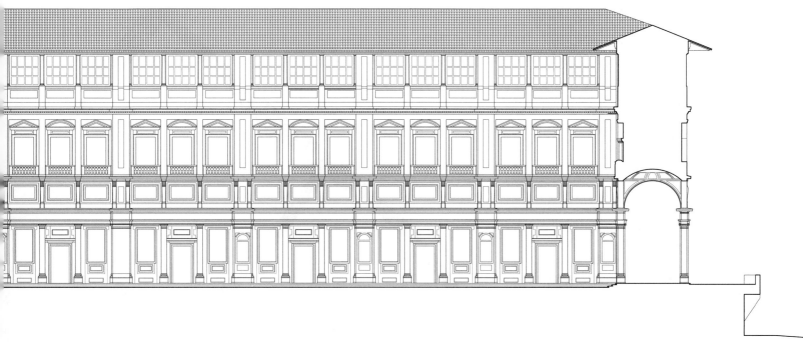

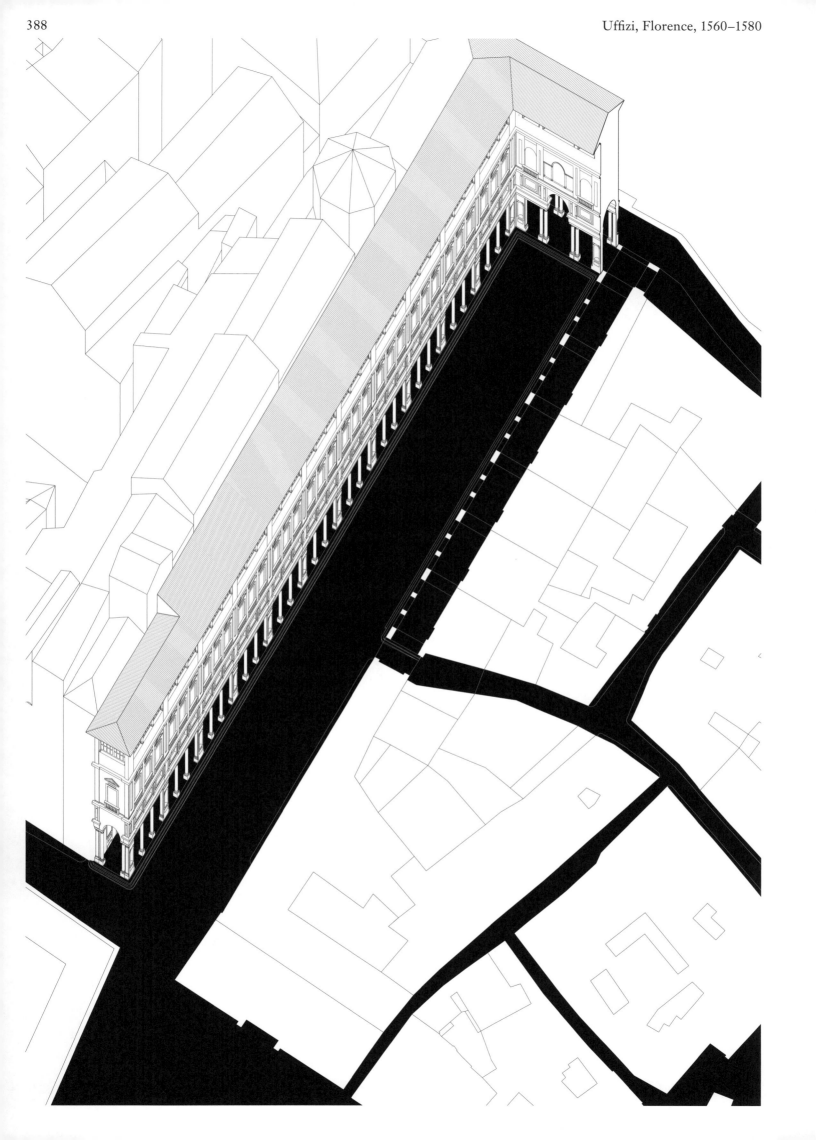

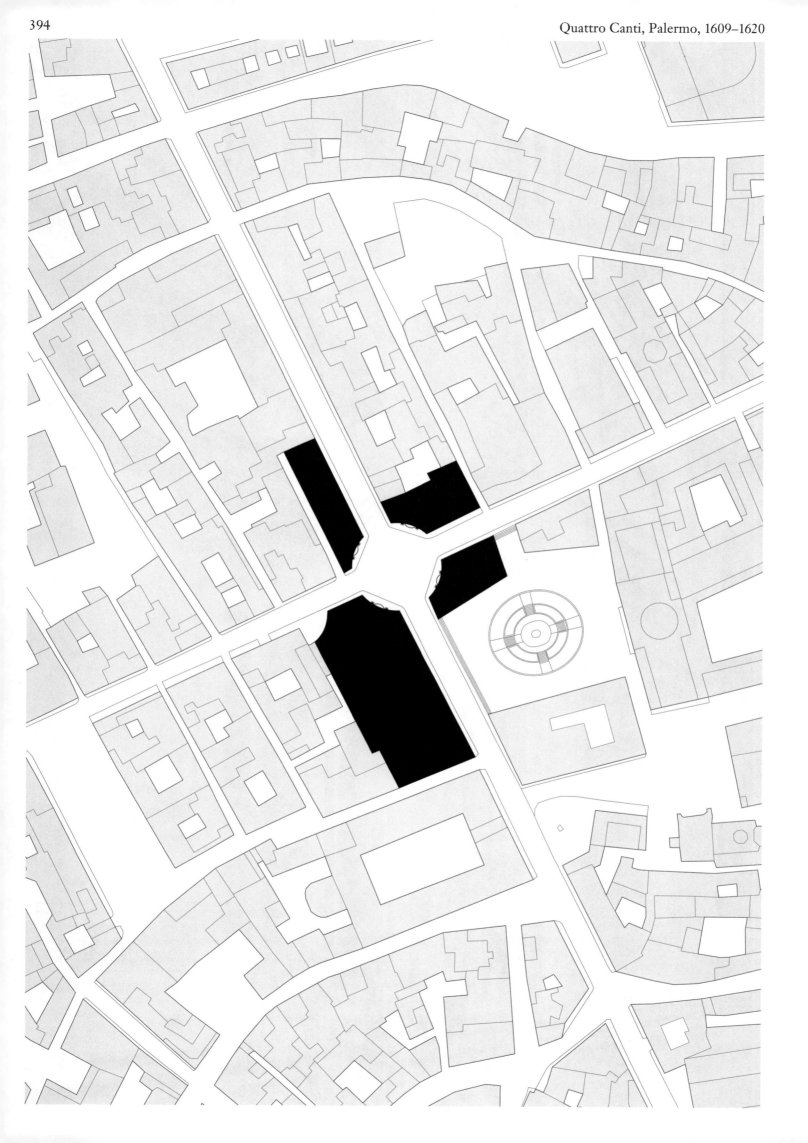

Quattro Canti, Palermo, 1609–1620   394–405

Piazza Villena in Palermo, also known as Quattro Canti or Ottagono del Sole, is an octagonal piazza at the intersection of the two main thoroughfares of the city: Via Maqueda, parallel to the coast, and Via Vittorio Emanuele, perpendicular to it.

The organization of the square, clearly based on the Quattro Fontane in Rome, is a monumental tribute to the crossroads between Via Maqueda, the axis of growth of the city built towards the end of the 16th century, and the ancient Cassaro, the road dating back to the foundation of the city in the 7th century BC, retraced in the 16th century.

The design of the square was assigned by the Spanish viceroy, Marquis Don Juan Fernandez Pacheco de Villena y Ascalon, to the Florentine architect Giulio Lasso in 1608; the work was completed in 1620, under the supervision of Mariano Smiriglio.

The four elevations of the piazza offer a sweeping overview of the history and age-old traditions of the city; paced by the presence of architectural orders, they are all organized on multiple levels with decorative motifs whose themes are based on a principle of ascent from nature towards the heavens. At the lower level there are four fountains that represent the rivers of the old city—Oreto, Kemonia, Pannaria, Papireto—and, framed by a Doric order, the allegories of the four seasons, represented by Aeolus, Venus, Ceres, and Bacchus. The second level, with an Ionic order, displays statues of Charles V, Philip II, Philip III, and Philip IV. Finally, in the upper order, there are the four patron saints of Palermo: Agatha, Ninfa, Olivia, and Christina.

Each elevation measures about 12 meters in width and 26 meters in height.

Piazza Villena marks the point of intersection of the four historic quarters of Palermo—also known as *mandamenti*—each protected by one of the saints represented on the four elevations: the Albergheria district, also known as the district of the Palazzo Reale, which contains the oldest nucleus of the city; the Capo district; the Loggia district that hosts the Vucciria market; and, finally, the Tribunali area, which locals indicate with its Arabic name, Kalsa.

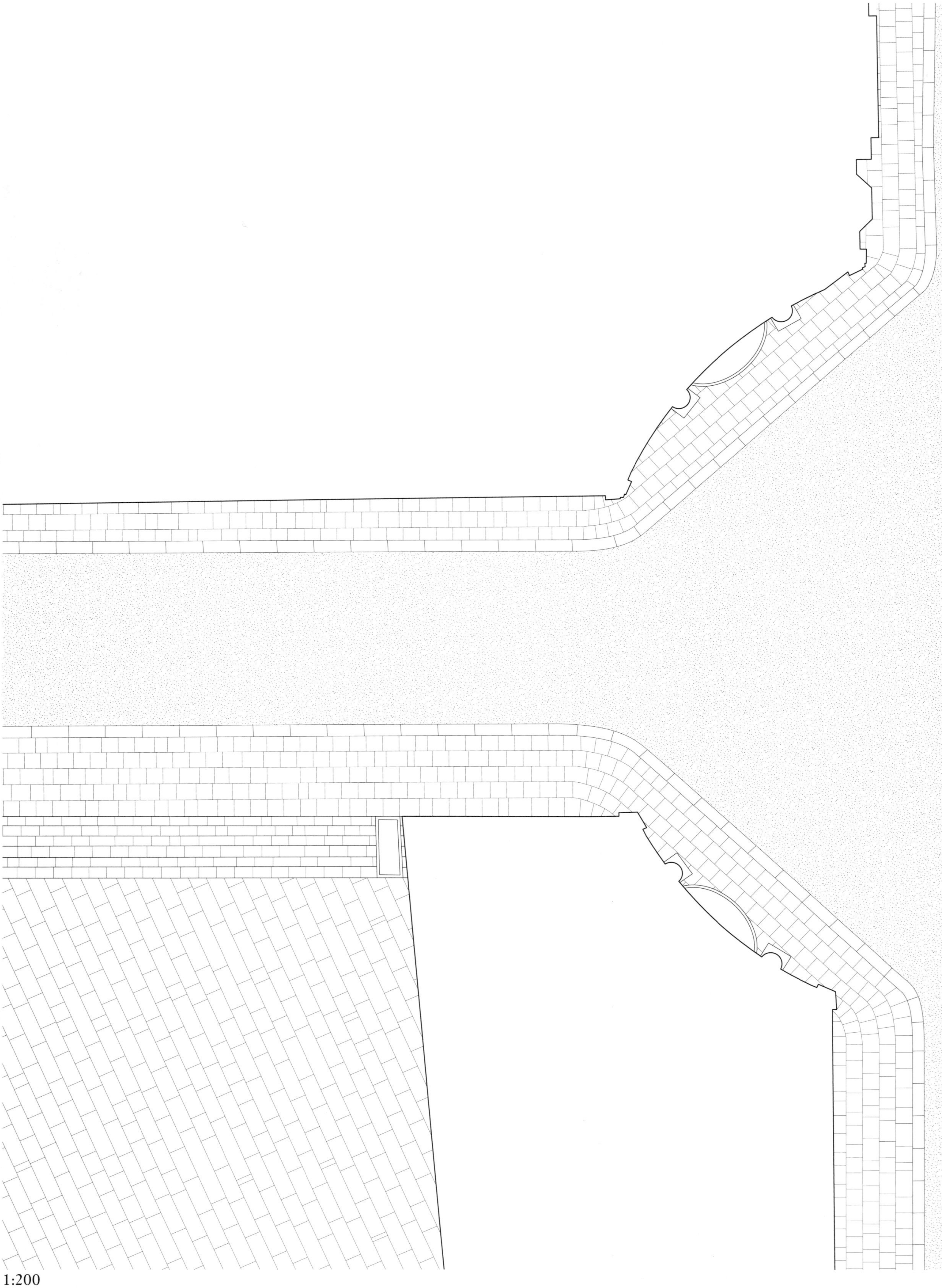

1:200

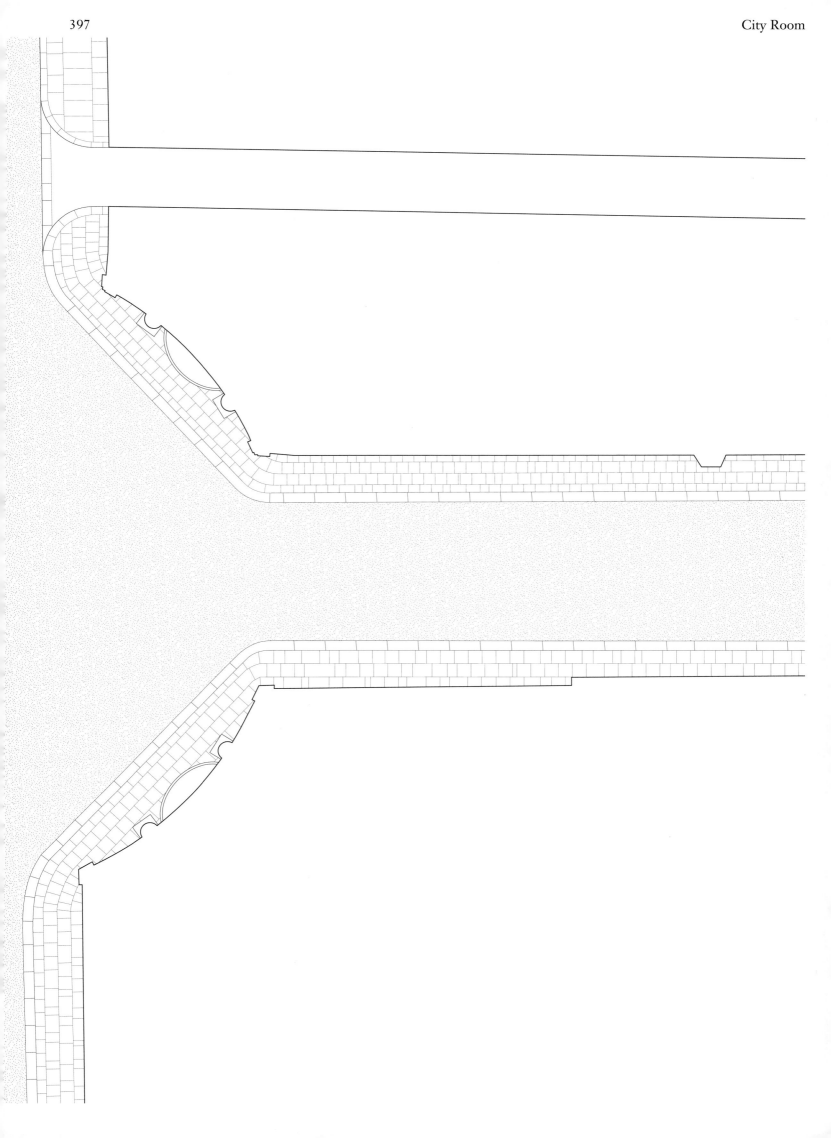

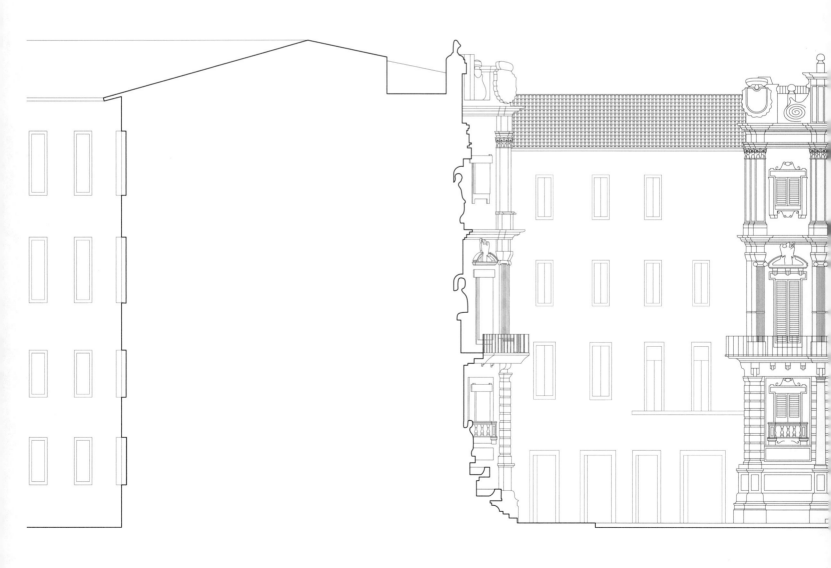

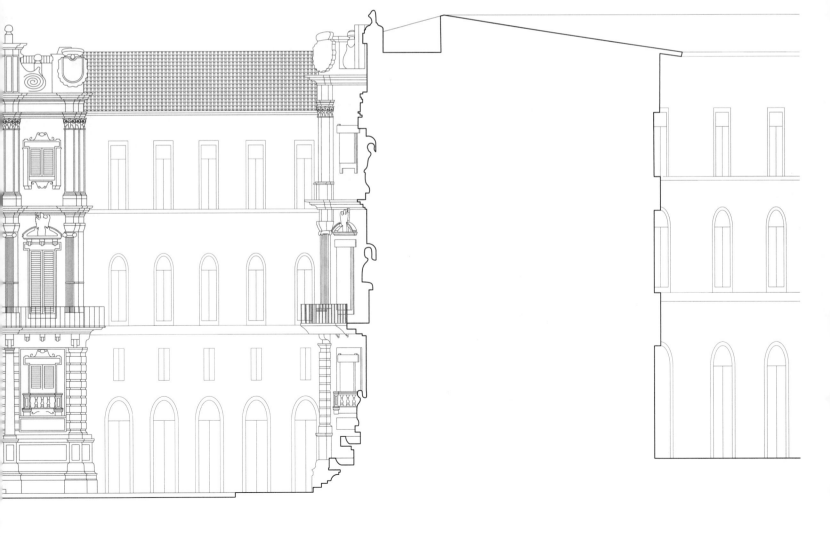

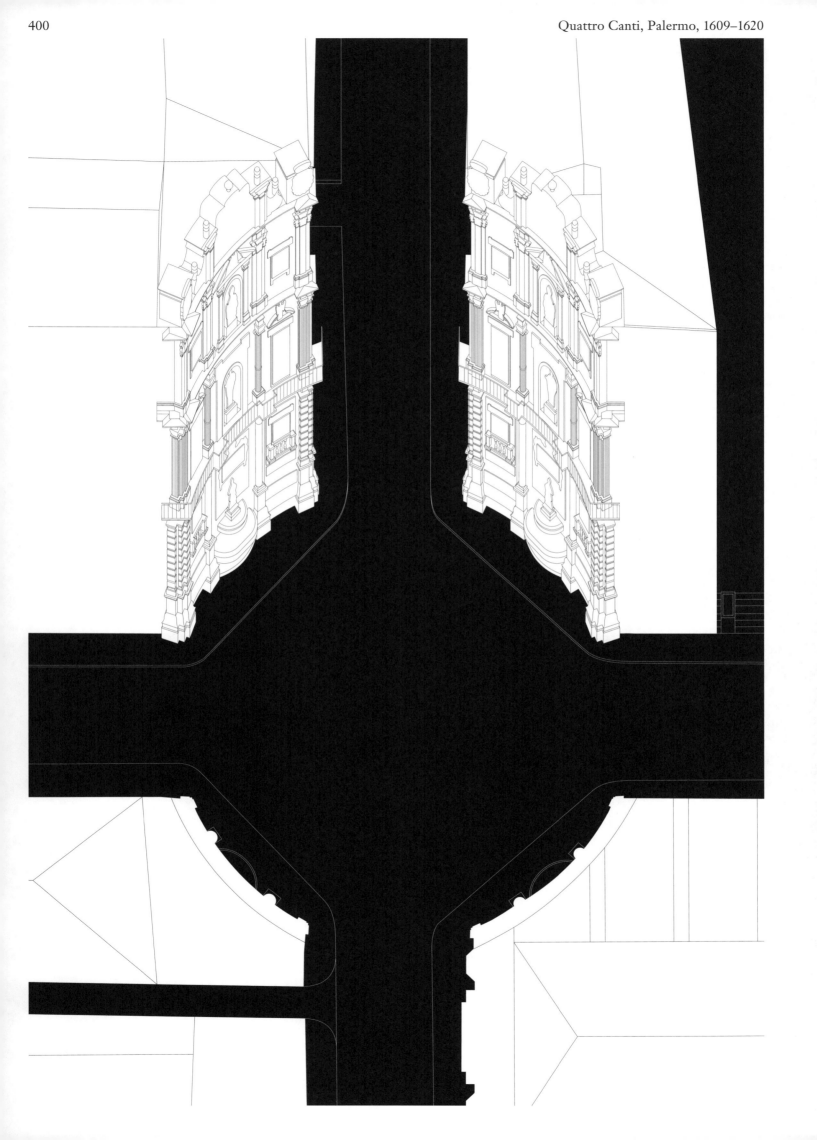

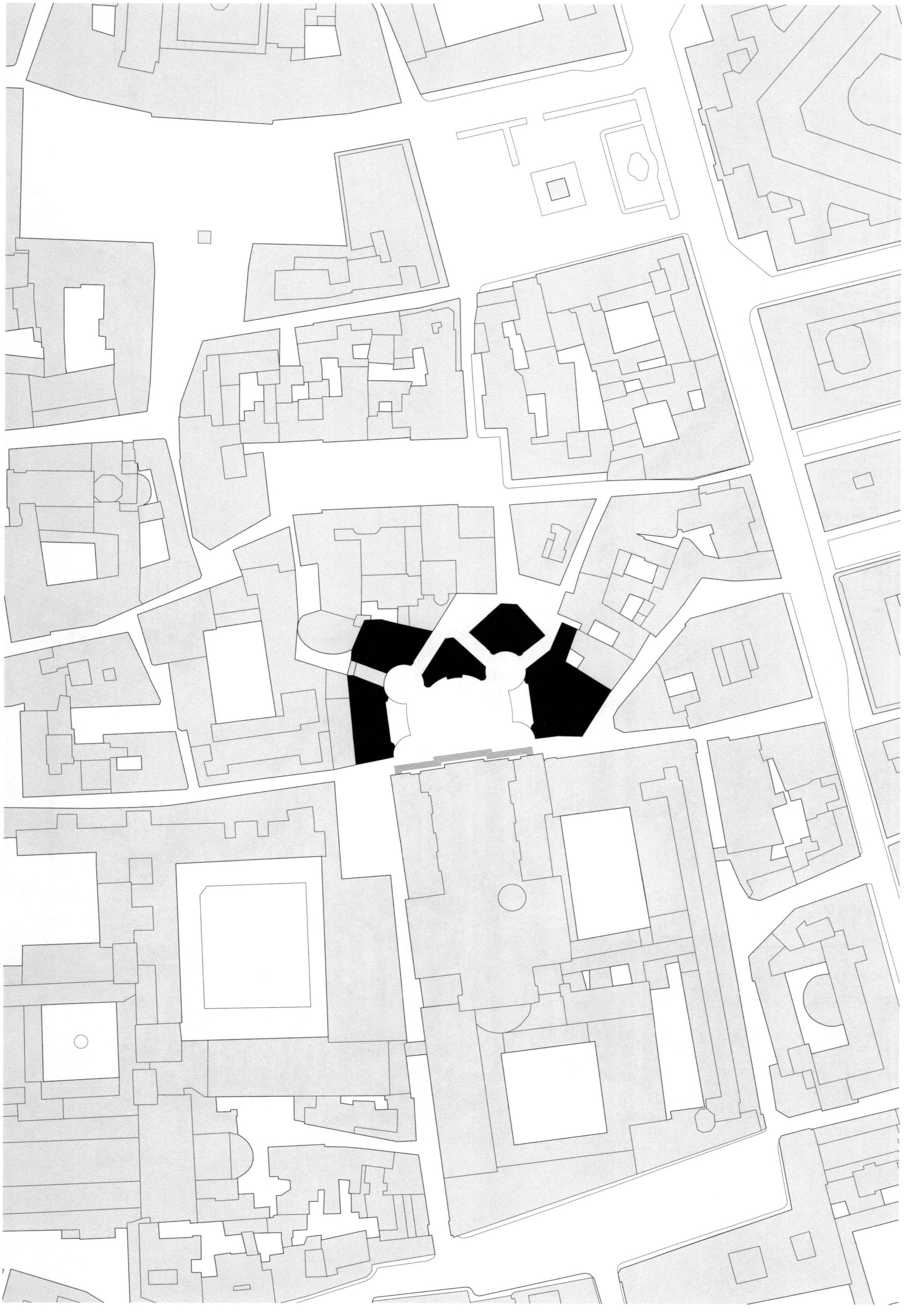

Piazza Sant'Ignazio, Rome, 1727–1728   406–417

Located in the historical center of Rome, Piazza Sant'Ignazio is in front of the church dedicated to Saint Ignatius of Loyola, founder of the Society of Jesus.

Through the alternation of full and empty portions, and thanks to rigorous, skillful use of geometry, the set of buildings on Piazza Sant' Ignazio forms an enveloping space that in spite of its small scape is able to compete with the much larger dimensions of the church faced by the square.

The need for the construction of a piazza became clear immediately after the completion of the church of Sant'Ignazio (1626–1650), accentuated by the strident contrast between the scale and magnificence of the new church and the dilapidated condition of the buildings in front of it.

The project was commissioned by the Jesuits, the owners of the church, to Filippo Raguzzini in 1727, with the express desire to build rental housing that would bring financial income. The area for the project was obtained through the demolition of most of the structures facing the church.

In order to respond to the impressive façade of the church, though working on buildings of a smaller scale, Raguzzini imagined a theatrical set organized in relation to the churchyard and around a square with a width of 45 meters and a depth of 25 meters; envisioned as theatrical wings on staggered planes, Raguzzini created three new buildings and three voids of circular form with a radius of 12 meters.

The final result stands out for its extraordinary and original compositional unity, based on a complex geometric scheme of concave and convex figures and diagonal axes that originate in the design of the neighboring church.

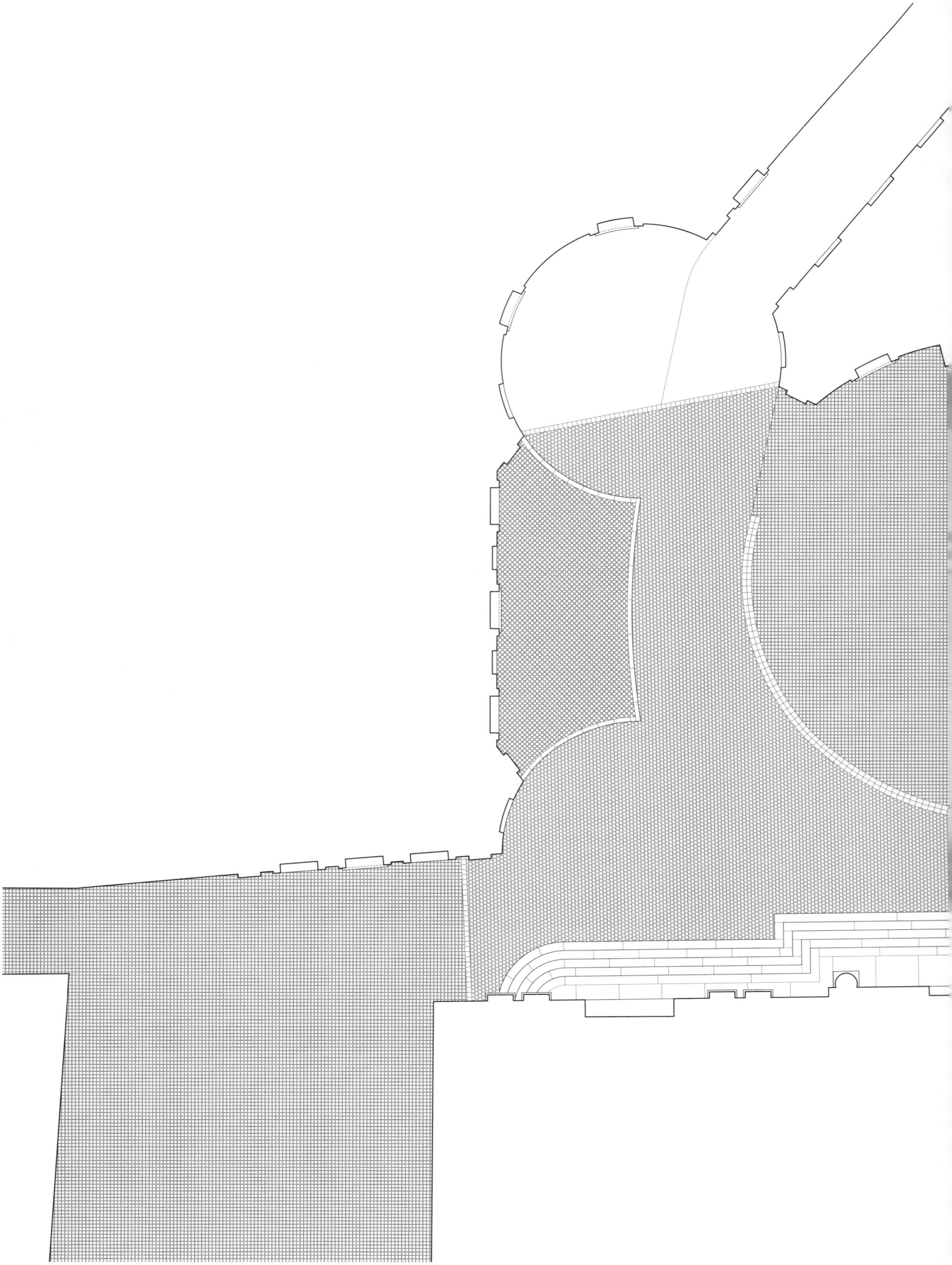

1:150

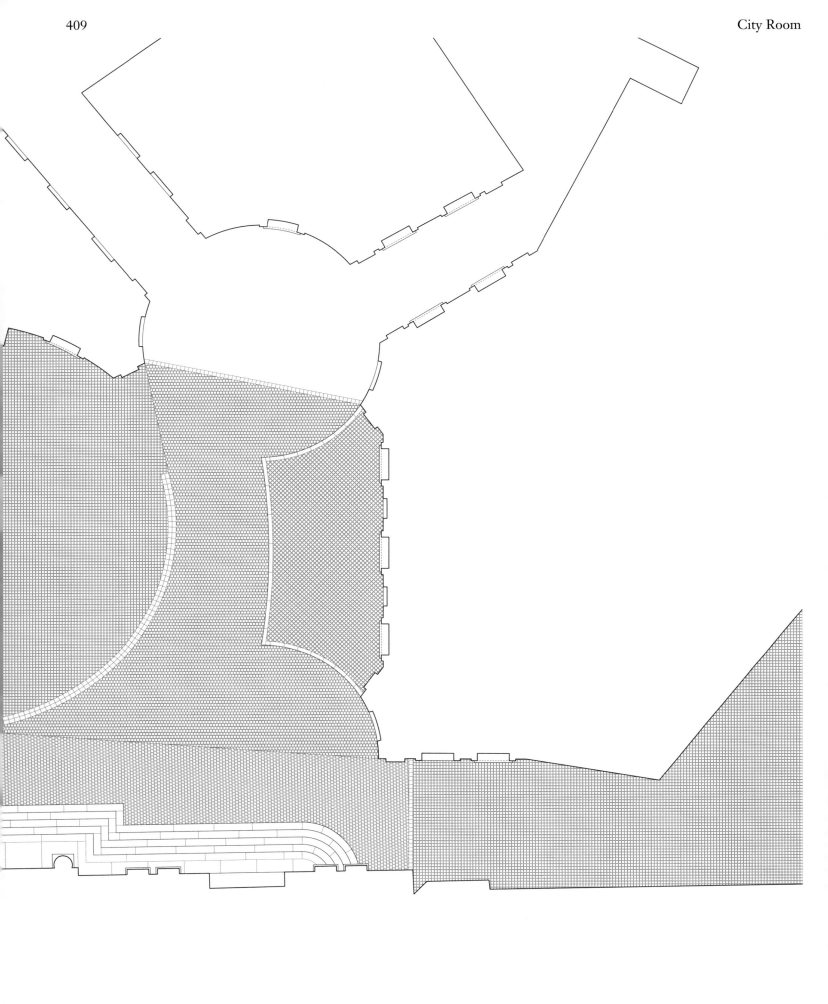

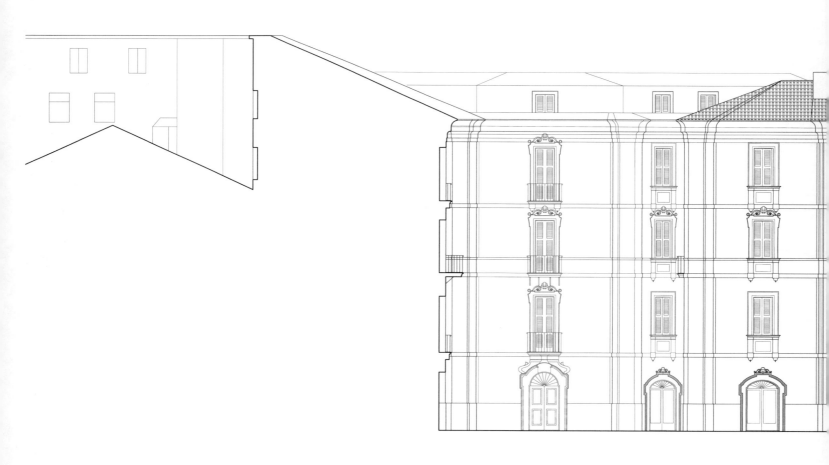

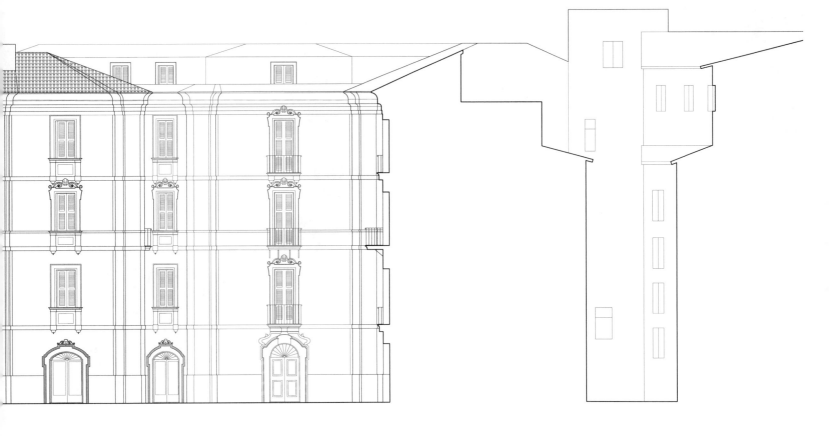

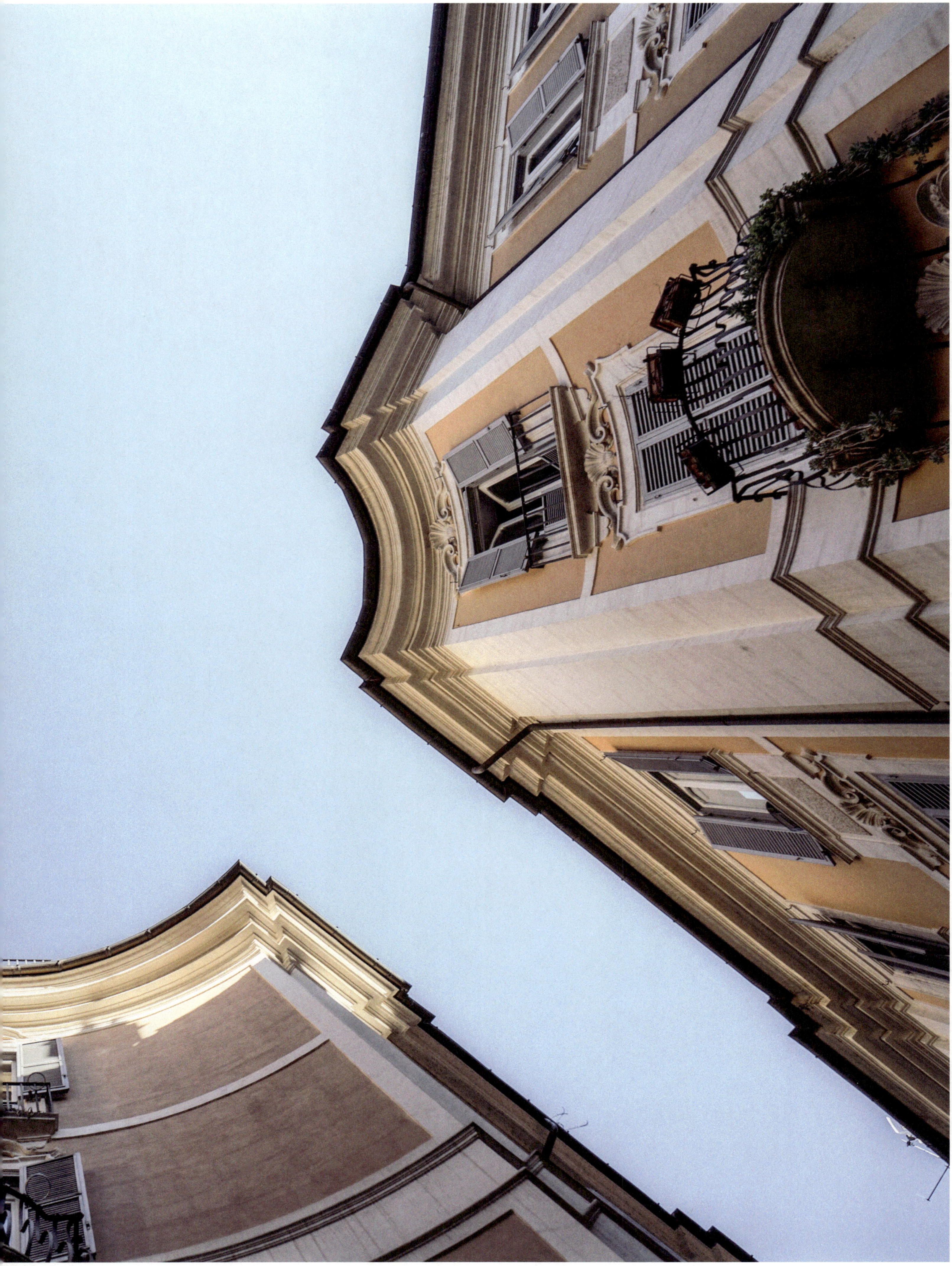

A device through which a building, protruding from its profile, extends over a street or a public space.
In other words, when a building is able to enhance a public space through formal devices that provide order.

A device through which a building, protruding from its profile, extends over a street or a public space.
In other words, when a building is able to enhance a public space through formal devices that provide order.

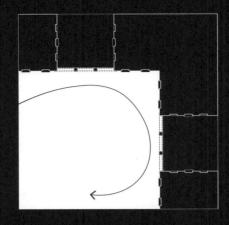

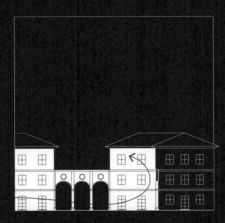

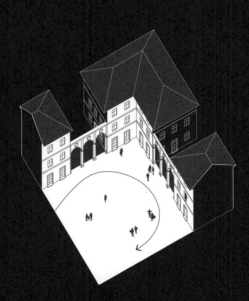

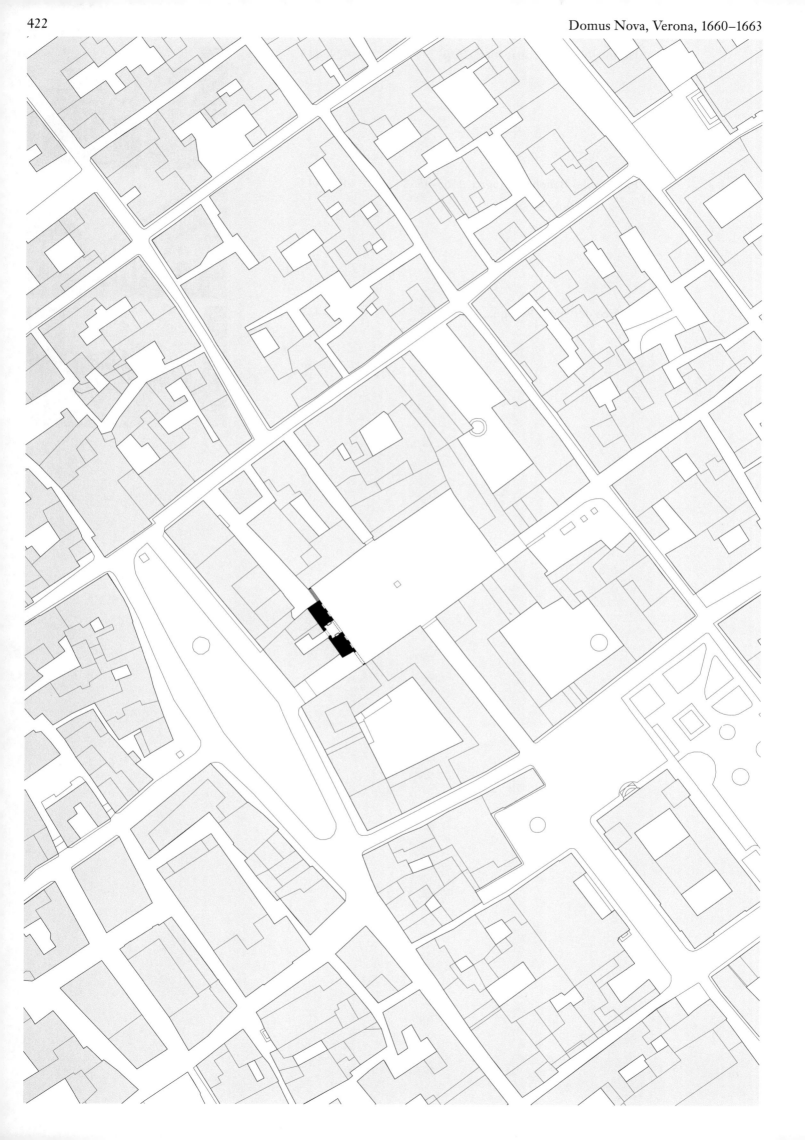

Domus Nova, Verona, 1660–1663   424–433

The Domus Nova, also known as Palazzo dei Giudici, is a residential building of medieval origin that was refurbished in the 17th century, located between two of the main squares of Verona: Piazza delle Erbe and Piazza dei Signori.

Through the redesign of the façade on Piazza dei Signori and the construction of two arches for connection to the neighboring buildings in the 17th century, the Domus Nova reinforces the perimeter of the square in front of it, providing it with clarity and spatial identity.

The dating of the building is uncertain, though we do know that it already existed in 1277, at the time of the renovation of Piazza delle Erbe. Separated at street level from the adjacent structures, it was connected to them by means of elevated passages; in particular, a first bridge connected it with the older Palazzo del Comune to the south, while at a later time a bridge was added for connection to the upper levels of the Mazzanti houses to the north. Initially used as residences and offices for the municipal government, the Domus Nova was later a residence for judges, explaining why it is also known as "Palazzo dei Giudici." Over the centuries, the building has undergone various damages, as a result of earthquakes, requiring various repairs and renovations. Given the location at the center of the political and administrative powers of the city, in the second half of the 17th century the municipal government made firm efforts to regenerate the building itself and Piazza dei Signori.

The chosen project leading to the current situation was to involve not only the building, but also the entire southwestern side of the piazza, by constructing three large round arches: the one at the center corresponded to the main entrance of the building, while the two lateral arches connected to the neighboring buildings through portals. The construction, from 1660 to 1663, was supervised by the master builders Stefano Panizza and Francesco Marchesini. Work on an upper addition to the Domus was completed in 1731, commissioned by the Muselli brothers, the owners of the complex.

The project has an overall length of 36 meters on the southwestern side of Piazza dei Signori. The façade of the building, 24 meters long, features the presence of a large central round arch with a diameter of 5.6 meters, flanked by two arches of equal size at the sides of the façade.

The elevation is organized in three main horizontal parts; each level contains two orders of openings—main and mezzanine windows—arranged symmetrically with respect to the central arch. On the upper level, at the position of the central arch, the motif can be seen of a tetrastyle temple with a triangular tympanum.

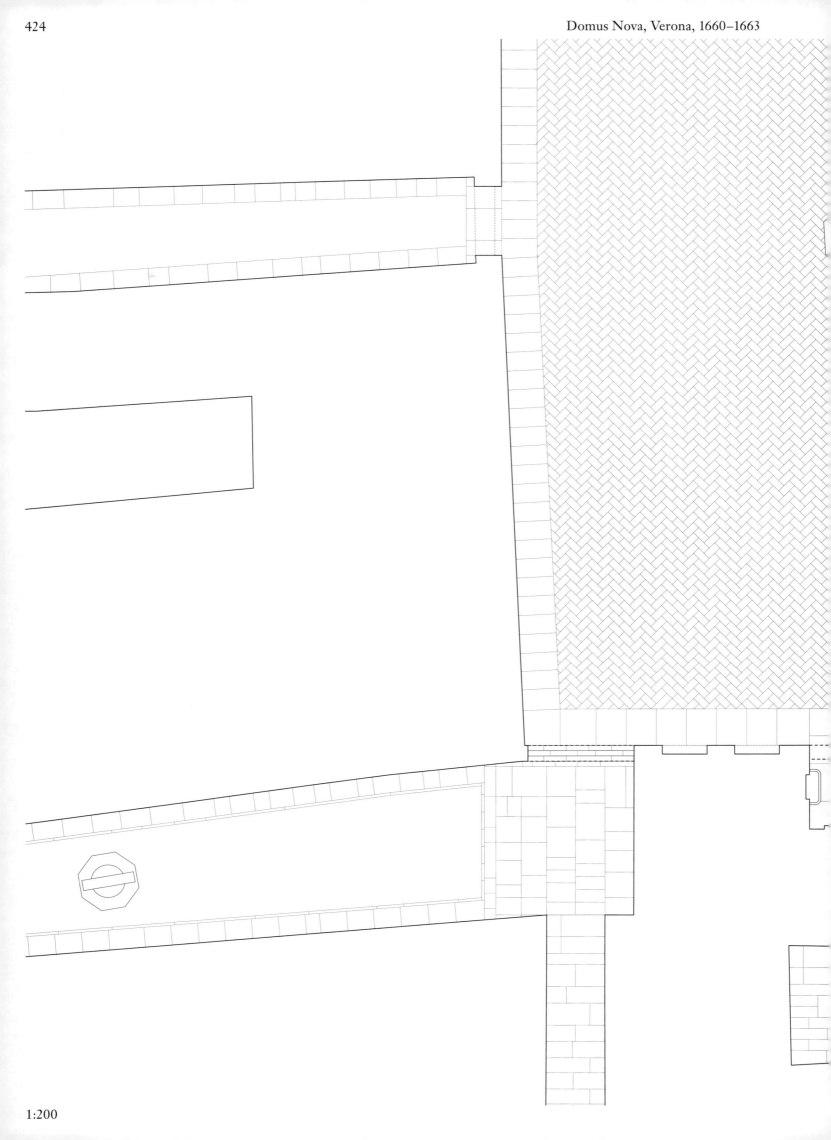

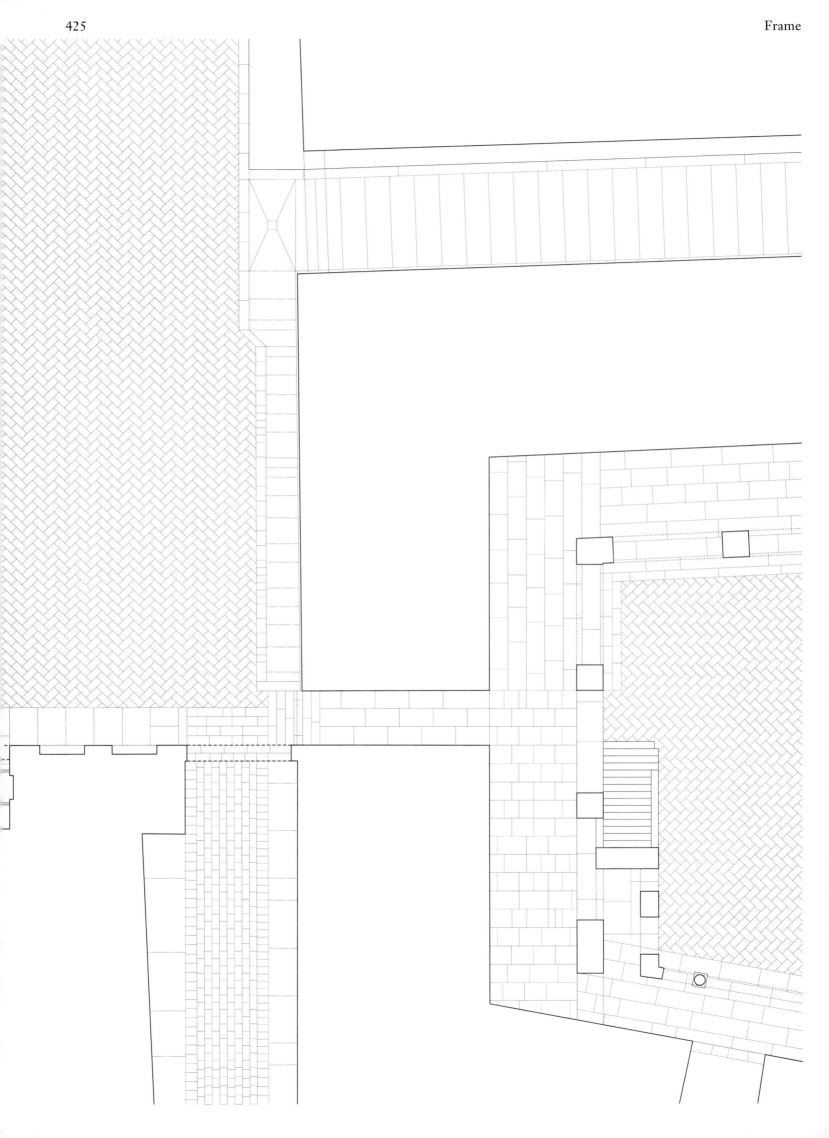

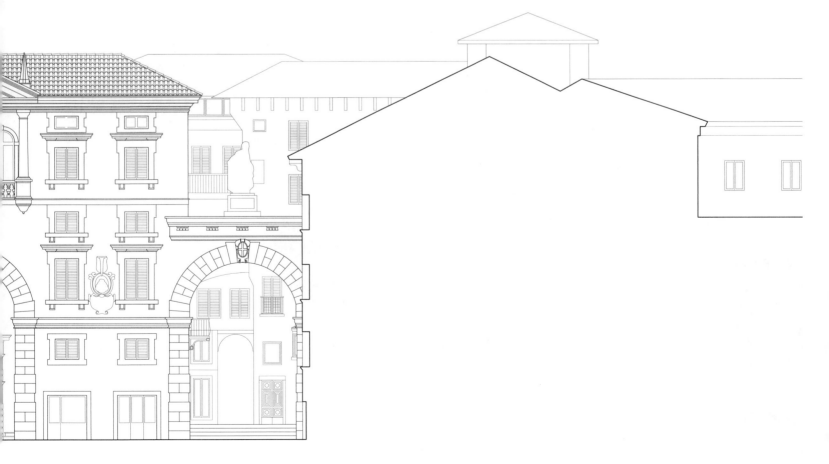

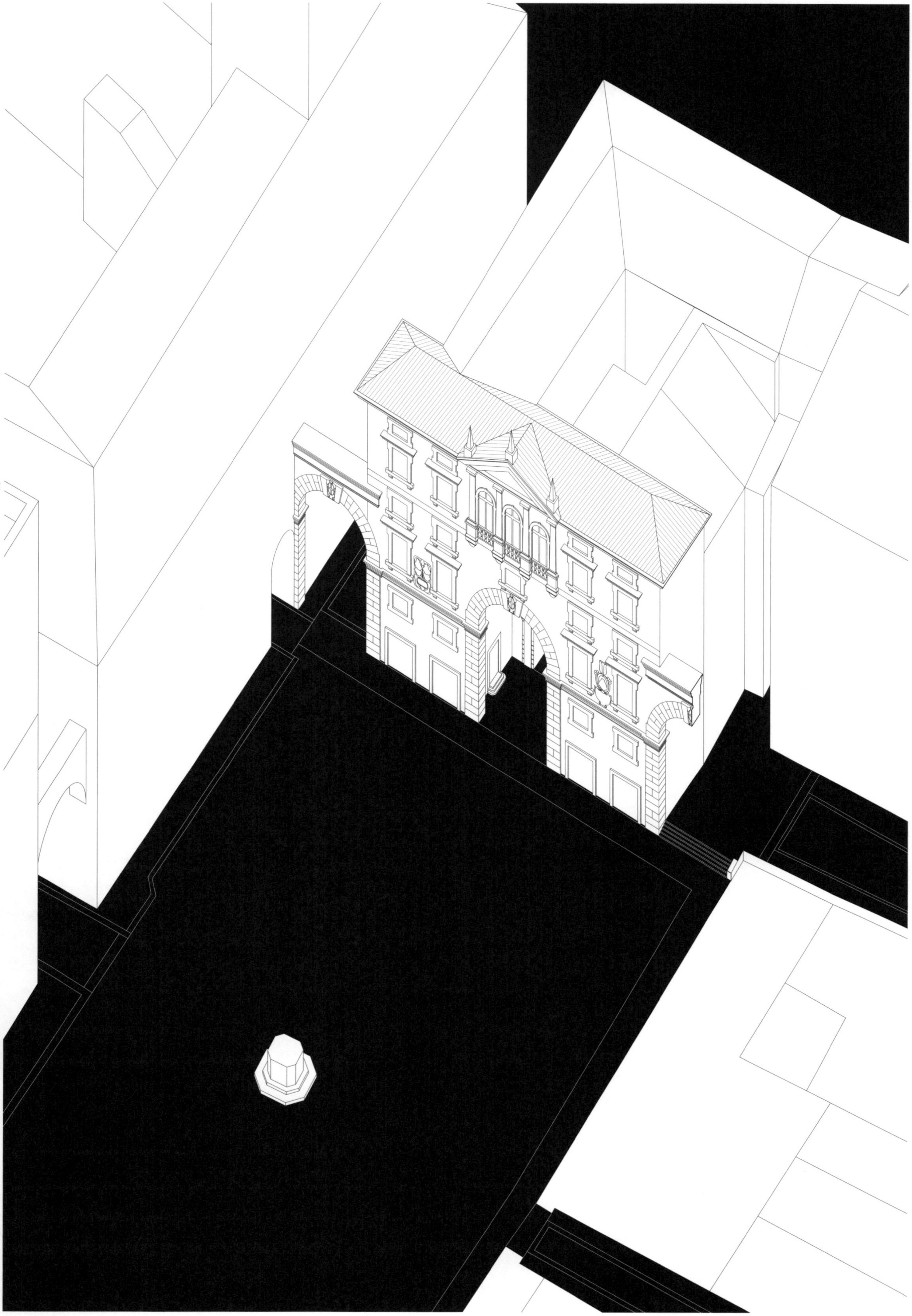

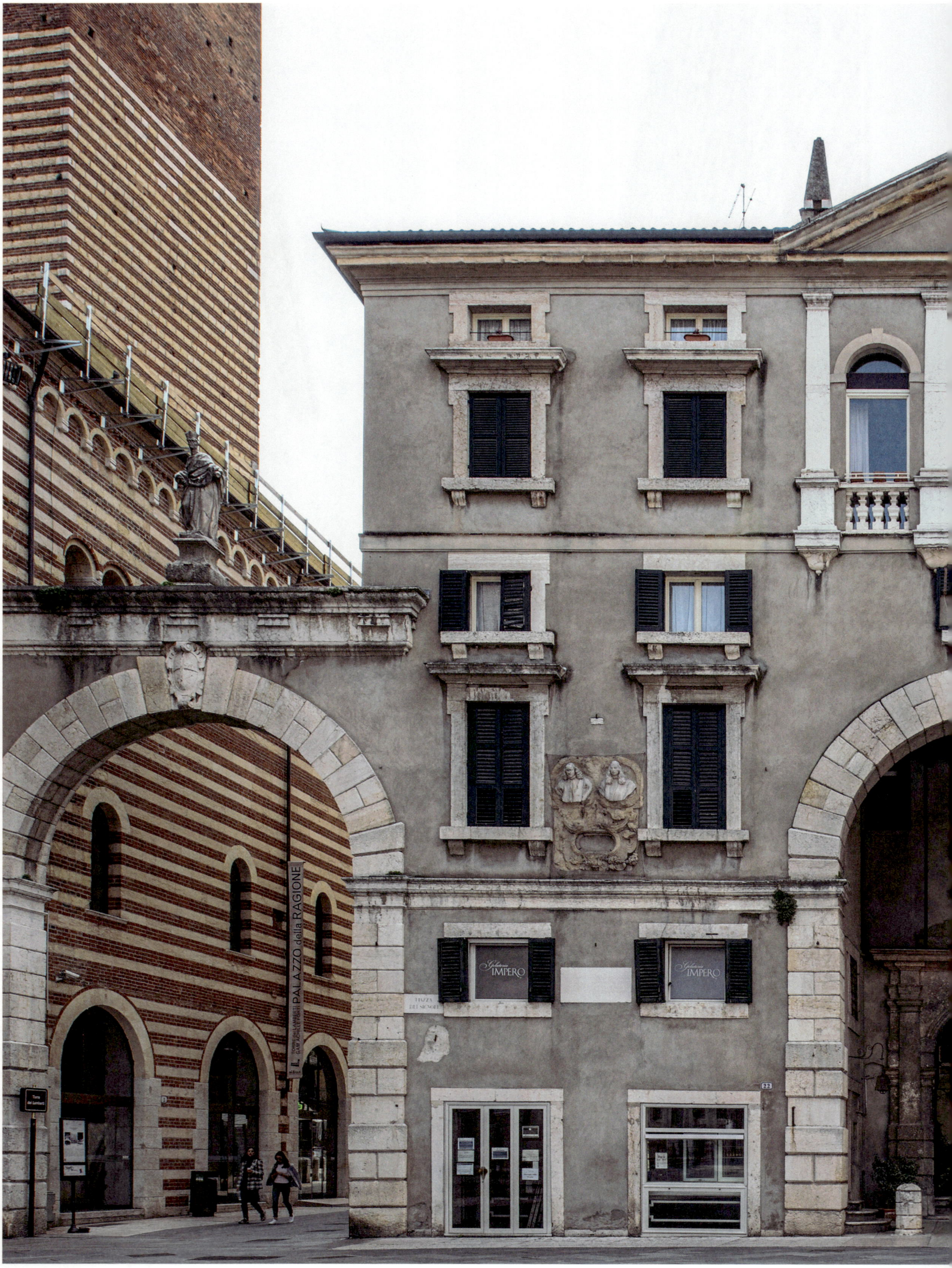
PALAZZO della RAGIONE
IMPERO
IMPERO

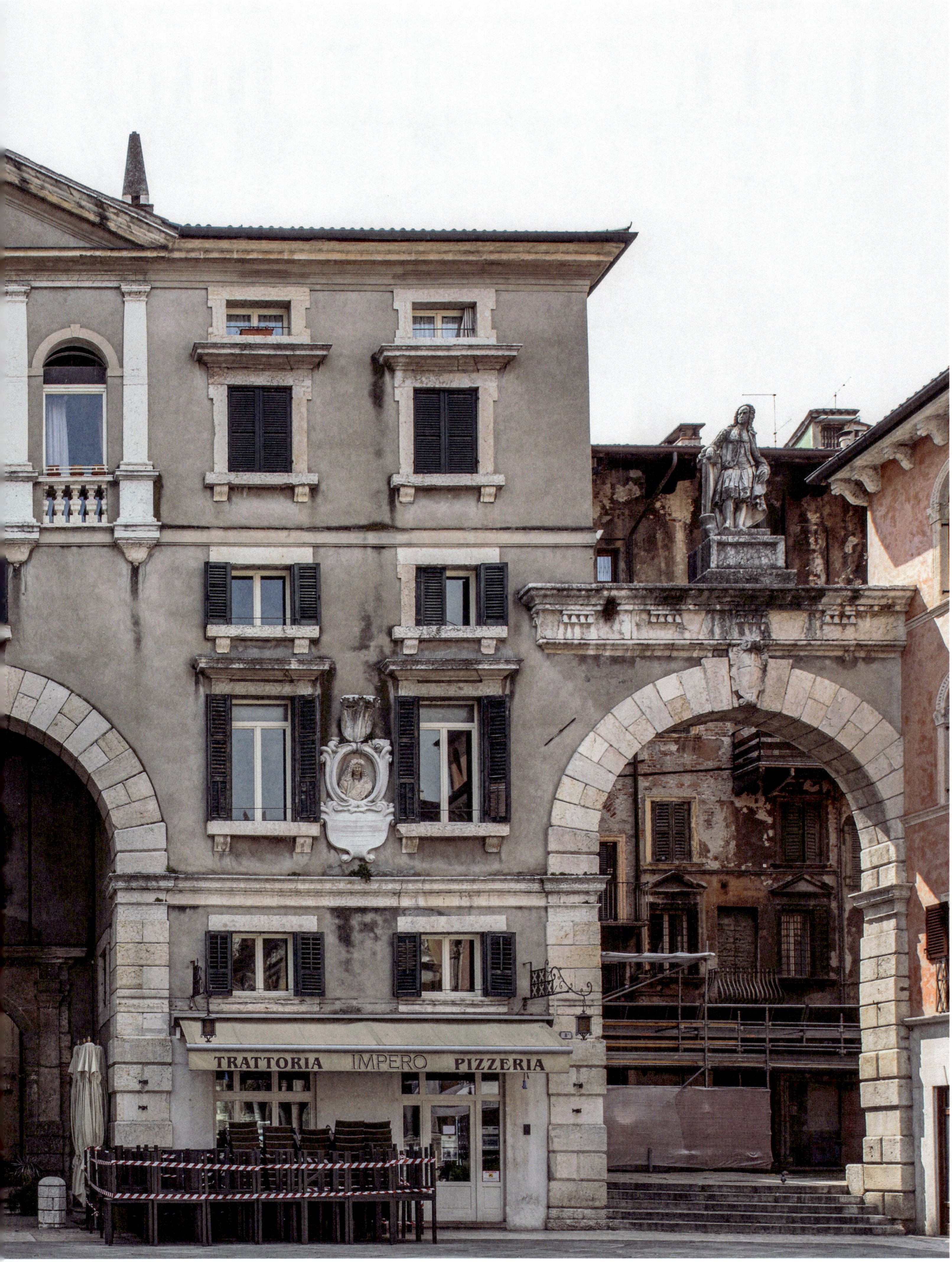
TRATTORIA IMPERO PIZZERIA

Palazzo dei Banchi, Bologna, 1565–1568   434–445

Palazzo dei Banchi, located on the eastern front of Piazza Maggiore, takes its name from the presence of banks or currency exchanges in the 15th and 16th centuries.

With a single unifying gesture based on forceful accentuation of the compositional elements of the façade—pillars, pilaster strips, and cornices—Jacopo Barozzi da Vignola reinvented the eastern side of Piazza Maggiore, designing a structure that acts as mediation between the monumental scale of the piazza and the minute scale of the surrounding urban fabric.

Construction of the building began in the second decade of the 15th century, and it owes its present configuration to the project implemented in 1565 and 1568 by Vignola, who redesigned the façade and the portico to provide a suitable backdrop on the eastern side of the piazza faced by the city's most important church, the basilica of San Petronio. The new elevation had the task of bringing harmony to the old buildings on this side of the piazza, while masking the two accesses of the market at the back in a single composition.

The new façade, though it references certain elements of the neighboring Palazzo del Podestà, stands out for a more intense vertical rhythm and a clearly Renaissance language. Subdivided into two levels by an overhanging stringcourse, the façade has a lower level in a giant order that frames the round arches of the portico, topped by a tripartite attic; an upper level, also in three parts, is framed by stylized pilasters that fully merge into the architrave.

The new elevation designed by Vignola has a length of 95 meters with a total of 15 bays. The round arches have a diameter of 4.4 meters and are supported by pillars that pace the façades at intervals of 6 meters. At the position of the two streets connecting the piazza to the adjacent Mercato di Mezzo, wider arches occupy the height of the entire lower level up to 9 meters, indicating the presence of the narrow streets from the inside of the piazza.

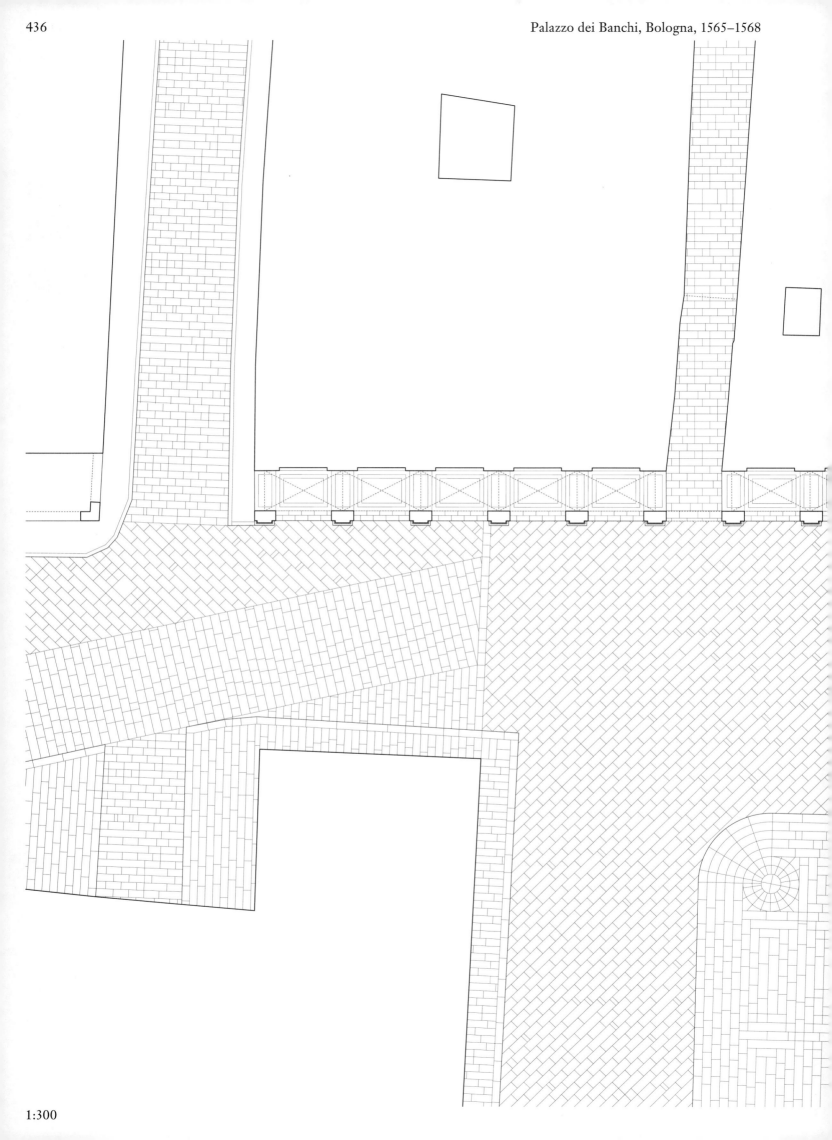

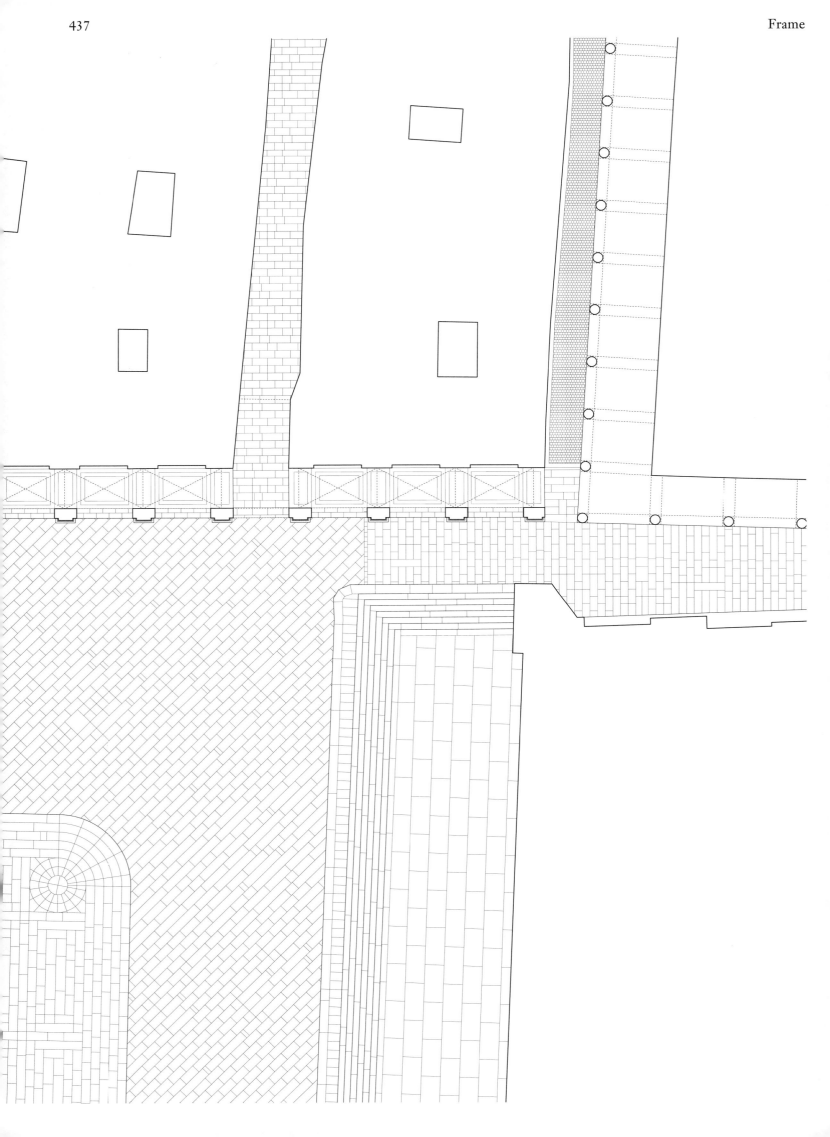

1:300

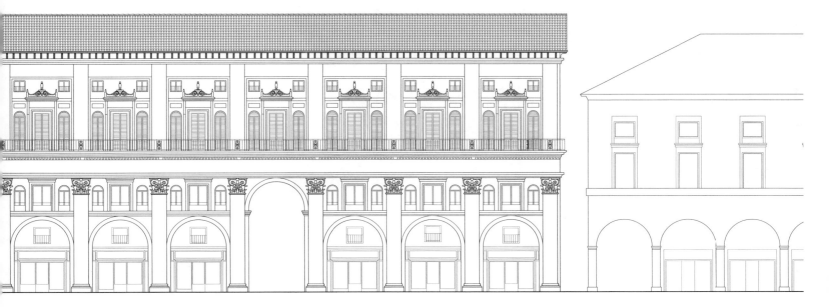

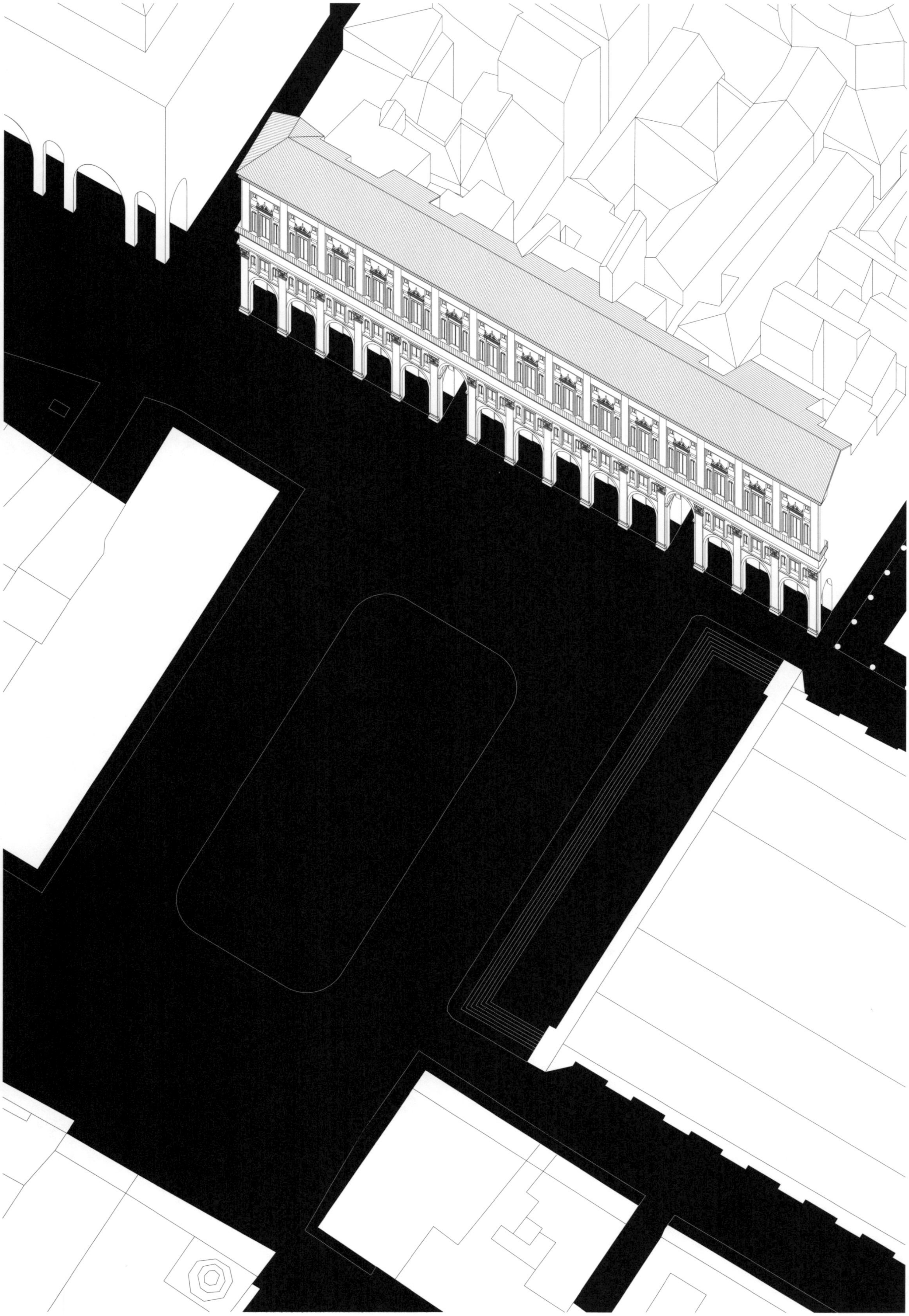

Portico dei Servi, Bologna, 1392–1864   446–457

The Portico dei Servi, built from the 14th to the 19th centuries, is a portico with four sides connected to the basilica of Santa Maria dei Servi.

Part of the urban portico system of the city, the structure is organized as a continuous path that determines the space in front of the basilica; unlike the traditional porticos, normally placed on the ground level of a building, the system of porticos of Santa Maria dei Servi extends into the city, taking on its own formal autonomy and at the same time constituting a threshold between two outdoor spaces. The portico extends to the east along Strada Maggiore and is connected at the south to the porticoes of Via Guerrazzi.

The history of the portico cannot be separated from that of the basilica of Santa Maria dei Servi, for which it constitutes the space of the parvis. The first place of worship, at the service of the Order of Servants of Mary, was completed in 1383; but already, in 1386, work began on its expansion and embellishment, based on a design by Padre Andrea Manfredi da Faenza, general of the Order. Starting in 1392, also with design by Manfredi, construction began for the creation of the portico next to the left side of the church, along Strada Maggiore. Other arcades were gradually added, in various phases, in 1492, 1515–21, and in the 17th century, until finally reaching the present appearance in the form of a quadriporticus in 1864, with a project by Giuseppe Modonesi, who for the purpose ordered the demolition of the church of San Tommaso.

The portico, whose depth is equal to 6 meters—the deepest in the city—is composed of a total of 51 nearly identical bays, of which 32 are located along Strada Maggiore, 7 on Via Guerrazzi, and 12 in the inner portion. The round brick arches, built in keeping with golden ratio, are supported by slender columns in Verona marble with composite capitals. The inner flooring is in Venetian terrazzo, a recurring feature of porticos in Bologna.

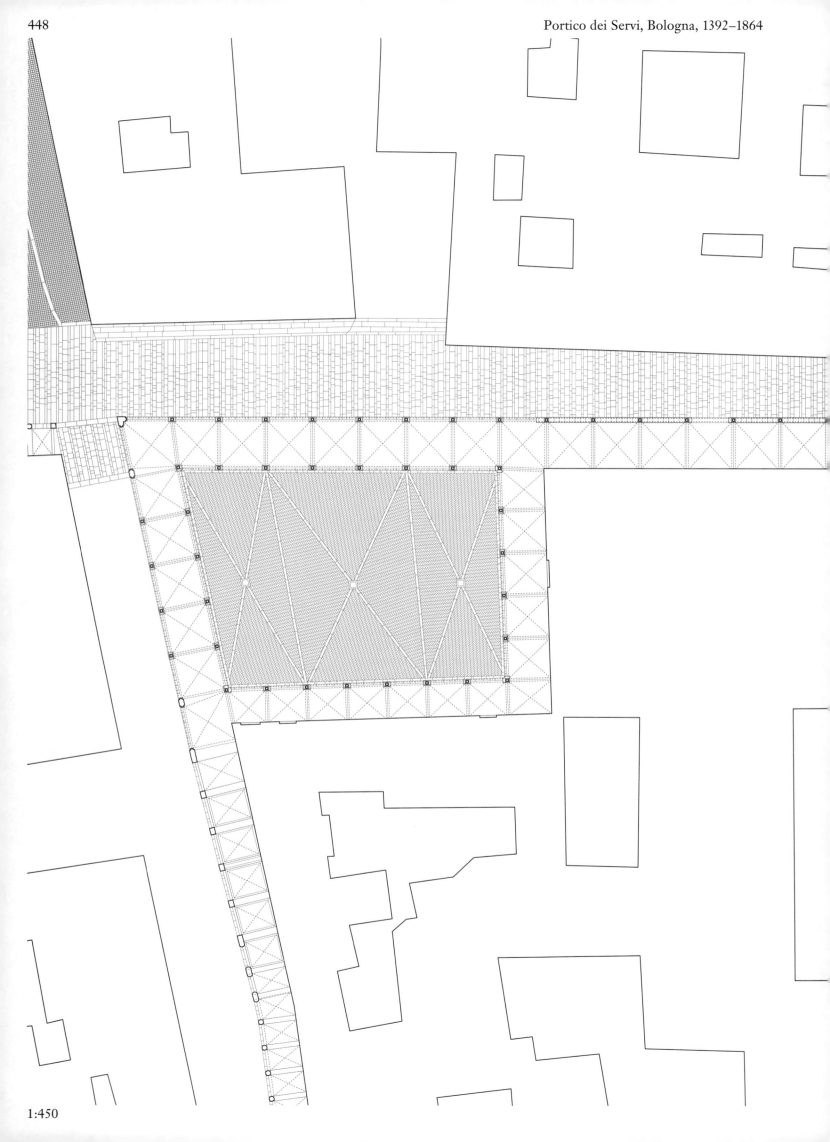

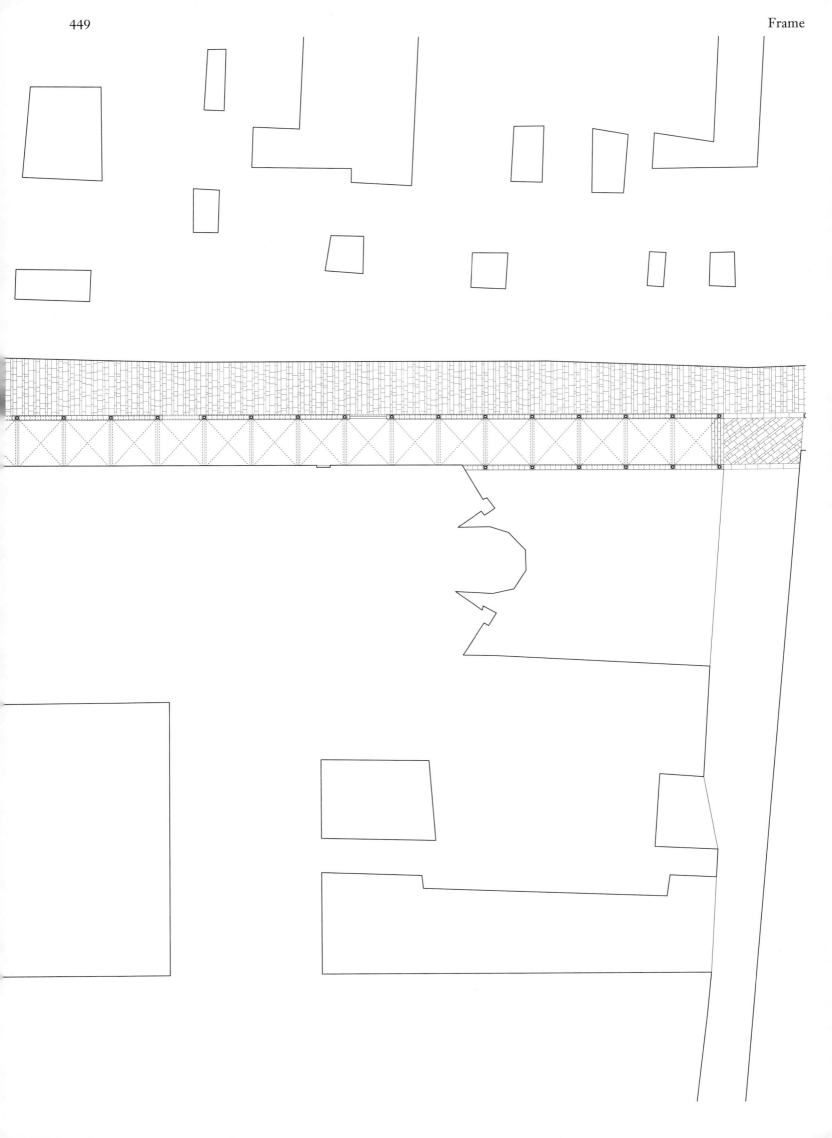

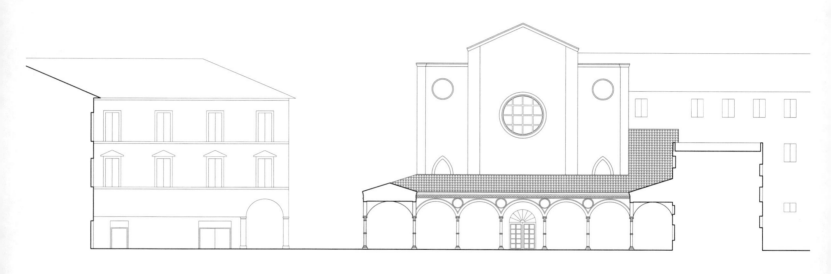

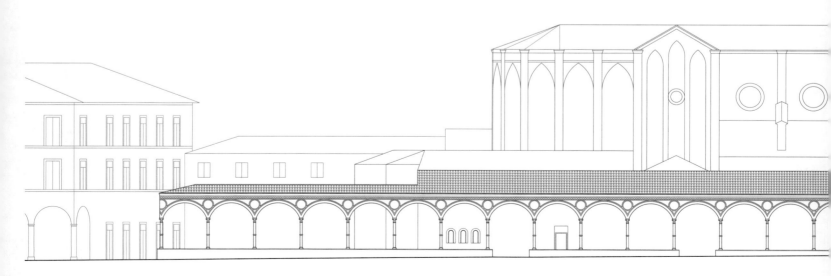

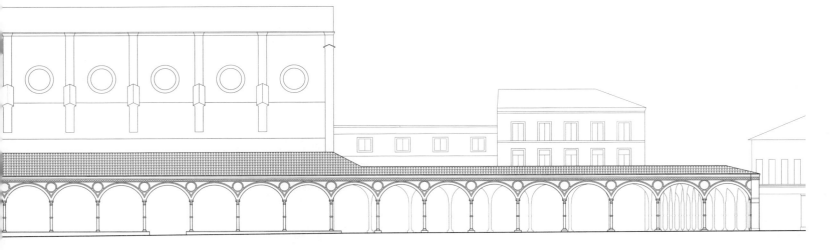

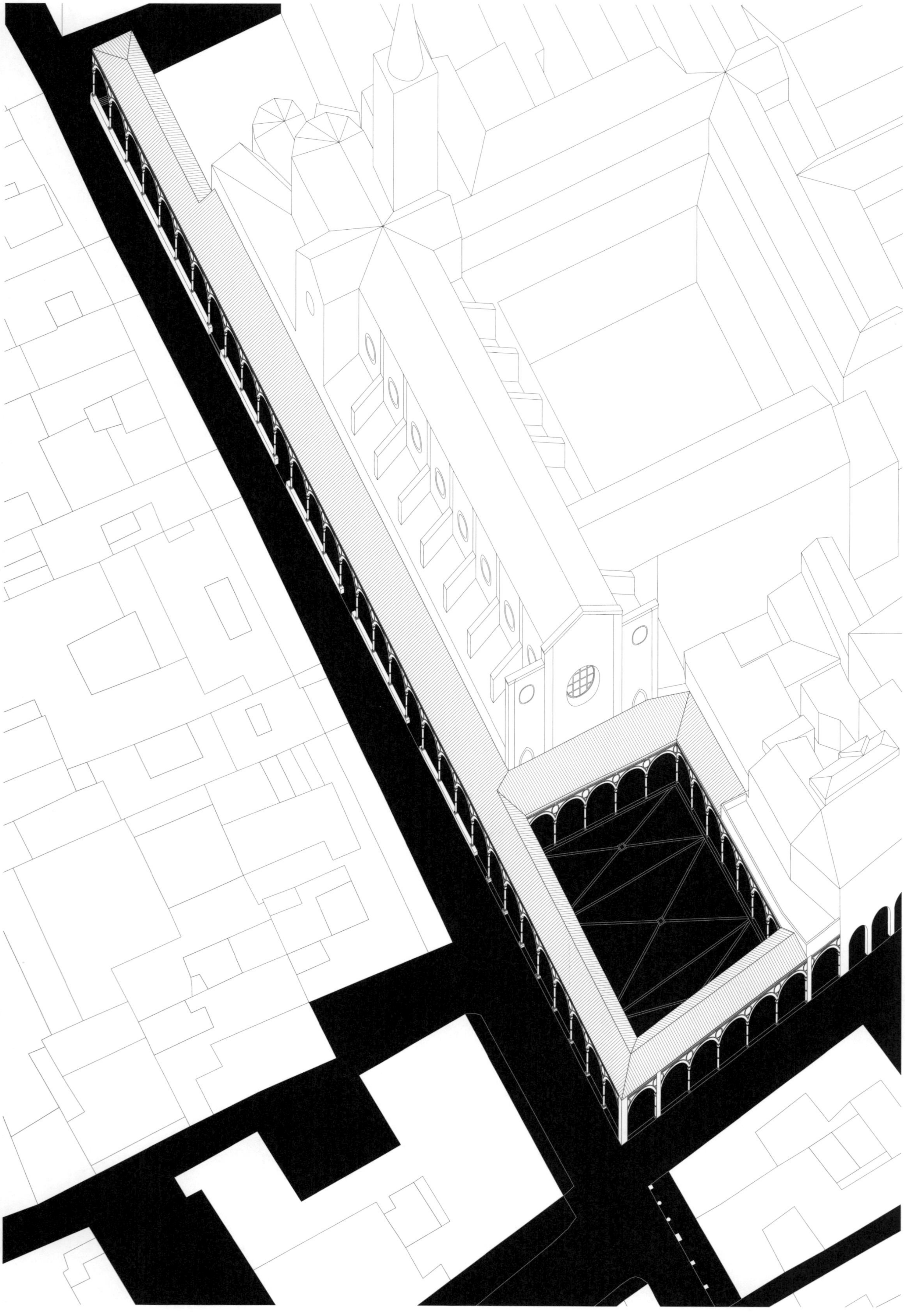

ECCE CIVITAS
Marco Biraghi

Why Italy's historic cities have such good architecture

Historic Italian cities (their names resonate in our ears like trade-marks of nearly inestimable value—Rome, Florence, Venice—but the same is also true for minor centers like Ferrara, Vigevano, Noto, just to mention a few) stand before us as a warning, or even a real certainty: there is *something* here, something that *takes place*. It is the event of a beauty that cannot be grasped in this object or that one, this building or another. A widespread, plural beauty, of many faces, but a single countenance.

We usually refer to this beauty in vague, idealistic terms, as if it were a miracle whose accomplishment has happened in circumstances and ways that do not seem to rely on human interven-tion. This was precisely the way Gabriele D'Annunzio understood the monuments gathered around a meadow in Pisa. Men in remote eras probably observed the spectacle of nature, such as that of a starry sky, with a similar sensation of witnessing an awesome, inexplicable wonder.

But in concrete terms, what constitutes the beauty of a context composed of artifacts made in various moments by various people? What is the secret binder that holds together such a multiplicity of phenomena? We have to try to answer these questions in order to assert that we have at least approached the mystery of Italian cities; we have not simply avoided their enigmas and merely admired their results.

An initial response to the queries raised here might be the one provided by the time—by definition "happy" and "perfect"— in which these "miracles" took place. For a certain perspective on Italian art, architecture, and culture in general, they are all seen as belonging to the Renaissance: a magical, evocative word, on a par with the names of the cities to which it refers in an imprecise (or at times even improper) manner. The Renaissance, from this viewpoint, is not only a real historical period, with its extraordinary developments, but it also has its contradictions and limits. It is a grand tent richly decorated with fabrics under which to place the entire set of products of Italian civilization, as in the painting *Madonna del Parto* by Piero della Francesca. A protective super-cloak that assigns a uniform identity to everything within its sheltering reach.

Nor will it suffice—to justify this conceptual tendency, widespread above all among English-speaking historians—to identify the Renaissance as a long-term phenomenon. In fact, while in the United Kingdom and other parts of Europe, historical-artistic time seems to linger (or maybe that is the impression produced by historians who are too phlegmatic to even bother sharpening their gaze), in Italy it generates an "avalanche effect": an uninterrupted chain of social forms, individual figures, works of art that, from the communal age to the 1700s and beyond, parade without stopping to make anything like a single, unified historical framework. Instead it creates an entire collection of historically determinant frameworks, each of which is highly recognizable and distinct from the others. The public spaces illustrated in this book belong to this crowded gallery: spaces that although they seem to be part of the same vital phase of Italian cities, are actually scattered from the start of the 13th century to the 1930s.

After all, the very concept of "Italy" has changed across this very extended time span—in phases of fragmentation and unification—in a quantity of different ways, without disturbing its clearly recognizable and well-known geographical form. But for those who want to get beyond a superficial vision of things, the Italian reality offers an interesting lesson. Because a common denominator does exist, shared by the albeit different public spaces that punctuate the different cities: something that goes beyond specific circumstances, functions, makers, periods; something that this book, not by chance, interprets not so much in terms of linguistic aspects or decorative implementations, but through the instrumentation of drawing in plans and sections, and even more through the analysis of the particular syntax of the space (the relationships between inside and outside, open and closed, full and empty, the connection with the street, the layout of the passages, the shifts of level). These analyses not only allow us to more precisely identify the various typologies in which the spaces can be inserted, each corresponding to a given spatial arrangement, but above all they reveal a factor that becomes clear on closer examination, on which only the difficulty of recognition of the pure evidence could cast any doubt: rather than isolated or isolable constructions, to a great extent the public spaces examined herein are "urban devices," inextricably grafted and combined in the fabric of the city. One emblematic example is that of the portico (though the same considerations could apply to all the other selected types). In the methodical way it is deployed in a city like Bologna—but also in its more rhapsodic use in many other cities—the portico constitutes an element of urban organization, of its overall structuring, a "system," as it is called, in fact, in the case of Bologna, which totally transcends the individuality of the building. If anything, the portico enters the building as a fundamental, inseparable part of it, though without determining the rest of its characteristics. In this interpretation, the portico represents the connection point between architecture and city, the physical location in which the necessary specificity of one becomes the necessary generic character of the other. It becomes a fully public space, available for use by all. And the same thing happens with loggias, urban courtyards, covered squares, inhabited bridges, galleries, steps, urban terraces, city rooms, and frames.

The extraordinary nature of this mode of mutual relation of architecture and city could go unnoticed only by the eyes of those who have completely forgotten how much they can differ from what we are accustomed to considering them: namely, respectively, a finished, self-defining object, conceived exclusively to perform a function, and a concentration of objects of various kinds destined as a whole to ensure the carrying out of human actions in the most thorough way possible. The relationship that is established between these entities is, in the end, the same one that exists between numbers (or terms) of addition and the total sum: while on the one hand the summed elements do not produce any entirety; on the other, the total in no way conserves the memory of the single addends. Thus we have a mechanical aggregation, which therefore is purely cumulative.

To the contrary, in Italian cities the existing link between the whole and the parts is exactly the same one that can be found in a living body: each organ provides its specific contribution, and together the organs cooperate towards a shared goal: to the "common good," as it was insistently called, especially starting from the 13th century.

Nevertheless, to try to delve a bit deeper into the architectural miracle of Italian cities, it will not suffice to rely on the facile solution provided by the *passepartout* of the organicism; we have to try to break up that apparently inseparable pairing represented by "public space," and hence also try to dispel the mythical aura of irreplicability it has taken on in the present era. In other words, we have to question what it means in the light of the fact of being "public" and of being "space."

The first phantom from which to break free has to do with the concept of "public" and its usual opposition to the concept of "private." This does not mean that such a duality does not exist in the cities of past centuries. In fact, as we have seen, in certain cases there was a true "conflict between private interests and public powers for the control of urban spaces."[1] The history of Italian cities is one of continuing negotiations—not always pacific—between secular (political) power, ecclesiastic power, and particularly strong patrician families for the "sharing out" or for the exercise of specific "rights" or privileges related to the use of certain urban spaces. And while the medieval cities were still—at least to a certain extent—"communitarian" organisms whose size did not generally exceed a radius of one mile (a space that could be crossed on foot in a few minutes), inside which the citizens enjoyed certain rights (though not always unanimously, in practice), the Renaissance cities instead represent the domain of the nobleman, meaning that their spaces are an expression of the hierarchy of powers imposed in the new social order. This, in any case, makes "public" spaces into the three-dimensional manifestation of clearly defined affiliations, namely just the opposite of a generic equality or lack of distinction between their users. The paradigm of an abstract generic and neutral character of the space is countered by the model of concrete spaces for concrete citizens, engaged for various reasons in the carrying out of collective functions (just consider the Loggia della Signoria in Florence, originally purposed for the assemblies of the populace of the Florentine Republic).

In this sense, we should not forget that in historical terms the community was the form of a precise social composition, involving equally specific interests; every member, far from being a citizen without other attributes, was part of a noble family, a military order, a merchant or craft guild, a religious confraternity, or he/she was still a salaried worker (and in this case ran the risk of having no rights of citizenship). Furthermore, each member belonged to a certain spatial aggregation (*quartiere, sestiere, gonfalone,* or *contrada*), zones that were distinguished from each other by particular characteristics, identified by means of colors and crests. This made the members of the community into bearers of interests: shared, collective, and individual.

This organization of the community was immediately reflected in urban space; but to the same extent that it was "public," it was also a space of conflict. This aspect was and is fundamental to understand the concept of "public" in its effective dimension, outside the overly idealizing tent in which we continue to enclose it; the public status of those spaces covered not only the peaceful coexistence of the parties, but also their disagreement and antagonism. And while this certainly does not attenuate the opposition between public and private, it nevertheless introduces a dialectic in that very concept of public, which can help us to redefine its nature in our perspective.

Perhaps this type of rethinking can allow us to ward off two other phantoms from the notion of "public": the one that makes us erroneously equate what is public with something "belonging to everyone," rather than something to which each person should make a contribution; and the phantom—which is even more bothersome and stubborn—that prompts us to match the term "public" with the term "space," like some kind of faithful but useless servant. In reducing it to a simple qualifying adjective, in fact, it winds up losing substance, thus making it empty into a *fait accompli.*

To come to the other half of the manner of speaking we are trying to unpack, what is the space of the *civitas* (space as such, free of the burden of the "public" label), if not the expression of the special condition of freedom enjoyed by citizens inside the urban walls? A freedom that should not be confused with the political status they may or may not have had, and instead should be understood as freedom *from* the dangers that arose when one was *extra moenia*. If, in fact, the commune made a commitment (at least in its intentions) to establish peace and justice inside the city, "outside it was quite another matter…"[2] Freedom, then, that corresponds to the very state of urbanization (in the face of which, to the exact contrary, Dante's "rough and rustic mountaineer" is "bewildered."[3]

So before seeing it as the site of implementation of single and specific functions in the space of the *civitas*, we should note the materialization of the possibilities offered to citizens to create their own *mundus artificialis*, which is utterly other than the countryside or the rest of the territory. And in fact—again, over and above the implementation of single and specific functions—the spaces of the *civitas* are the physical translation of a few fundamental human actions: gathering, finding shelter, moving, lingering, exchanging, connecting. Spaces that because they are the result of these actions in various combinations cannot help but be the demonstration of a collective freedom—if not in the concrete use that is made of them over time, at least in the act of their original conception. Spaces that are forms of aggregated, shared life, that in turn generate architecture of aggregation, of sharing. An architecture that, having those simple actions inscribed within it, makes them clearly legible in the syntax it utilizes and the elements it deploys; hence, the arcading of porticos and loggias speaks of permeability, the vaults of galleries and covered squares speak of protection, the sequences of steps of staircases speak of interconnection, the pavements of piazzas, urban courtyards, and city rooms speak of extension and limits. Architecture, then, as *free* expression of the potentialities of the *civitas*.

This transparency of the meaning of Italian urban spaces has been grasped with extraordinary clarity during the course of the 20th century—certainly not by chance—by two foreign observers: the American George Everard Kidder Smith, in his famous book *Italy Builds: Its Modern Architecture and Native Inheritance,*[4] illustrated with the author's own photographs; and the Englishman Ivor De Wolfe (the pseudonym of Hubert de Cronin Hastings), in the beautiful volume featuring the photographic images of his wife Ivy De Wolfe (Hazel Rickman Garrard), *The Italian Townscape.*[5] In both cases, Italy is observed through the mirror of its cities (larger and smaller, without distinctions of rank), while the latter are analyzed through the mirror of their spaces and buildings. In these two works, what we can take away is the particular dynamic of those spaces and buildings, their way of forming inextricable nodes while each remaining perfectly distinct; in short, the way of asserting themselves as entities-pluralities in constant dialogue (*diá-logos*, a mode of relation that by definition is established between differences, between others).

But if all this has been possible, it is also by virtue of the unique character of the legal bases of the governments of Italian cities, where the influence and partial survival of Roman law is clearly not an extraneous factor. These bases were indeed different from those of the monarchies widespread in that moment in Europe, and they were also different from those of the subsequent lordships. We are looking at a mixed system of powers (*podestà,* council of the elders, captain of the people, just to mention a few of them), marked by extremely short terms of office and rigorous controls and cross-checking, often implemented through the involvement—particularly in the figure of the *podestà*—of *forestieri* (foreigners) who belonged to allied cities but at the same time had no direct interests in the management of the city's affairs. Institutions of laymen, secular in character, whose idea of human nature was as crude as it was exact and absolutely realistic; institutions that had nothing to do with modern pseudo-democracies, yet nevertheless fought strenuously for the implementation of *libertas* and *aequalitas*.

And it is emblematic to the utmost that precisely this system of government, in spite of the conflicts for which the *civitas* was the daily setting (or perhaps even by virtue of those conflicts), produced the most beautiful spaces and finest buildings in our past, those that best reflect democratic parameters, in today's perspective.

What remains overshadowed, in this discussion, is the individual contribution that multiple authors presumably made in the creation of spaces destined to represent the community, the *populus civitatis*, a contribution that varies, case by case, and could only be measured by means of much closer analysis. But apart from the individual cases, the explanation of the architectural miracle of the Italian cities is perhaps easier than we might have imagined: a simplicity that is the reversed image of the complex balances that sustained the *civitas*.

How today's cities can become what they should be

First of all: what are today's cities? And secondly: how can they become what they should be? Starting with the first point, in spite of the relative differences between them, today's cities remain abysmally distant from what was supposed to be indicated by the term. While the latter embodied an organism, though composed of parts or elements distinct from one another but deeply connected, today's cities take their founding image-myth from the idea of a mechanism, a machine of gigantic proportions and extraordinary complexity, though in many cases it is not very efficient.

This image-myth of the city-machine is a reference point not only for modernity and the ideology of rationalization that constitutes its essential principle, but also for capitalism, which adopts its logic. Based on this, how can we expect contemporary urban spaces to have anything in common, other than mere sharing of names, with those of the *civitas*? And how can we imagine, today, that it is possible not only to produce something vaguely akin to the collective spaces of the *communitas*, but also to continue to give life to already existing spaces?

On the other hand, to respond to those who complain of the present dearth of public spaces in the contemporary city, blaming it on the ineptitude of today's architects, we might remind them of the fact that many of those spaces still exist, though they have often been erased by layer upon layer of automobiles, or rendered useless by our preference for spending time in other, private places (our living rooms, for example, rather than public squares). The "public venues" that now occupy large portions of collective space are highly emblematic in this regard, since they are actually private businesses.

The situation of architecture purposed for shared functions is even more problematic, which in today's logic meets with a drastic reduction of demand, or is simply considered a useless waste of space (or, as they say nowadays, a matter of disadvantageous "land consumption").

These, then, are the cities. As to how they could become what they should be, there is the risk of total impossibility if the "should be" in question corresponds to the daydreams of an implausible return to "childhood." This risk increases every day, with the gradual widening of the distance between the dominant interests that hold sway in today's cities and the sense of mutual belonging that was characteristic of the *civitas*. Nor will isolated attempts on the part of players with "good intentions" suffice to reverse this trend, especially because they are actually nothing more than seductive smokescreens offered for the benefit of alleged "new metropolitan communities."

Nevertheless, it might be worthwhile to at least try to think about the conditions of possibility of such a *rapprochement*, difficult as it might be in practice. A small but significant signal in this direction is precisely that of the research conducted by Labics. There can be no illusion that on its own this can bring about any change of course. It can, however, be seen as an indicator that suggests the right direction. Not just due to its thematic content, but also for the general framework of meaning in which it is situated.

Labics is an Italian, Roman architecture firm, working on the international scene for years now; a studio that has seen and sees no lack of concrete project opportunities. Nevertheless, Labics' research activities constitute an indispensable area of work; research that is without immediate returns (meaning free of overly stringent design objectives, free of the constraints of fashion and the market), and is instead interested in exploring the field in the most comparable and exchangeable way possible. Getting beyond the usual tendency of architects towards individualism and self-centered reference, Labics attempts to make a contribution to collective reflections.

To indicate this specific research project as "exemplary" means acknowledging its ability to focus on the theme of the architecture of public space in historic Italian cities as an indispensable cognitive premise for those who wish to approach urban design today; without any empty hope that this will in itself lead to the solution of the problem, and rather with the conviction that study and analysis constitute the first step for the creation of a common ground.

In this perspective, even the single cases examined, no matter how interesting they may be, should all be taken back to the general gist of the question, for which each of them represents a demonstration, a confirmation—and, prior to this, the necessary recognition of the situation. The fact that a problem exists in our way of thinking about and making the contemporary city, this is the indispensable premise from which to approach it, if not yet to truly solve it. And it is in this direction, in fact—taking cues from this awareness—that the projects of Labics are moving: the addition and reorganization of several spaces of Palazzo dei Diamanti in Ferrara (2017–), the project for a Bio-Medical Campus of the University of Rome (with Topotek 1, 2018–), the reconstruction of the arena level of the Roman Colosseum (with Milan Ingegneria, Fabio Fumagalli, Consilium and CROMA, 2021–), just to mention a few. All these cases are attempts to give rise to spaces marked by outstanding permeability and openness, and by morphological principles that can be linked to an idea of city-*civitas*, though at the same time without any nostalgic attitudes. Because looking at history (the historical city, historical architecture) as something not purely archaeological or to be slavishly imitated, something from which to garner still timely lessons, is precisely the attitude that might enable us to make today's cities—at least within the limits of their possibilities of intervention—become "what they should be." Furthermore, since this attitude is not unique, but shared by a nevertheless limited number of other architects, the potentialities of that possibility could lead to a perhaps imperceptible, but in any case significant, augmentation.

Of course, as some might object, the architects are not the ones who decide, and major changes in the society are always the result of essentially social transformations. But if a sign is a "sign of the times" and not an isolated factor, then the appearance of architects who do not limit their role to merely supplying the system with what it wants, but instead attempt to productively transform it in the sense outlined above (though in a way that is only partial, for the moment), should be greeted as good news. After all, an architect genuinely deserving of that title is required, apart from specific forms of expertise, to have formulated a world view (*Weltanschauung*, it would be in German) that goes beyond the ability to execute to also include the ability to guide and to provide orientation.

All this said, there do not seem to be substantial reasons why Labics' attempt should not fail, as many others have failed in the past. In its favor, we can only point to the way it has been carried out: it is analytical, taxonomic, we might even say "scientific," although that adjective might suggest the idea of a detachment that is far from pertinent in this case; because, instead, this research project has deeply absorbed its makers, in spite of the fact that it is not—as we have seen—purely instrumental for their design activity. And it is precisely this disinterested condition, in the immediate sense, that makes Labics' investigation highly symbolic for a more structural, more objective reason (less arbitrary or questionable) than it might seem: in its way of getting beyond the limits of the "useful" it implies a more ambitious project, also beyond its cognitive objectives. It is here that its true interest lurks, which does not call for compensations and ignores advantages. To have the courage to spread a word that is not one's own, and not even associated with any direct benefits—to have the courage to propagate the truth of the *civitas* in a world dominated by the ironclad mechanical-mercantile rules of the city-machine—does not mean being driven by "good intentions." Instead, it means infringing values, being *destroyers*. It means pursuing a more profitable profit than the mere economic benefit offered today by capitalist city-societies to citizens as their only possible sustenance; a social gain, a human gain.

The pathway towards making today's cities become what they should be necessarily passes through the constructive destruction of the values on which they are based, in the arduous re-appropriation of the practices of the civilizing of the *civitas*. Those who offer help to proceed along this path can be given credit for something more than ability or expertise—namely, a world view.

1   Paolo Grillo, "Spazi privati e spazi pubblici nella Milano medievale," in *Studi Storici 39*, no. 1 (1998).
2   Mario Ascheri, *Le città-stato*, Bologna: Il Mulino, 2006.
3   *Purg.*, XXVI, lines 67–69.
4   George Everard Kidder Smith, *Italy Builds: Its Modern Architecture and Native Inheritance*, New York: Reinhold Publishing Corporation. 1955.
5   Ivor De Wolfe, *The Italian Townscape*, London: The Architectural Press. 1963.

Drawings

Marta Copetti:
La Rotonda, Badoere; Piazza del Duomo, Noto; Palazzo Comunale, Piacenza; Piazza Ducale, Vigevano.

Alessandro Esposito:
Piazza del Popolo, Faenza; Piazza delle Vettovaglie, Pisa; Palazzo and Piazza del Municipio, Ferrara; Galleria Sciarra, Rome; Galleria Vittorio Emanuele II, Milan; Steps of Ara Coeli, Rome; Ponte Vecchio, Florence.

Giovanni Fabbri:
Palazzo delle Logge, Arezzo; Loggia dei Lanzi, Florence; Loggia del Pesce, Florence; Loggia Vasariana, Castiglion Fiorentino; Palazzo della Loggia, Brescia; Palazzo della Ragione, Milan; Mercato del Pesce di Rialto, Venice; Rotonda Foschini, Ferrara; Piazza Grande, Gubbio; Bastione di Saint Remy, Cagliari; Ponte Vecchio, Bassano del Grappa; Trepponti Bridge, Comacchio; Uffizi, Florence; Piazza Sant'Ignazio, Rome; Domus Nova, Verona; Palazzo dei Banchi, Bologna; Portico dei Servi, Bologna.

Giulio Marzullo:
Galleria Subalpina, Turin; Galleria San Federico, Turin; Quattro Canti, Palermo; San Cerbone Cathedral, Massa Marittima.

Photographs

Cover photo: Labics

Maria Claudia Clemente
Photographs on pages: 60–61, 112, 202–203, 244–245, 266–267, 392, 416–417

Francesco Isidori
Photographs on pages: 45–49, 57–59, 81–85, 109–111, 113, 121–125, 133–137, 173–177, 201, 204–205, 213–217, 284–285, 293–297, 305–309, 321–325, 349, 361–365, 373–377, 389–391, 393, 429–433, 441–445, 453–457

Giulio Marzullo
Photographs on pages: 161, 189–193, 242–243, 253–257, 265, 269

Giovanna Silva
Photographs on pages: 69–73, 93–97, 149–153, 162–165, 229–233, 241, 268, 281–283, 333–337, 350–353, 401–405, 413–415

Maria Claudia Clemente (1967) graduated in architecture in 1992 and received her PhD in 1995, both from Università Sapienza in Rome. In 2022 she became an associate professor at the same university; since 2003 she has been responsible for a design studio investigating in particular public design. In 2003, 2008, 2011, 2014, 2018, 2020, and 2022 Maria Claudia served as a visiting critic at Cornell University in Rome and Ithaca, New York. In 2014 she was invited to be a visiting critic at IUAV (University of Venice).

Maria Claudia Clemente is regularly invited to give lectures on Labics' research and projects and to direct design workshops in a variety of Italian and international universities including Università La Sapienza, Università Roma Tre, Cornell University, the University of Iowa, Syracuse University, Tulane University, and the University of Hannover. She is the author, together with Francesco Isidori, of *Labics Structures* (Park Books 2018).

Francesco Isidori (1971) graduated from Università Sapienza in Rome in 1999; he received in 2006 a PhD in Architectural Composition and Theory from the same university. From 2002 to 2010 he was a visiting professor at Università Sapienza, conducting a studio on architectural design. In 2003, 2008, 2011, 2014, 2018, 2020, and 2022 he served as a visiting critic at Cornell University in Rome and Ithaca, New York. In 2014 he was invited to be a visiting critic at the University of Ferrara and IUAV (University of Venice).

Francesco Isidori is regularly invited to give lectures on Labics' research and projects and to hold design workshops in a variety of Italian and international universities, including Università Sapienza, Università Roma Tre, Cornell University, the University of Iowa, Syracuse University, Tulane University, IUAV, University of Ferrara, and the University of Hannover. He is the author, together with Maria Claudia Clemente, of *Labics Structures* (Park Books 2018).

Marco Biraghi (1959) is an architectural historian. He graduated in architecture in 1986, and received his PhD in 1990, both from Politecnico di Milano. He is now full professor of History of Contemporary Architecture in the same university. He lectured—among others—at Columbia University, Cooper Union, Harvard University, University of Houston, Berlage Institute, Queensland University, FAU São Paulo, China Academy of Art of Hangzhou, and Accademia di Architettura of Mendrisio.

Among his books: *Storia dell'architettura contemporanea* 1750–2023 (Einaudi 2008, 2023), *Project of Crisis. Manfredo Tafuri and Contemporary Architecture* (The MIT Press 2013), *Storia dell'architettura italiana 1985–2015* (with S. Micheli, Einaudi 2013), *L'architetto come intellettuale* (Einaudi 2019), *Questa è architettura. Il progetto come filosofia della prassi* (Einaudi 2021), *Post Western Histories of Architecture* (with P.M. Guerrieri, Routledge 2023). He also edited the Italian edition of *Delirious New York* by Rem Koolhaas (Electa 2001).

Concept: Maria Claudia Clemente
and Francesco Isidori
Translation: Stephen Piccolo
Proofreading: Christen Jamar
Graphic design: Samuel Bänziger,
Rosario Florio, Larissa Kasper
Lithography, printing and binding:
DZA Druckerei zu Altenburg GmbH,
Thuringia
Typeface: Janson Text LT
Paper: Fly Extraweiss

Park Books
Niederdorfstrasse 54
8001 Zurich
Switzerland
www.park-books.com

Park Books is being supported by the
Federal Office of Culture with a general
subsidy for the years 2021–2024.

ISBN 978-3-03860-311-5